ISLAND STORIES

AN UNCONVENTIONAL
HISTORY OF BRITAIN

DAVID REYNOLDS

**WILLIAM
COLLINS**

William Collins
An imprint of HarperCollins*Publishers*
1 London Bridge Street
London SE1 9GF

WilliamCollinsBooks.com

First published in Great Britain in 2019 by William Collins
This William Collins paperback edition published in 2020

1

A catalogue record for this book is available from the British Library

ISBN 978-0-00-828235-6

Typeset in Minion Pro by Palimpsest Book Production Ltd, Falkirk, Stirlingshire

Printed and bound in Great Britain by CPI Group (UK) Ltd, Croydon

'Lively, slender and timely'   *Foreign Affairs*

'The Normans to Nigel Farage: it's quite a journey . . . takes us from
the 12th-century chronicler Geoffrey of Monmouth, who saw the
Channel as "the straits to the south", an easy means of getting to
the mainland of Europe, through Edward I and the Plantagenets,
trying to hold on to their French lands, to English defeat in the
Hundred Years' War, after which the Channel became not a bridge,
but a barrier . . . Fascinating'   *Times*

'A witty and revealing look at long-term patterns in British history'
Kirkus

ALSO BY DAVID REYNOLDS

The Creation of the Anglo-American Alliance:
A Study in Competitive Cooperation, 1937–1941

An Ocean Apart: The Relationship between Britain and America
in the Twentieth Century (with David Dimbleby)

Britannia Overruled: British Policy and World Power
in the Twentieth Century

The Origins of the Cold War in Europe (editor)

Allies at War: The Soviet, American and British Experience, 1939–
1945 (co-edited with Warren F. Kimball and A. O. Chubarian)

Rich Relations: The American Occupation of Britain, 1942–1945

One World Divisible: A Global History since 1945

From Munich to Pearl Harbor: Roosevelt's America
and the Origins of the Second World War

In Command of History: Churchill Fighting
and Writing the Second World War

From World War to Cold War: Churchill, Roosevelt
and the International History of the 1940s

Summits: Six Meetings that Shaped the Twentieth Century

America, Empire of Liberty: A New History

FDR's World: War, Peace, and Legacies
(co-edited with David B. Woolner and Warren F. Kimball)

The Long Shadow: The Great War and the Twentieth Century

Transcending the Cold War: Summits, Statecraft, and the
Dissolution of Bipolarity in Europe, 1970–1990
(co-edited with Kristina Spohr)

The Kremlin Letters: Stalin's Wartime Correspondence with
Churchill and Roosevelt (with Vladimir Pechatnov)

We have got all we want in territory, and our claim to be left in the unmolested enjoyment of vast and splendid possessions, mainly acquired by violence, largely maintained by force, often seems less reasonable to others than to us.

Winston Churchill, 10 January 1914

Trade cannot flourish without security.

Lord Palmerston, 22 April 1860

Unless we change our ways and our direction, our greatness as a nation will soon be a footnote in the history books, a distant memory of an offshore island, lost in the mists of time, like Camelot, remembered kindly for its noble past.

Margaret Thatcher, 1 May 1979

Vote Leave. Take Back Control.

Brexit campaign slogan, 2016

Contents

List of illustrations

Introduction

Brexit Means . . . ?

On 23 June 2016, the British electorate voted to leave the European Union. The margin was arithmetically narrow, yet politically decisive: 51.89 per cent 'Leave' and 48.11 per cent 'Remain'. 'Leave' meant 'out' but nobody in the governing class, let alone the country, had a clear idea where the country was going. No contingency planning for a 'Leave' vote had been undertaken by David Cameron, the Prime Minister who had called the referendum. And Theresa May, who succeeded Cameron after he abruptly resigned, lacked any

coherent strategy for exiting an international organisation of which the UK had been a member for close to half a century. Her mantra 'Brexit means Brexit' initially sounded cleverly Delphic, but it became a sick joke. Even after her successor Boris Johnson finally took the UK out of the EU on 31 January 2020, there was still no clear idea what Brexit meant. The country's future seemed more uncertain than at any time since 1940.

And not just its future; also its past. How should we tell the story of British history in the light of the referendum? Had the turn to 'Europe' in 1973 been just a blind alley? Or was the 2016 vote mere nostalgia for a world we (thought we) had lost? Bemused by both future and past, Brexit-era Britons feel challenged about their sense of national identity – because identity has to be rooted in a clear feeling about how we became what we are.

This is not a book about Brexit – its politics and negotiations: these will drag on for years. Instead, I ponder how to think about Britain's history in the light of the Brexit debate. Because the country's passionate arguments about the European Union raised big questions about the ways in which the British understand their past. About which moments they choose to celebrate and which to blot out. And about how to construct a national narrative linking past, present and future. Or, more exactly, national narratives – plural – because a central argument of this book is that there is no single story to be told – whatever politicians may wish us to believe.

For a century, there *was* a dominant national narrative: about the expansion of Britain into a global empire. In 1902 – after victory over the Boers in South Africa – the poet A. C. Benson added words to Edward Elgar's *Pomp and Circumstance* 'March No. 1', extolling the 'Land of Hope and Glory':

> Wider still and wider shall thy bounds be set,
> God, who made thee mighty, make thee mightier yet

But after two world wars and rapid decolonisation, the 'ever-mightier' imperial theme rang hollow. In 1962, Dean Acheson, the former US Secretary of State, declared that Britain had 'lost an empire' but 'not yet found a role'.[1] Over the next decade British leaders – Tory and Labour – tried to join the European Economic Community. But two French vetoes from President Charles de Gaulle blocked their way and it was not until 1973 that the UK (together with Ireland and Denmark) eventually became a member of the EEC. Even though Britain was always an 'awkward partner'[2] – protesting about the size of its budget contributions and the EEC's obsession with farm subsidies – for the next four decades or so the narrative did seem clear: the British had lost a global empire but found a European role.

But in 2016 that new role suddenly also seemed to be lost. During the referendum debate, various historical precedents and patterns were invoked to help frame Brexit Britain's historical self-understanding. Much cited was 'Our Finest Hour' in the Second World War. Leaving the EU 'would be the biggest stimulus to get our butts in gear that we have ever had', declared billionaire Peter Hargreaves, a financier of Brexit. 'It will be like Dunkirk again . . . Insecurity is fantastic.'[3] Developing the 1940 theme, Tory politician Boris Johnson asserted that the past 2,000 years of European history had been characterised by repeated attempts to unify Europe under a single government in order to recover the continent's lost 'golden age' under the Romans. 'Napoleon, Hitler, various people tried this out, and it ends tragically,' he claimed. 'The EU is an attempt to do this by different methods.' The villains of the piece, in Johnson's view, were once again the Germans. 'The Euro has become a means by which superior German productivity is able to gain an absolutely unbeatable advantage over the whole Eurozone.' He depicted Brexit as 'a chance for the British people to be the heroes of Europe and to act as a voice of moderation and common sense, and to stop something getting in my view out of control . . . It is time for someone – it's almost always the British in European history – to say, "We think a different approach is called for".[4]

Also touted as a historical guide for Britain's future was the idea of the 'Anglosphere' – influenced by Winston Churchill's *A History of the English-Speaking Peoples* from the 1950s – and even the concept of an 'Imperial Federation' with the 'White Dominions', as proposed by Joseph Chamberlain in the 1900s. Churchill biographer Andrew Roberts was one of those advocating CANZUK – a confederation of Canada, Australia, New Zealand and the UK – as potentially 'the third pillar of Western Civilisation', together with the USA and the EU. He argued that that 'we must pick up where we left off in 1973' when the 'dream of the English-speaking peoples' was 'shattered by British entry into the EU'. Theresa May spoke in a similarly expansive vein when outlining her government's vision of Brexit. 'June the 23rd was not the moment Britain chose to step back from the world. It was the moment we chose to build a truly Global Britain.' Although stating that she was 'proud of our shared European heritage', May insisted: 'we are also a country that has always looked beyond Europe to the wider world. That is why we are one of the most racially diverse countries in Europe, one of the most multicultural members of the European Union.'[5]

Here were hints of how Brexit might be seen in historical perspective: as the latest attempt to resist a continental tyrant, or as the chance to resume a global role that had been rudely interrupted by joining the EU. But neat historical analogies are not adequate. Nor are simplified benchmarks like 1940 or 1973. We need to probe more deeply what is still often called 'our island story' – and to do so with greater geographical breadth and over a longer time span – in order to gain some perspective on the Brexit malaise.

* * *

Our Island Story was the title of Henrietta Marshall's best-selling *History of England for Boys and Girls*, first published in 1905. In 2010 the education secretary Michael Gove told the Tory party conference that he would 'put British history at the heart of a revived national curriculum', so that 'all pupils will learn our island story'. In 2014 Prime Minister David Cameron lauded Marshall's stirring account of the country's inexorable progress towards liberty, law and parliamentary government.[6] But today a simple 'Whiggish' narrative is implausible. This is a book about 'stories', plural – about different ways in which to see our complicated past. In particular, we need to move beyond the idea of a self-contained 'island', portrayed as adopting various roles over the centuries – empire, Europe, the globe – as if these could be tried on and then taken off, like a suit of clothes. In reality, 'we' have been 'made' by empire, Europe and the world as much as the other way round.

And the 'we' – the United Kingdom – has also been a shifting entity, a historically conflicted archipelago, comprising more than six thousand islands, and not a unitary fixed space occupied by a people whom many in England still tend to call, interchangeably, 'British' or 'English'.[7] In particular, 'our island story' omits Ireland – 'John Bull's Other Island', as George Bernard Shaw entitled his satirical comedy of 1904 about an English con man who dupes Irish villagers into mortgaging their homes so he can turn the place into an amusement park. Ireland was brought under English rule in the Norman period but never really subdued, despite the Acts of Union in 1801. Its centuries of turmoil and tragedy, in turn, had a profound impact on the island of Britain.

This, then, is a book about history, framed by geography. But it is also a book about ways of thinking, because being 'islanded' is a state of mind.[8] The English Channel did not always seem a great divide: for four centuries the Anglo-Norman kings ruled a domain that straddled it and treated water as a bridge rather than a barrier.

The sense of 'providential insularity' came later, as a product of England's Protestant Reformation, followed by several centuries of war against the continental Catholic 'other', embodied in Spain and then France. As the power of Protestantism waned in twentieth-century Britain, providential insularity was given a new lease of life by two wars against Germany, and especially by the way that 1940 has become inscribed in national history and popular memory.

Nor would the 'island' narrative have proved so enthralling had medieval English kings not created such a strong state, which they then tried to impose by force on their neighbours. The Welsh were incorporated in the 1530s, the Scots not until 1707, but thereafter – during the eighteenth, nineteenth and most of the twentieth centuries – the London government effectively directed the whole of 'our' island of Britain. Yet making the 'other island' across the Irish Sea 'British' as well proved a far more difficult task. The English failed to do so, but the struggle ebbed and flowed for centuries, costing several million lives through war and famine. At points along the way the 'Irish Question' also tested the unity of Britain itself – in the 1640s, for instance, when it was the catalyst for civil war, and in the Home Rule crisis before 1914. In 1920, after the brutal war of independence, it resulted in the partitioning of the island of Ireland in two between an independent Catholic state and an embattled, Protestant-dominated Ulster clinging on to its Britishness within the UK.

In the mid-1960s the rancorous issues of partition and sectarianism escalated into the three-decade long 'Troubles' in Northern Ireland, whose brutal violence was quelled only by the Good Friday agreement of 1998. This brought a ragged peace to Ulster and also redefined the political geometry of Ireland, opening up the border between the two states. Yet during the EU referendum debate, the Conservative and Unionist Party closed its eyes to recent history.

Only after the vote to leave the EU did it start to grapple with the profound implications that Brexit would have for Northern Ireland, the peace process and the unity of the UK.

By the end of the twentieth century, both the Good Friday agreement and the institution of devolved governments in Scotland and Wales presaged a different set of relationships between and within the two main islands. In England the apparent indifference of London to the socio-economic problems of the regions, especially in the north, played a significant part in the Leave victory in 2016, and the failure of the Westminster Parliament to resolve – or even address – the challenges of Brexit aggravated this sense of alienation. Yet the saga of Britishness – forged by war and burnished by retelling – continues to exert immense power, whether deployed by politicians or dramatised in movies. Equally potent are the individual national stories of the Scots, Welsh and Irish – even of the English without the others[9] – all reinvigorated by the crisis of the Union. In a struggle for the future, the past really matters. Yet not just the past of the two islands and their tangled relations with continental Europe. The global dimension is equally important.

Developing as a seafaring nation from the sixteenth century, the English used their relative security from the Continent as both a sanctuary and a springboard. Exploiting their growing naval reach they were able to prey on foreign rivals, profit richly from the slave trade, open up markets and create settlements – first in the Caribbean and North America; later in the Indian subcontinent, Australasia and Africa. The wealth thereby generated played a critical part in Britain's precocious industrial revolution. It also drew the country gradually and messily into a patchwork of formal empire, which the British then struggled to rule on the cheap in the face of bigger and stronger international challengers. By the 1970s, after two world wars and an often violent process of decolonisation, the British Empire has disappeared. But the UK remained a global economy, shaped by its commercial and financial past, and the stories of global greatness, now somehow disconnected from the empire project, still appealed to political and public nostalgia. More problematic legacies of empire, such as the slave trade or mass immigration, tended to be ignored in the grand narrative of our island's worldwide reach.

Those simple words 'island' and 'stories' are, therefore, worthy of close examination. To do so we need to engage with 'big history' and the *longue durée* in ways which do justice to the English stamp on these islands' histories without being narrowly Anglocentric. And although *Island Stories* has been prompted by the Brexit imbroglio, it reflects deeper concerns. There is now a profusion of innovative and detailed scholarly research, based on analysis of new sources and fresh insight into old sources. But much of this work takes the form of micro-histories, addressing narrow topics for an academic audience, and a good deal of it has been shaped by the 'cultural turn' – which privileges food, dress, and gender relations and frowns on political history as being antiquated and irrelevant. As a result, big-picture narratives have been left to popular writers skimming the surface, or to politicians advancing their own agenda. This short book is an attempt by one professional historian to start filling this gap, at a time when political and international history really matter.

The four main chapters outline and probe four alternative, if overlapping, ways of telling our island stories in the era of Brexit. They draw on some of the narratives that have been offered by famous voices of the twentieth century, such as Joseph Chamberlain, Winston Churchill, Hugh Gaitskell and Margaret Thatcher, and also by politicians of our own time including Boris Johnson and Jacob Rees-Mogg. But the chapters range far beyond the problems and personalities of the twentieth century, and offer some very long views to offset the national fixation with 1973 and 1940.

Each chapter explores an overarching theme, reflecting on the history of the last millennium. The first chapter 'Decline' looks at how and why Britain's place in the world has changed in recent centuries, and whether the turn to Europe represented realistic statesmanship or a failure of national will. I also consider the country's assets – both 'hard' and 'soft' power – in the Brexit era and the powerful hold of 'heritage' in the national culture. The second chapter looks more closely at Britain's engagement with Europe, going back beyond the Protestant Reformation to the Anglo-Norman kings, and exploring that ambiguous role of the Channel as both barrier and bridge. The third chapter turns to the long history of Britain, tracing the impact of English empire-building on the archipelago and assessing the two Acts of Union in 1707 and 1801 that brought Scotland and then Ireland into the United Kingdom. The chapter also discusses the impacts of two world wars, 1990s devolution and the Brexit vote on the unity of the Union. The fourth chapter, 'Empire', emphasises the role of slavepower as well as seapower in making Britain great, but also examines how the ideology of freedom both promoted the empire and eroded it. In the last section of this chapter, 'The Empire comes home', I offer a historical context for the impassioned Brexit debate on immigration and reflect on a post-imperial country in which racist attitudes coexist with multiculturalism.

In the concluding chapter, 'Taking Control of Our Past', I reflect more generally on what the political feuding since 2016, and the 2020 Covid-19 pandemic, reveal of Britain's deeper problems in dealing with Brexit and also in coming to terms with its past. This is, of course, a personal view – on topics that are highly contested, for history has become an integral part of the country's Brexitoxic political argument. *Island Stories* is a contribution to that fevered debate. And by taking a long view, it also offers an unconventional history of Britain.

1

Decline

Of every reader, the attention will be excited by an history of the decline and fall of the Roman empire, the greatest, perhaps, and most awful scene in the history of mankind.

Edward Gibbon, 1788[1]

Thus began the final paragraph of Edward Gibbon's magnum opus *The History of the Rise, Decline and Fall of the Roman Empire.* Volume one had appeared in 1776, just as the American colonies declared independence from Britain and proclaimed themselves a republic. The sixth and last volume was published in 1788, a year before *ancien régime* France was engulfed by revolution. Its fratricidal anarchy would spawn Napoleon's continental empire.

Gibbon's chronicle of the *Pax Romana* became a literary classic during the nineteenth century, as Britain saw off the Napoleonic challenge and grew into a global power – spanning the world from India to Africa, from the Near East to Australasia. By the end of the century the term *Pax Britannica* had entered the vernacular. But there were also creeping fears of imperial mortality – captured by Rudyard Kipling, the bard of empire, in his *fin de siècle* poem 'Recessional':

Far-called, our navies melt away;
On dune and headland sinks the fire:
Lo, all our pomp of yesterday
Is one with Nineveh and Tyre![2]

BULL AND HIS BURDENS.

An 1879 Punch *cartoon by John Tenniel shows John Bull the ox carrying the world's woes on his back – Russia, Afghanistan, Egypt, Scotland (a recent financial scandal in Glasgow), a striker and a gleeful African warrior from the costly Zulu Wars.*

Britain's Victorian and Edwardian leaders sought strategies that might save their unlikely empire from a Roman fate. How best to deal with jealous rivals? By military confrontation, or selective appeasement? The first could sap the nation's wealth and power; the latter risked letting in the barbarians by the back door. They also wrestled with the Roman tension between *libertas* and *imperium*, of civic virtues supposedly corrupted by militarism and luxury. Would British imperialism undermine political liberty at home? Conversely, would a freedom-loving people have the backbone to resist the jackals of the global jungle? These dilemmas became acute during the era of the two world wars.

On a larger canvas, Gibbon's Rome has provided a template for telling the story of Britain's changing place in the world over the last five centuries in terms of a great empire's rise, decline and fall. This held a perennial, almost mesmeric fascination for a political class that modelled itself on imperial Rome. Under this narrative, however, lurk problematic notions of empire. Should it be understood as a clearly defined possession – eventually 'lost' or 'surrendered'? Or was it like an increasingly outmoded and ill-fitting suit of clothes, which was finally tossed aside? This chapter looks more closely at Britain's changing global role and at related shifts in the country's power and prosperity – arguing that the Gibbonian concept of 'decline' is deeply misleading. In doing so, it also highlights a recurrent pattern of British political rhetoric from the late nineteenth century right up to the present. Politicians have frequently couched their campaigns to change national policy within a dramatic 'declinist' narrative of the recent past. Here are a few examples.[3]

Ideologists of 'decline'

Joseph Chamberlain has been described by historian Peter Clarke as Britain's 'first leading politician to propose a drastic method of averting the sort of national decline' that he 'saw as otherwise inevitable'. Chamberlain was also the first to do so in a style of populist nationalism crafted for an era of mass politics. He and his followers posed a 'Radical Right' challenge to mainstream Toryism, preaching what has been called a gospel of 'messianic catastrophism'.[4]

Chamberlain was a self-made Birmingham businessman who got rich as a manufacturer of screws, before moving into politics in the 1870s as a reforming Mayor of Birmingham ('Radical Joe') and then as a member of W. E. Gladstone's second Liberal Cabinet. His ego and energy splintered not one but two parties – first the Liberals in 1886 because of his opposition to Home Rule for Ireland, and then the Conservatives in 1903 over 'Tariff Reform'. Quite what that phrase meant was almost as elusive as 'Brexit' in our own day, but at its core was Chamberlain's conviction that the rise of competitors such as Germany and the United States must be met by abandoning the Victorian precepts of 'free trade' and imposing tariffs in order to protect British industry and to consolidate the empire. Only this strategy could save 'the weary Titan' who 'staggers under the too vast orb of its fate.' He told the colonials, 'We have borne the burden for many years. We think it is time that our children should assist us.' The alternative was decline into 'a fifth-rate nation' – another Venice or Holland. 'All history is the history of states once powerful and then decaying,' Chamberlain told a political rally in 1903. 'Is Britain to be numbered among the decaying states: is all the glory of the past to be forgotten? . . . Or are we to take up a new youth as members of a great empire, which will continue for generation after generation the strength, the power and the glory of the British race?'[5]

Chamberlain's aim was to shore up Britain's power base in an era of rival empires by protecting its existing manufacturing industries. For him, structural economic change was unacceptable: it would mean replacement by 'secondary and inferior' industries, causing 'individual suffering' to the working man without 'any real compensation to the nation'. 'Your once great trade in sugar refining is gone,' he declaimed mockingly in another speech in 1903: 'all right, try jam. Your iron trade is going; never mind, you can make mouse traps.'[6] But although Chamberlain's populist crusade for tariff reform briefly caught the public imagination, it soon burnt out. The main effect was to divide the Conservatives and pave the way for the Liberal landslide of 1906. Chamberlain died, bitter and disillusioned, in July 1914 – a month before the Great War began. Ironically, during the 1920s and 1930s, the very restructuring and diversification he deplored would transform the Birmingham area. Chemicals and electrical engineering, aviation and motor vehicles not only rejuvenated the Midlands economy but also prepared Britain to wage a second world war in the era of airpower.[7]

Winston Churchill was another politician who, in later life, became obsessed with Britain's decline – doing so, like Chamberlain, when in opposition and with one eye on gaining power. Conviction and calculation conjoined. After a spectacular political rise on either side of the Great War, culminating in Chancellorship of the Exchequer at the age of 50, the premiership seemed within Churchill's grasp. But then, for a decade from 1929, he was cast out into the political wilderness, regarded as a wilful opportunist too mercurial for inclusion in the National Governments of Ramsay MacDonald, Stanley Baldwin and Neville Chamberlain – Joe's son. To attract attention he campaigned loudly on various causes, from Edward VIII in the Abdication Crisis to air rearmament against Germany. It is the latter for which Churchill's 'wilderness years' are now best remembered. But the underlying issue for him – and the one that sustained the rest of his life – was Britain's decline as a great power.

Churchill's crusade, however, took a very different form from Chamberlain's. He was and remained a staunch Free Trader who had broken with the Tories over tariff reform. Churchill's vision of Britain's greatness centred not on the white-settler colonies that Chamberlain wanted to weld into an imperial economic bloc, but on India, which young Winston had experienced first-hand as a soldier fighting for his Queen Empress. In 1931 the Conservative party adopted a policy of giving India 'dominion status' within the British Empire – potentially setting it on a course of devolution and independence similar to that already conceded to Canada, Australia, New Zealand and South Africa. Incensed, Churchill broke with the party leadership and embarked on a four-year crusade against what became the Government of India Act of 1935. Now virtually forgotten in British history, this was the biggest parliamentary struggle of the 1930s – eclipsing in time and passion even the issues of Germany and rearmament – for which Churchill rolled out some of his most extravagant rhetoric.

Inveighing in February 1931 against the 'nauseating' sight of 'Mr Gandhi, a seditious Middle Temple lawyer, now posing as a fakir of a type well known in the East, striding half-naked up the steps of the Viceregal palace . . . to parley on equal terms with the representative of the King-Emperor,' Churchill claimed that India was 'no ordinary question of party politics' but 'one of those supreme issues which come upon us from time to time', like going to war against Germany in 1914. A month later he warned that 'the continuance of our present confusion and disintegration will reduce us within a generation, and perhaps sooner, to the degree of States like Holland and Portugal, which nursed valiant races, and held great possessions, but were stripped of them in the crush and competition of the world. That would be a melancholy end to all the old glories and recent triumphs.'[8] The root problem, in Churchill's opinion, was a failure of national will since the Great War. 'The British lion, so fierce and valiant in bygone days, so dauntless and unconquerable through the agony of Armageddon, can now be chased by rabbits from the fields and forests of his former glory. It is not that our strength is seriously impaired. We are suffering from a disease of the will. We are the victims of a nervous collapse, of a morbid state of the mind.'[9]

If willpower alone was what counted, Winston would have won

the battle over India. But he led a diehard minority within the Tory party. What's more, his vehemence and obduracy not only estranged him from the party leadership; it also undermined his credibility on more consequential matters. His description of the Indian nationalist leaders as 'evil and malignant Brahmins' with their 'itching fingers stretching and scratching at the vast pillage of a derelict empire' was striking, but it was 'not likely to make comparable descriptions of genuinely evil men credible'.[10] Churchill's hyperbole about India helped keep him in the political wilderness. Only with the onset of a second German war was he brought back into government.

Churchill never modified his opinions about India, empire and decline. Even in the darkest days of the Second World War in April 1942 – as Hitler's Afrika Korps advanced on Cairo and the Japanese conquered Burma – he deplored any concessions to Indian nationalists. When President Franklin D. Roosevelt breezily informed Prime Minister Churchill that the British should concede self-government to India, on the lines of the Articles of Confederation under which the new United States had initially been run after independence in 1783, Churchill replied that he 'could not be responsible' for such a policy and even threatened to make it a resignation issue.[11] In November 1942 he warned defiantly: 'We mean to hold our own. I have not become the King's First Minister to preside over the liquidation of the British Empire.'[12]

On this, Churchill proved as good as his word. But not because liquidation did not happen; only that he did not have to preside over it. For that lucky escape, he had the British electorate to thank: they voted him out of office in July 1945. What one might call his 'second wilderness years', from 1945 to 1951, allowed him to watch from the sidelines and criticise with impunity Clement Attlee's Labour Government for its 'scuttle' from India and Burma in 1947. Some of his predictions had prescience – for instance that 'any attempt to establish the reign of a Hindu numerical majority in India will never be achieved without a civil war' – but, as in the 1930s, they were blunted by his jeremiad of decline and his lamentations about lack of will. 'It is with deep grief that I watch the clattering down of the British Empire with all its glories, and all the services it has rendered to mankind. I am sure that in the hour of our victory now not so long ago, we had the power to make a solution of our difficulties which would have been honourable and lasting. Many have defended Britain against her foes. None can defend her against herself.'[13]

In similar vein, campaigning for the premiership again in October 1951, Churchill denounced Attlee's six years as marking 'the greatest fall in the rank and stature of Britain in the world' since 'the loss of the American colonies two hundred years ago.' He asserted that 'our Oriental Empire has been liquidated' and 'our influence among the nations is now less than it has ever been in any period since I remember.'[14] Back in office, however, the ailing Churchill did not fight the tide. He saw little choice but to approve the withdrawal of British troops from the Suez Canal Zone in 1954, arousing the anger of a new generation of Tory diehards, which opened the door to Egypt's nationalisation of the Canal two years later.

Although Tories have been particularly prone to narratives of decline, something of the sort also underpinned Labour's election victory of 1945. The party's manifesto 'Let Us Face the Future' was rooted in a historical narrative of lost greatness – this time not about empire, but about social promise betrayed by wilful politics.[15] 'So far as Britain's contribution is concerned', the manifesto argued, 'this war will have been won by its people, not by any one man.' (The Tory campaign featured Churchill.) The Great War had similarly been a people's victory, Labour went on, but afterwards the people had allowed 'the hard-faced men who had done well out of the war' (Stanley Baldwin's famous phrase) to craft 'the kind of peace that suited themselves'. And so, despite winning the war, 'the people lost that peace.' By which Labour meant not only the Treaty of Versailles, but also 'the social and economic policy which followed the fighting'.

In the years after 1918, those 'hard-faced men' and their political allies kept control of the government, and also the banks, mines, big industries, most of the press and the cinema. This, said Labour's manifesto, happened in all the big industrialised countries. So, 'The great inter-war slumps were not acts of God or of blind forces. They were the sure and certain result of the concentration of too much economic power in the hands of too few men.' They acted solely in the interest of their own private monopolies 'which may be likened to totalitarian oligarchies within our democratic State. They had and they felt no responsibility to the nation.'

Similar forces were at work now in 1945, the manifesto warned. 'The problems and pressure of the post-war world threaten our security and progress as surely as – though less dramatically than – the Germans threatened them in 1940. We need the spirit of Dunkirk and of the Blitz sustained over a period of years. The Labour Party's programme is a practical expression of that spirit applied to the tasks of peace.' On election morning, 5 July, the pro-Labour *Daily Mirror* told readers: 'Vote on behalf of the men who won the victory for you. You failed to do so in 1918. The result is known to all.' The paper devoted most of its front page to reprinting a Zec cartoon first published on VE Day in May. This showed a weary, battered soldier holding out a laurel wreath labelled 'Victory and Peace in Europe'. The caption read: 'Here You Are – Don't Lose it Again.'[16]

This narrative of the lost peace, torn from the hands of the people by greedy capitalists, was sharpened by bitter memories of mass unemployment during the 1920s and 1930s. Together they informed Labour's campaign of nationalisation after its triumph in 1945. The flagship policies of bringing the commanding heights of the economy – industries such as coal, steel, utilities and railways – into public ownership and providing a stronger social safety net through the welfare state and the National Health Service were presented as repayment to the people for their sacrificial efforts during two world wars in a quarter of a century.

Once built, however, Labour's edifice became a central target of the declinist narrative of another Tory three decades later: Margaret Thatcher, Prime Minister from 1979 to 1990. She outlined her stark version of history in the introduction to her memoirs, *The Downing Street Years*: 'Britain in 1979 was a nation that had had the stuffing knocked out of it' over the course of the previous century. In economic terms, Thatcher acknowledged that some degree of relative decline was inevitable, once rivals such as America and Germany caught up with Britain's head start. But, she argued, the country had 'failed to respond to the challenge effectively. We invested less; we educated and trained our people to a lower standard; and we allowed our workers and manufacturers to combine in various cartels that restricted competition and reduced efficiency.' Most serious of all, after 1945 the country had indulged in a protracted and disastrous experiment with socialism. This 'represented a centralising, managerial, bureaucratic, interventionist style of government', which 'jammed a finger in every pie' on the principle that 'the gentleman in Whitehall really know better what is good for the people than the people know themselves.'[17]

Breaking the hold of Labour statism was not merely a domestic priority. Thatcher argued that 'Britain's weakened economic position meant that its international role was bound to be cramped and strained as well.' She cited the failure of the Suez expedition of 1956 as a turning point – in her opinion a military victory undermined by 'political and economic weakness' because Anthony Eden's government withdrew the troops that had regained the Canal after a run on the pound encouraged by Washington. 'Whatever the details', she continued briskly (and evasively), this defeat 'entered the British soul and distorted our perspective on Britain's place in the world.' Thanks to the 'Suez syndrome', as she called it, 'having previously exaggerated our power, we now exaggerated our impotence.'[18]

Her account of history was not just retrospective wisdom. Reversing decline was almost the leitmotif of Thatcher's politics. 'Britain's prestige in the eyes of the world has gone down and down,' she had declared during her very first election campaign in 1950, when she was 24: 'We Conservatives are not afraid to face the future whatever problem it entails, because it is our earnest desire to make Great Britain great again.'[19] Such rhetoric was certainly at the heart of her message in the 1979 campaign. 'I can't *bear* Britain in decline. I just can't,' she exclaimed to a BBC interviewer. 'We who either defeated or rescued half Europe, who kept half Europe free, when otherwise it would be in chains. And look at us now!'[20] She told an audience in Bolton: 'Unless we change our ways and our direction, our greatness as a nation will soon be a footnote in the history books, a distant memory of an offshore island, lost in the mists of time, like Camelot, remembered kindly for its noble past.'[21] This was her refrain right to the end. 'Let me give you my vision,' she declaimed in her final election broadcast. 'Somewhere ahead lies greatness for our country again; this I know in my heart.'[22]

Thatcher shared with Joseph Chamberlain and Churchill a Napoleonic belief in the capacity of a great leader to transform history through sheer willpower. Indeed, in her memoirs she applied to herself the famous words of William Pitt the Elder, during the Seven Years' War of 1756–63: 'I know that I can save the country and that no one else can.'[23] And she employed her formidable will and conviction to cover inner insecurities and get her way in an overwhelmingly male world. Not only did she seem happiest when 'up against a wall', biographer Hugo Young observed. But 'when she wasn't actually embattled, she needed to imagine or invent the condition: embattled against the cabinet, against Whitehall, against the country, against the world'.[24]

" We can fly the Union Jack instead of the white flags in Britain, too ! "

After Margaret Thatcher's victory in the Falklands War, Cummings in
the Daily Express *(16 June 1982) shows her waving the Union Jack*
in triumph while white-flag merchants from the Foreign Office
and the Labour party – Tony Benn (middle) and party leader
Michael Foot (right) – lie flat on their backs.

Indeed one can say that her grand narrative of those Downing Street years was constructed around two triumphant battles royal against 'decline': the Falklands War in the spring of 1982 and the miners' strike of 1984–5. Argentina's shock capture of the Falkland Islands, which it claimed as the Malvinas, provoked a cross-party wave of anger in Parliament on 3 April, but Thatcher made the operation to liberate the 1,800 British islanders from Argentine rule into her own personal crusade. And she used the eventual victory over General Leopoldo Galtieri's military junta to make a larger point. 'When we started out, there were the waverers and the fainthearts,' she told a Tory rally in Cheltenham on 3 July 1982. 'Those who believed that our decline was irreversible – that we could never again be what we were.' But now, she proclaimed, 'We have ceased to be a nation in retreat . . . Britain found herself again in the South Atlantic and will not look back from the victory she has won.'[25] Or more pithily, to a jubilant crowd singing 'Rule Britannia' outside 10 Downing Street: 'Great Britain is great again.'[26] Almost as if the mission she had set herself in 1950 had now been accomplished.

In June 1983 the 'Falklands Factor' helped her to win a landslide election victory and in 1984–5 she was ready to take on Arthur Scargill and the striking miners in their last-ditch effort – under the slogan 'jobs, pits and communities' – to stop what was effectively the closure of their industry. For Thatcher, however, the miners became the centrepiece of her struggle to break up the unprofitable and bureaucratic state monopolies and she treated Scargill as the domestic equivalent of General Galtieri. Notes for a speech to Tory backbenchers in July 1984 read:

> Since Office
> Enemy without – beaten him
> & strong in defence
> Enemy within –
> Miners' leaders . . .
> – just as dangerous

Biographer Charles Moore writes that Downing Street staff prepared for the miners' strike as if it were another war. 'Instead of names like Bluff Cove, Goose Green and Mount Longdon, they became familiar with pits like Shirebrook, Manton and Bilston Glen. And once she had vanquished Scargill just like Galtieri, Thatcher won the election of 1987 on the slogan: 'Britain is Great Again. Don't Let Labour Wreck It.'[27]

Yet there were limits to Britain's 'greatness'. Margaret Thatcher was also the Prime Minister who, having liberated 1,800 British subjects from the Argentine junta, in December 1984 signed over 5.5 million other British subjects in Hong Kong to the rule of China – a communist state to boot. Like Churchill over the Canal Zone, she saw no choice given the realities of power. Under the 'one nation, two systems' principle enshrined in the Sino-British Joint Declaration of 1984, British sovereignty would end in 1997 but Hong Kong was to be a 'Special Administrative Region' enjoying 'a high degree of autonomy' for another fifty years, with its social and economic system 'unchanged' and civil and property rights 'protected by law'. Even before the handover in 1997, however, these guarantees were called into question by the Chinese government's brutal repression of the pro-democracy movement in Tiananmen Square in June 1989. And nothing the British government said or did could influence Beijing.

The rhetoric of reversing 'decline' by the assertion of willpower has also been at the heart of the Brexit narrative. Take, for instance, the speech delivered by Tory MP Jacob Rees-Mogg, a leading Brexiter, who took pride in his nickname 'the Honourable Member for the Eighteenth Century'.[28] That, he claimed, was the century in which 'the seeds of our greatness, sown long before in our distinguished history, sown conceivably by Alfred the Great, began to grow and to flourish in a way that led to our extended period of good fortune and greatness.' But Rees-Mogg said that he also wanted to be the 'Honourable Member for the Twenty-First Century' because this was the century in which the country would 'regain its independence' and 'rediscover the opportunities of a truly global Britain'.

'How we came to join the European Union is an important part of understanding our Island story,' Rees-Mogg explained. 'We won the war and were full of optimism about our place in the World, but then came Suez.' In his opinion, the debacle of 1956 had a profound and debilitating effect, permanently undermining the nation's self-confidence. 'Margaret Thatcher tried to break away from that, but it was such a strong feeling that once she had gone it seeped back again.' As a result of Suez, 'the Nation's view of itself changed and the Establishment, the Elite, decided that its job was to manage decline, that the best they could do was to soften the blow of descending downwards, soften the effect on the Nation of being less successful than it had been in the past, and recognise that we would not be able to keep up with other countries. This led to the notion that it was Europe or bust.' But that, he argued, was a false contrast because Britain had ended up with both: in Europe and also bust. The country made the mistake of joining flagging, low-growth economies so that the process of 'managing our decline' became 'part of managing the decline of the whole of the European Union by putting a fortress around it'.

So, he asserted, the 2016 referendum was a vote 'by people who believed in democracy' and 'voted to take back control'. And any attempt by those he derided as 'cave-dwellers' to keep Britain in the EU – in fact if not name – 'would be Suez all over again. It would be the most almighty smash to the national psyche that could be imagined . . . an admission of abject failure . . . that we were not fit, that we were too craven, that we were too weak to be able to govern ourselves . . . Although countries across the Globe can govern themselves, poor little Blighty cannot.' But if, on the other hand, Britain embraced Brexit wholeheartedly, there was 'a world of opportunity ahead of us' as we took 'charge of our own destiny protected by our own laws' and 'setting our own direction' in international affairs rather than 'hiding behind the skirts of the German Chancellor'.

This, then, was Jacob Rees-Mogg's take on contemporary history: the 'brave British people' asserting themselves against the establishment's 'managers of decline', and scorning the nanny state across the Channel. His fixation with 1956 echoed Thatcher's 'Suez syndrome'. His drama of goodies versus baddies paralleled the tone, though not the content, of Labour's 1945 manifesto. And the elevation of willpower was a feature of all these anti-declinist narratives of betrayal. But the spin on Brexit was all his own.

A remarkable rise

On the face of it, decline might seem a plausible description of Great Britain's changing place in the world over the last century or so. In the 1870s, the country possessed more battleships than the rest of the world combined. It directly controlled about a fifth of the earth's surface, including India, Canada and Australasia. It was the world's largest economy, accounting for over 20 per cent of global manufacturing output and a similar proportion of global trade. The first industrial nation had become the greatest power the world had ever seen. A century later, however, Britain had lost nearly all its overseas territories; it accounted for a mere 4 per cent of world manufacturing and about 7 per cent of world trade. The first post-industrial nation was struggling to find its post-imperial role.

Membership of the EEC from 1973 was supposed to resolve that identity crisis – the loss of an outmoded global empire would be offset by a new European dynamic. But in the wake of the 2016 referendum, Brexiters claimed that 'Europe' had been a blind alley and that leaving the EU in 2019 was the way to reverse national decline and retrieve Britain's global greatness.

Yet this preoccupation with Britain's 'decline' can mislead. More historically remarkable is the coutry's rise. That, indeed, had been Gibbon's thesis in the case of Rome: 'The rise of a city, which swelled into an empire, may deserve, as a singular prodigy, the reflection of a philosophic mind. But the decline of Rome was the natural and inevitable effect of immoderate greatness.' Similarly, observed a more recent historian, François Crouzet, 'it is a mistake to think that England's original supremacy was normal and her decline abnormal.'[29] On the contrary, what really needs explanation is the original 'supremacy'.

To put it simply, Great Britain stood in the forefront of the great surges of European expansion that shaped the world between 1700 and 1900: commerce and conquest in the eighteenth century, industry and empire in the nineteenth century. All these movements were intertwined with the lucrative Atlantic slave trade – half of all Africans carried into slavery during the eighteenth century were transported on British vessels – and the profits from that trade lubricated Britain's commercial and industrial revolutions.[30] The country's principal advantage was a relatively secure island base during what was still the era of seapower. Unlike rivals such as France and Prussia/Germany, who shared land borders with belli-cose neighbours, Britain could shelter behind the English Channel – what Shakespeare called the country's 'moat defensive', its 'water-walled bulwark'. Or, to quote Gladstone in 1870, 'the wise dispensation of Providence has cut her off by that streak of silver sea . . . partly from the dangers, absolutely from the temptations, which attend the local neighbourhood of the Continental nations.'[31] Insularity did not guarantee immunity – in 1588, 1804 and 1940 the threat of invasion seemed acute – but it did mean that the British did not require a large standing army of the sort that became normal on the Continent. The Royal Navy, however, was popular and also necessary, not just for direct defence but also because, as an island, increasingly dependent on the import of food and raw materials, Britain needed to protect its seaborne commerce from peacetime privateers and wartime enemies.

Britain's insular position left it ideally placed to capitalise on five great bouts of warfare against France. Whereas French leaders from Louis XIV to Napoleon Bonaparte had to fight their primary battles on land against continental foes, Britain was able to divert more of its resources into the struggle for trade and colonies. The Seven Years' War of 1756–63 left the British in control of most of North America and although thirteen colonies won their independence during the next world war of 1776–83, Britain held on to what became Canada and the British West Indies. The Revolutionary and Napoleonic Wars of 1793–1815 was a period of extended crisis, during which Britain endured long periods of economic isolation, but, in the end, the country won a total victory. French seapower had been destroyed and Britain was left as the world's main colonial power, paramount in India but also increasingly entrenched in Australasia and parts of Africa. Its fleet, previously based mostly at home and in the Baltic and Mediterranean, was now spread around the globe. The Royal Navy's ability to command the seas depended on holding what Admiral Sir John Fisher, First Sea Lord at the start of the Great War, called the 'five strategic keys' that 'lock up the world' – the great British bases at Dover, Gibraltar, Alexandria, the Cape of Good Hope and Singapore.[32]

Established at strategic points around the globe, able to project power through a strong navy and merchant fleet, Britain after 1815 also enjoyed the huge advantage of becoming the world's first industrial nation. The country's initial manufacturing surge had been driven by the cotton trade. All the raw material was imported and most of the production was for export. By 1830, cotton goods accounted for half the value of British exports and raw cotton made up 20 per cent of net imports. After the cotton boom subsided, iron and steel became the new growth sector, stimulated by the railway-building mania of the 1830s and 1840s, and then sustained by British dominance in the financing and construction of railways around the world. By 1860, a country with only 2 per cent of the world's population was producing half the world's iron and steel and accounted for 40 per cent of world trade in manufactured goods. It had the highest GDP in the world and its population, despite vast inequalities of wealth, enjoyed the highest average per capita income.[33]

During much of the Victorian era, therefore, Britain did seem truly great as the leading colonial empire, the world's industrial giant and the dominant sea power. In the decades after 1815, the Royal Navy appeared to rule the waves, driving piracy from the Indian Ocean and the China Seas, confronting slave traders in the Caribbean and South Atlantic, and aggressively promoting Britain's commercial interests – particularly in the Opium War of 1839–42 to open up China to British trade. Many foreign leaders had no doubt that British power was decisive. 'Only England, mistress of the seas, can protect us against the united force of European reaction,' exclaimed Simón Bolívar, the liberator of South America, as he contemplated the danger of Spanish reconquest. Muhammad Ali, the Ottomans' unruly viceroy of Egypt, remarked that 'with the English for my friends I can do anything: without their friendship I can do nothing'.[34] The analogy between the *Pax Britannica* and the *Pax Romana* did not sound far-fetched. Like Rome, Britain seemed to rule or shape much of the world, and was what the poet Alfred Tennyson rhapsodised in 1886 as

> . . . the mightiest Ocean-power on earth
> Our own fair isle, the lord of every sea.[35]

The country's global power was on flamboyant display during celebrations for Victoria's Diamond Jubilee in June 1897. A week of martial
festivities culminated in a vast naval pageant off the Isle of Wight
when the Queen reviewed 165 of her warships manned by 40,000
sailors. The highpoint was 22 June when Her Majesty processed in
state along six miles of London streets amid cheering crowds. Speaking
for most observers, the *Manchester Guardian* described the theme of
the celebrations as 'the world-wide Empire of Britain . . . the exultant
expression of a power the greatest in the world's history'. Onlookers
were particularly intrigued by contingents of troops from the Queen's
domains all over the globe. A reporter for the new popular newspaper
The Daily Mail could hardly contain his patriotic fervour as he
described them marching up Ludgate Hill to St Paul's:

> white men, yellow men, brown men, black men, every colour,
> every continent, every race, every speech – and all up in arms for
> THE BRITISH EMPIRE AND THE BRITISH QUEEN. Up they
> came, more and more, new types, new realms at every couple of
> yards, an anthropological museum – a living gazeteer of the British
> Empire. With them came their English officers, whom they obey
> and follow like children. And you begin to understand, as never
> before what the Empire amounts to.[36]

Much of the rhetoric from that week in June 1897 was similarly
extravagant, often preposterous. A jubilee mug, inscribed with
portraits of the 78-year-old monarch, carried the legend *The Centre
of a World's Desire*. A Canadian poet penned his own tribute:

> Here's to Queen Victoria
> Dressed in all her regalia
> With one foot in Canada
> And the other in Australia.[37]

A truly remarkable posture, but not one that could be sustained for long. In fact, the world we have lost was one that we were bound to lose. Britain's global power was always more limited than appearances suggested. A closer look at the nature of that power – economic, international and imperial – will help explain why.

The changing relativities of wealth and power

It is a precept of international affairs that wealth is needed to underpin power: to quote historian Paul Kennedy, there is 'a very significant correlation *over the longer term* between productive and revenue-raising capacities, on the one hand, and military strength, on the other'.[38] The British case certainly fits that broad argument. In 1880, Britain produced nearly 23 per cent of the world's manufactured goods; only 10 per cent in 1928 when Churchill was Chancellor of the Exchequer and a mere 4 per cent in 1980, around the start of Thatcher's premiership. As a trading nation Britain's slide was slower but the end result was similar. In 1899 Britain accounted for 33 per cent of the world's exports of manufactured goods, 25 per cent in 1950 and less than 10 per cent in 1980.[39] While Britain's share of the world's wealth gradually diminished, the cost of armaments rose exponentially. In the 1980s, for instance, 385 Tornado fighters for the RAF cost more in real terms than all the 21,000 Spitfires produced before and during the Second World War.[40] Yet a nation that fell behind in the spiral of technological sophistication risked eclipse as a first-rank power, especially if others overtook it in economic capacity.

And this was bound to happen. Britain's Victorian-era economic supremacy was in a sense artificial, given the country's size and population. Britain's comparative advantage was certain to be reduced once the process of industrialisation spread to countries with larger populations and greater resources – Germany in the late nineteenth century, America during the twentieth century and China in the twenty-first. The United States and the People's Republic were both countries the size of a continent, blessed with a booming workforce, abundant natural resources and a vast tariff-free internal market. Apart from being disadvantaged in the long run by relative size, Britain was also susceptible to the 'catch-up' phenomenon. Once countries had crossed a basic socio-economic threshold, they could copy an economic leader's technological innovations, rather than having to learn by trial and error. And the growth rates of previously underdeveloped countries always look particularly spectacular – the 'Asian tigers', for instance, in the 1960s, and China during the last quarter-century.

The predominant British response to economic catch-up was to consolidate existing advantages. One of these was its naval-industrial complex – based on integrated steel/armament/shipbuilding firms such as Vickers, Armstrong-Whitworth and John Brown, as well as the Royal Dockyards – which later diversified into military aircraft and tanks. In the early 1930s, Britain and France shared half of global trade in armaments almost equally between them; in 1938, Hawker-Siddeley advertised itself 'the leading aircraft organisation in the world'. The British arms industry was boosted by the two world wars and sustained by the Cold War. Even though the 'warfare state', like the slave trade, is now largely omitted from general narratives about the British economy, it matters as much in the history of modern Britain as the 'welfare state'.[41]

Even more important were financial and commercial services – another aspect of Britain's economy often neglected by narratives of rise and decline that focus on heroic industrialism. This service sector coexisted with the development and mutation of industrialisation; indeed these processes were often complementary because goods can be derived from services just as much as services from goods – exemplified by innovations across the centuries ranging from bills of exchange and actuarial tables to barcoding and computerised trading.[42] Britain's merchant navy, most of it serving non-British customers, headed the list of 'invisible' earnings, supported by insurance and banking. Together with profits from overseas assets such as railways, plantations, utilities and oil concessions, these earnings were equivalent to around 75 per cent of the earnings from exports of domestic merchandise in the 1890s.[43] These more than covered the gap between Britain's imports and exports, and they provided a 'war chest' on which British governments drew in both world wars. Indeed, during the 1930s, the Treasury referred to Britain's financial position as the 'fourth arm' – as central to waging a future war as the three armed services.

The other response to sharper economic competition was to shift from free trade to protectionism. In the 1900s, Joseph Chamberlain may have failed in his campaign for tariff reform, but in 1932, at the nadir of the world depression after Britain had abandoned the gold standard, his son Neville – then Chancellor of the Exchequer – steered it through the Commons with Joe's widow watching proudly from the gallery. In a trading economy now protected by tariffs, 'Imperial Preference', meaning preferentially lower rates, was accorded to countries of the British Empire. An embryonic Sterling area was also formed during the 1930s, and then consolidated during the Second World War. This overlapped with Imperial Preference but was not coterminous. Canada, though enjoying preferential tariffs, was outside the Sterling Area; countries in Latin America and Scandinavia belonged to the latter but not the former. Between 1913 and 1938 the empire's share of British exports rose from 22 per cent to 47 per cent, and during the interwar years the empire attracted far more new British foreign investment than non-imperial countries – a contrast with the pre-1914 story.[44] The empire/Commonwealth and the Sterling Area became the framework for British foreign economic policy – a privileged market for goods and capital which tried to insulate the domestic economy from international competition from the thirties to the late sixties.

The end of imperial preference and Britain's entry into the EEC broadly coincided with the demise of the Sterling Area, the onset of the oil crisis and the collapse of the post-war boom. The long 1970s recession accelerated the process of deindustrialisation for all Western European countries, but Britain's experience of it was exacerbated by the ferocity of class politics in the Thatcher era. Within this complex nexus of global economic change, it is no simple task to isolate the historical consequences of joining the EEC. Suffice to say here that a crude declinist narrative fails to take account of the country's adaptive economic changes since the 1970s: an accelerating shift into services and the success of the financial sector, which adjusted particularly well to the post-imperial era.

'As the good ship sterling sank, the City was able to scramble aboard a much more seaworthy vessel, the Eurodollar.'[45] This term signified dollar assets held not in the USA but in Europe – starting with those created by Middle Eastern states from the profits of the 1970s oil shocks. They were attracted to the City of London by the tax benefits on offer and by the deliberately more relaxed regulatory environment than Wall Street. But this was not the 'old' City, geared to sterling and the British economy, but a 'new' City, 'externally orientated' and 'foreign-owned' (dominated by US, Japanese and continental European banks) and which 'flourished as long as it was left alone by the authorities'.[46] This externalisation process accelerated when the Thatcher government ended exchange controls in 1979 and encouraged the 'Big Bang' deregulation of the stock market. In 1981 only 3.6 per cent of the UK stock market was owned by foreigners but the proportion then rose to 43.1 per cent in 2010 and 53.9 per cent in 2016. There are, of course, still plenty of British players in this business – Jacob Rees-Mogg, for instance, made his multimillion fortune as a hedge-fund manager – but in large measure the City had adapted to change by becoming an immensely lucrative offshore banking sector through which foreigners, not least post-Soviet Russian oligarchs, could move their money without too many questions or impediments.[47]

So the erosion of Britain's relative advantage in manufacturing did not mean that the country became a minor feature of the world economy. On the contrary: today it is the tenth-largest global exporter and fifth-largest global importer; it ranks second or third in both inward and outward direct foreign investment. In economic terms Britain is roughly where one might expect for a country of its size, resources and historic commercial expertise. What has changed is that Britain's *relative* power internationally has diminished because, over the last century, other states have generated economies that are equal or superior to it.

What mattered even more for the country's place on the world stage was the changing nature of geopolitics. International rivalries intensified from the 1860s, after a half-century of peace since the defeat of Napoleon. And then revolutions in the technology of warfare over the subsequent century negated many of the benefits of Britain's insular position.

Despite what is a common belief, 'European peace in the nineteenth century did not derive to any great degree from Britain's maintaining a continental balance.'[48] That equilibrium stemmed from the exhaustion of Europe in 1815, after more than two decades of ruinous war, and the acceptance of the post-Napoleonic peace by all the continental powers except defeated France. Rather than the *Pax Britannica* sustaining the peace it was peace that sustained the *Pax*. Indeed Britain was almost a free rider – allowed to concentrate its resources on global expansion because of the unusual tranquillity of Europe, which was in marked contrast to the eras of Philip II, Louis XIV and Napoleon.

When continental states once more resorted to war as an instrument of policy – resulting in the unification of Italy and then Germany between 1859 and 1871 – Britain could do little to affect the outcome. Its trump card, the Royal Navy, was largely impotent in the face of fast-moving crises in the hinterland of Europe, and the British did not adopt the continental practice of large standing armies sustained by military conscription. In 1871, during the Franco-Prussian war, Lord Salisbury reckoned that whereas the Austrians and the Germans could each put over a million men into the field, and the Russians 1.5 million, Britain's 'utmost strength' for 'foreign action' was 100,000. Little wonder that Otto von Bismarck, the Prussian chancellor, reportedly scoffed that if the British army landed on the German coast, he would send the local police force to arrest it.[49] Bismarck's new German Empire – created through successive victories over Denmark, Austria and France – became the greatest military power on the continent, dominating Central Europe. Benjamin Disraeli called the Franco-Prussian War of 1870–1 'a greater political event than the French Revolution . . . The balance of power has been entirely destroyed and the country which suffers most . . . is England.'[50]

Even more important for future geopolitics was the outcome of the American Civil War. At the start, in 1861, Britain declared its neutrality: 80 per cent of Britain's cotton imports came from the Confederacy, supporting a textile industry that employed 4 million people. And the ethical issues looked confused: the Federal government claimed to be fighting to preserve the Union, not to abolish slavery, and many English liberals saw the Confederate cause as a war for national liberation, like the recent secession of the Italian states from the Habsburg Empire. In October 1862 Gladstone told an audience in Newcastle that the 'leaders of the South have made an army; they are making, it appears, a navy; and they have made what is more than either, they have made a nation.' Indeed, he welcomed the potential break-up of the Union because it was 'in the general interests of Nations that no State should swell to the dimensions of a continent.'[51]

But talk of possible British mediation in the conflict was a passing phase. By April 1865, the North, with its far superior resources, had defeated the 'Rebellion' and the United States of America regained its unity 'from sea to shining sea'. The implications of a country the size of a continent were not lost on Europeans. In 1866 the French economist Michel Chevalier urged Europe to unify in the face of 'the political colossus that has been created on the other side of the Atlantic'. And in 1882, as the pace and intensity of economic development accelerated throughout America's vast and now peaceful single market, the German writer Constantin Frantz considered it 'hardly preventable' that 'the New World will outstrip the Old World in the not far distant future'.[52]

What is more, the balance of force across the whole world was shifting against Britain. After the post-1815 lull, imperial rivalries renewed with the scramble for Africa in the 1880s and 1890s and the attempted partition of China at the turn of the century. Britain's naval supremacy had by then been undermined. In 1883 the Royal Navy boasted 38 battleships; the rest of the world had 40. By 1897 Britain was outnumbered: 62 against 96.[53] By this time the Russian Empire had expanded across Asia to the Pacific, creating friction along the borders of British India. And other non-European powers were emerging. Japan had industrialised and turned its economic strength into military might, defeating China in 1894–5 and Russia in 1904–5.

In the first half of the twentieth century, the British therefore tried to defend a global position that had been consolidated during a rare half-century of European peace and stability after 1815. And they had to do so against rivals which had caught up with Britain, and even surpassed it, in economic and military capability. France remained a competitor in the 1920s and 1930s, and the Japanese threat was acute in 1937–42. But the most momentous and sustained challenge came from the German Reich.

Unified Germany's first bid for hegemony, in 1914–18, was stopped but at great cost. Britain and the empire lost one million dead, as well as nearly 15 per cent of the country's total assets. The war also saw a geopolitical shift to the Pacific as both Japan and America – wartime allies of Britain – developed into major naval and economic powers. And although the Habsburg and Ottoman Empires disintegrated under the strain, Russia survived revolution and civil war to re-emerge under Bolshevik leadership. This posed a double danger for Britain, because traditional rivalries with Russia in Asia were now coupled with the ideological challenge of a Soviet state officially dedicated to world revolution.

Round two of the German challenge assumed a more menacing form for Britain because of the collapse of France in June 1940. Throughout the Great War the French, with increasing British support, had sustained a Western Front against Germany. But in four weeks Hitler achieved what the Kaiser's best generals had failed to do in four years – knocking France out of the war and winning a continental empire. Hitler was now free to turn against the Soviet Union years earlier than expected. Germany's amazing victories emboldened Italy and Japan to press their own bids for empire in North Africa and East Asia respectively – with British possessions as the main target.

Thanks to its own resources and those of the empire, Britain avoided defeat in 1940. There is no doubt that this was a moment of global significance. Had Britain surrendered, like France, or been knocked out the war, Hitler would have been free to devote all Germany's manpower and resources on his war against the Soviet Union, while the United States would probably have pulled in its horns and concentrated on defending the Western Hemisphere.

Instead, British defiance encouraged Roosevelt to extend material support and then enter the war. Britain became the essential base from which the Western Allies could eventually mount a cross-Channel assault to help liberate Europe.

So Britain's 1940 really mattered. But whatever Churchill declaimed then about 'victory at all costs', overcoming Hitler's Reich was beyond its own capabilities once there was no French army or Western Front in Europe, and when the Royal Navy faced challenges in the Mediterranean and the Pacific as well as in home waters. Britain therefore had no choice but to rely on new allies to win the victory – above all the USA and the USSR. By May 1945, after five years of total war, Hitler was dead and his Thousand-Year Reich lay in ruins, but he had brought down the old Europe with him. Such was the extent of Germany's early success in 1940 that the Führer had, in effect, called the superpowers into existence to redress the balance of the Old World. After the D-Day landings in Normandy in June 1944, the United States dominated the campaign in Western Europe, while the Red Army's long and bloody fightback from Stalingrad to Berlin left it in control of most of Eastern Europe. By the time the Germans surrendered, the armed forces of the USA and USSR each numbered between 11 and 12 million men, more than double the British figure.

Had the world reverted to the pattern of the previous post-war era after 1918, with American and Russian withdrawal from Europe, the power shift would not have been so pronounced. But out of this war there developed a bitter Soviet–American rivalry, which not only divided Germany and Europe into two military blocs but also became truly global and fiercely ideological. Although Britain was still a major power in the immediate post-war period – third in military and industrial terms around 1950, thanks in part to the total defeat of Germany and Japan – it could not match the two superpowers, despite maintaining until 1960 the policy of peacetime conscription. In 1953, Britain's peak post-war year, its armed forces totalled 900,000 compared with 3.5 million for the USA and 4.75 million in the case of the USSR.[54] Nor, in the age of nuclear weapons and inter-continental missiles, could it hope to keep up in the Cold War arms race with the Big Two. Since the 1960s, Britain's continued existence as a nuclear power has depended on its 'special relationship' with the United States.

This does not mean that Britain is no longer of any military consequence. It remains the only European member of the Western Alliance, apart from France, to maintain a capacity for power-projection outside the NATO area. But its days as a major global presence are over. As with the economic story, others have surpassed its precocious early lead – reducing Britain to the position that one might expect for a state of its size, population and resources. In power, as in wealth, what is historically striking was 'rise', not 'fall'.

Empire, power and greatness

Britain would never have risen so high but for the 'multiplier' effect of empire. It was the empire which made Britain great. At the start of the twentieth century Britain and Ireland had only 42 million people, whereas the population of the USA was 76 million and of Tsarist Russia 133 million. When the inhabitants of Britain's overseas territories were included, however, the arithmetic looked different. At its peak after the Great War, the British Empire covered nearly a quarter of the earth's land surface and encompassed a similar proportion of its population, over 500 million in all. France accounted for only 9 per cent of the earth's land surface and 108 million of its people.[55] At times of crisis the empire could serve as a vast resource of material and manpower. During the Great War the British government mobilised 6.7 million men from Britain and Ireland, but 3 million more came from the empire – nearly half of these from India.[56] In 1939–45 the imperial contribution was yet more pronounced: while the UK mobilised 5.9 million, the so-called 'white dominions' – Canada, Australia, New Zealand and South Africa – raised nearly 2.5 million and India over 2 million.[57]

Mindful of such statistics, some historians have castigated British leaders for 'losing' the empire, because that diminished the country's ability to compete with the continent-sized superpowers. Correlli Barnett, for instance, argued that if the British had not lost their nerve, they could have held on to India by 'resolute autocracy'.[58] Yet it was not willpower but hard power that mattered. And, to quote again the German commentator Constantin Frantz in 1882, Britain was really 'an artificial worldpower' (*eine künstliche Weltmacht*) because 'the territorial base of this power was just a European country' and its resources came from colonies spread out across the oceans which were tied to Britain only 'through the threads of the fleet' and 'these threads could all be broken or cut'.[59] This was not a vast continental empire commanding adjacent terrain, unlike the United States and the Soviet Union after each had surmounted its crisis of civil war – in 1861–5 and 1917–22 respectively.

This lack of a contiguous continental empire was Britain's basic weakness as a world power. But almost as significant was the diversity of its colonial territories. The empire emerged haphazardly, with little coordination from London. There were leftovers in Canada and the Caribbean from the pre-1776 American colonies; spoils from the wars against France, of which India was the most important; the fruits of creeping imperialism in West Africa as weak tribal governments caved in before the advance of European commerce, conquest and culture; pre-emptive strikes in South and East Africa in the late nineteenth century to block European rivals; and the carve-up of the decaying Ottoman Empire before and after the Great War, including territories such as Egypt astride the Suez Canal, oil-rich Iraq and the poisoned chalice of Palestine.

Nor did Britain truly 'own' these diverse 'possessions'. British control was usually superficial. In colonies settled by white emigrants from the UK, who dominated the indigenous population, successive London governments gradually followed the path of increasing devolution. This pattern began in Canada in the 1840s and was extended to the other white-settler colonies in Australasia and southern Africa during the late nineteenth and early twentieth centuries. By 1931, when the London Parliament's residual authority was abrogated, the Dominions – as the white-settler colonies were known – were effectively independent in all domestic affairs. Although still dependent on Britain for defence, the main bond linking them with Britain was that of loyalty to the country from which many of them, or their parents, had only recently emigrated in the early decades of the twentieth century. This 'Britannic nation-alism' was a potent force in mobilising support for the 'mother country' in the two world wars. In the 1930s, for instance, over 95 per cent of Australians and nearly 50 per cent of Canadians were of British stock.[60]

This policy of measured devolution was adopted in colonies where there was a large British settler community and also the capacity for fiscal independence. 'Non-white' colonies were treated differently because, until well after 1945, they were generally thought incapable of self-government. In these cases the British employed more autocratic and paternalistic methods, with an unelected government headed by a British Governor exercising certain devolved powers under supervision from London. Much of the dependent empire was run in this way as Crown Colonies. Even where there seemed little benefit to Britain – as in West Africa, the West Indies or the Falklands – London clung on for fear that a rival power might acquire the territories or because these lacked a natural ethnic or political viability. At the same time the British tried to minimise the costs of continued rule, thereby turning a blind eye to the problems of poverty and underdevelopment unless, as in the 1930s Caribbean, these colonies exploded in serious disorder. This was empire on the cheap: Britain was getting little out but putting little in.

Between the Dominions and the Crown Colonies stands the special case of India. There Britain supplanted the Mughal emperors as the paramount power. In what was called British India they ruled directly through the Indian Civil Service, headed by a European elite of only 1,300. In some six hundred princely states, covering a third of the sub-continent, they ruled indirectly through hereditary lords who handled all but defence and foreign policy under the eye of a British 'Resident'. British influence over a population numbering over 300 million in 1900 essentially depended on alliances with local landed and commercial leaders and on the Western-educated Indians who filled the clerical grades of British administration. Despite early Victorian waves of evangelical and reforming zeal, Indians – as elsewhere in the empire – were largely left to their own religious, social and cultural practices, except when order was threatened or British interests jeopardised.

In India, those interests were substantial. Around 1900 Britain provided 60 per cent of India's imports – particularly textiles, machinery and iron and steel products – and used the surplus generated to balance its deficits on trade with continental Europe and North America. Even more important was the Indian army. In 1914, its strength of 160,000 fighting troops – one-third of them British – represented half of Britain's peacetime military strength: vital manpower for a country with no tradition of military conscription. And this was also a cut-price army: India, in Lord Salisbury's phrase, was 'an English barrack in the Oriental seas from which we may draw any number of troops without paying for them'.[61]

More precisely, the Government of India paid out of its own tax revenues for the peacetime army in India and for the basic costs of troops serving overseas. During the Great War, 1.3 million Indian troops were sent abroad – from France to Gallipoli to East Africa – and they played a particularly significant role in the defeat of the Ottoman Turks, bringing Palestine and Iraq under British control.

Looking back now, the great British Empire seems like a bit of a con. How could so many be ruled for so long by so few? Admittedly, there *were* positive forces promoting acceptance of British imperial rule: the ties of 'Britishness' in the settler colonies, for instance, and the networks of clientage in India and elsewhere. But ultimately empire rests on force, or the threat of force, and for much of the Victorian era this could be exerted through superior British military technology. The Royal Navy may have faced growing European challengers, but it needed only a few steam-driven gunboats to overwhelm the Chinese junks and open up that country to European trade in the mid-nineteenth century. The British army may have been comical as far as Bismarck's Europe was concerned, but it was quite sufficient to handle most threats on the imperial periphery. At the battle of Omdurman in 1898, General Horatio Kitchener's army – including the young Winston Churchill – won control of the Sudan at the cost of only 368 men. His adversary, the Khalifa, lost 11,000: massacred by 3,500 shells and half a million bullets. In the pithy couplet of Hilaire Belloc:

> Whatever happens we have got
> The Maxim Gun, and they have not.[62]

Underpinning superior force was the potency of racial prestige – a point underlined by the colonial administrator Frederick Lugard. In Africa and India, he said in 1890, 'the native looks on it as a sacrilege to touch a Sahib, and also expects little short of death from the Sahib if he should try conclusions. To this prestige the white man owes his ascendancy, and it *must* at any price be maintained, just as one would with a brute beast.'[63] Acute awareness of these 'intangibles' of prestige and credibility was voiced by Sir Alexander Cadogan of the Foreign Office during the Czech crisis with Germany in September 1938. 'I *know*', he wrote in his diary, 'we are in no position to fight: but I'd rather be beat than dishonoured. How can we look a foreigner in the face after this? How can we hold Egypt, India and the rest?'[64]

In the nineteenth century, Britain struck out. In the twentieth century the empire struck back, especially in the era of the two world wars which opened up extensive opportunities for anti-colonial nationalists. In many British dependencies, new political organisations took shape, extracting concessions from the colonial authorities, which in turn gradually reduced their control over local policy and resources. The pattern of Dominion devolution was replicated, reluctantly, elsewhere – with the Indian case being especially important. Fiscal autonomy, conceded after serious disturbances in 1919, allowed the Indians to construct a tariff wall against British goods; this helped to ruin the Lancashire textile industry. When war began again in 1939, London agreed to pay for the extraordinary costs of using Indian troops; this resulted in a £1.3 billion British debt to India, equivalent to roughly one-fifth of Britain's GDP.[65] All this changed the cost-benefit analysis of holding on to India. At the same time the diffusion of military technology evened up the military imbalance between rulers and ruled. In 1946, for instance, less than half a century after Omdurman, a bunch of Jewish insurgents, using seven milk churns filled with TNT, blew up the King David Hotel in Jerusalem – the nerve-centre of British power in Palestine. Ninety-one perished, and with them much of Britain's determination to hang on to its troubled Mandate. Ties with the white Dominions also weakened after 1945, as British migration tailed off; other ethnicities flowed in, and a keener sense of national identity was created. Australia led the way, but this was true even in New Zealand, previously the most 'loyal' of Dominions. In South Africa the bonds had always been weaker because of the dominance of the ex-Dutch Afrikaners, while in Canada the Francophone community and the neighbouring USA had long exerted their own countervailing pulls.

For Tories such as Margaret Thatcher and Jacob Rees-Mogg, Suez in 1956 was a crucial moment in Britain's 'decline' – sapping the will to power – and also an episode that (in ways that that neither chose to specify) could have turned out differently. In reality, however, Suez – though making a big splash politically, especially within the Tory party – was 'little more than an eddy in the fast-flowing stream of history'.[66] Prime Minister Anthony Eden's military operation to regain control of the Suez Canal was an act of desperation by a sick man, who was often running a temperature of 105 because of a botched operation on his gall bladder. He deliberately excluded most of Whitehall, including the Foreign Office, Treasury and Joint Intelligence Committee. It was also at odds with underlying post-war verities of British foreign policy. Collusion with Israel – supposedly covert but in fact embarrassingly transparent – ran against traditional British cooperation with the Arab states, while the failure to consult the United States, leading to a Washington-induced run on sterling, breached the basic post-war axiom of keeping in step with the Americans.

By the 1950s, ministers and officials recognised that defence commitments had outstripped national income and also that, in the thermonuclear era, British security depended on its role as junior partner in a 'special relationship' with the United States. Suez was therefore an aberration from the pattern of post-war British foreign policy – a contingent moment reflecting the personality of a particular leader, rather than a fundamental turning point in

British history. At most, it dramatised to the world – and to the British public – the limitations on British power that were already common knowledge in Westminster and Whitehall.

If one is looking for a moment that was both psychologically traumatic and geopolitically significant, it is necessary to go back to the Second World War. Not, however, to 1940 – that 'finest hour' enshrined in national myth and movies – but to early 1942 when Britain's Southeast Asian Empire crumbled in the face of a Japanese blitzkrieg. The attack on Pearl Harbor formed the curtain-raiser to an audacious series of combined operations by Japan's land, naval and air forces that not only evicted the British from Hong Kong, Malaya and Singapore in a few weeks, but did so in a way that dramatically undermined key fundamentals of Britain's global position. The supremacy of modern airpower over traditional seapower was demonstrated in December 1941 when Britain's only two capital ships guarding its Asian Empire, *Prince of Wales* and *Repulse*, were sunk in a couple of hours by Japanese torpedo-bombers. 'In all the war I never received a more direct shock,' wrote Churchill in his memoirs. 'As I turned over and twisted in bed the full horror of the news sunk in upon me.' Across the Pacific and Indian Oceans 'Japan was supreme, and we everywhere were weak and naked.' That nakedness was then totally exposed by the fall of Singapore in February 1942 to inferior Japanese forces. Some 80,000 British and empire soldiers marched off into captivity in what Churchill called 'the worst disaster and largest capitulation in British history'.[67] For some weeks India and Australia seemed in danger.

Churchill himself admitted the extent of Britain's global overstretch in 1941–2, telling the Commons: 'There never has been a moment, there never could have been a moment, when Great Britain or the British Empire, single-handed, could fight Germany and Italy, could wage the Battle of Britain, the Battle of the Atlantic and the Battle of the Middle East and at the same time stand thoroughly prepared in Burma, the Malay Peninsula, and generally in the Far East against the impact of a vast military empire like Japan.'[68]

Although the Japanese tide was eventually turned – largely by the US Navy – and Britain regained most of its Asian Empire, the damage done in 1942 proved lasting. Newsreel film and press photos of British officers in their baggy shorts signing the articles of surrender in Singapore and then marching off into Japanese prisoner-of-war camps were beamed around the world, shattering the image of racial superiority that, as Lugard had rightly asserted, was so essential to British power. No longer could imperial loyalty be assumed. And the panic offer of independence to India in the crisis of 1942, though not enacted then, had to be honoured after the war – beginning the domino-like process of decolonisation.

In short, 1940–2 – from the fall of France to the fall of Singapore – was nothing less than a 'strategic catastrophe' for Britain's global position. It constituted the 'real turning point',[69] forcing the British into the expedient of peacetime conscription that was not sustainable in the long term, and into dependence on a force-multiplier alliance with the American superpower. The standard national narrative emphasises 1940 – heroic evacuation from Dunkirk and victory in the battle of Britain – while 'the import of the imperial disasters of 1941–2 has been obscured'.[70] In the country's global history, however, Singapore matters far more than Suez.

Affluence, heritage and history

Britain's current position in the world rankings of wealth and power does not compare with what it was 150 years ago. As has been suggested, this is hardly surprising: the country's rise was remarkable but not the diminution in its standing when more populous and resource-rich states caught up and global decolonisation took hold. Yet this is not the whole story.

'The British Empire declined; the condition of the people improved': that was A. J. P. Taylor's verdict on 1914 to 1945.[71] Taking the twentieth century as a whole, observes David Cannadine, the 'age of decline' was also 'the age of affluence'.[72] Notwithstanding periodic hand-wringing about British economic performance, the country remains one of the richest in the world. At the end of the twentieth century, in income per head, Britain was 'right in the middle of the range among big Western European countries (a little higher than Germany and Italy, a little lower than France), but on a world scale plainly very rich'.[73] Whatever the country's changing place in world rankings, since the Industrial Revolution the British have been 'beneficiaries of developments which in every generation' have left them 'richer than their predecessors'.[74]

The problem is: which British? The fruits of affluence have not been evenly shared across the population. Over the last century, the British economy has undergone radical restructuring. Just as Britain was in the vanguard of industrialisation – the shift of labour from the primary sector (farming, mining) to the secondary (the manufacturing industry) – so it also led a further shift to service industries (the tertiary sector) which today accounts for around 80 per cent of GDP. Even though there remains in some quarters an assumption that 'manufacturing' in more traditional forms such as steel, ships and motor vehicles is the mark of a great nation, this process of 'tertiarisation' is the norm for most developed Western countries. The USA, Germany and France are all around the 80 per cent level, but 'in Britain the process of deindustrialisation has gone further and faster than just about anywhere else'.[75]

And the human cost has been considerable, especially at two points during the twentieth century. First, in the 1920s and 1930s, a whole generation of workers in staple industries such as coal, steel, textiles and shipbuilding experienced long-term structural unemployment. Their iconic protest was the Jarrow March from Tyneside to London in October 1936. And then the even more precipitous slump from the 1970s in what was left of those sectors and across heavy industry as a whole. Between 1971 and 1999 the proportion of workers in manufacturing halved, from 34 per cent to under 16 per cent, while employment in the service sector rose from 54 per cent to 72 per cent – with most of that growth coming in financial and business services: up from 6 per cent to over 18 per cent of the workforce.[76] In both phases, deindustrialisation was mainly the result of sharp foreign competition from lower-wage developing economies, but it has been accentuated by the policy decisions of various British governments – privileging the gold standard in the 1920s, sticking to monetary targets and breaking union power in the Thatcher era. The consequence in each case was high levels of unemployment and enduring social deprivation in regions that had been heavily dependent on a single economic activity or enterprise – a coal mine, steel mill or car factory, with the old industrial heartlands of northern England, South Wales and Clydeside hardest hit. This process has tended to exacerbate the sense of a North–South divide – with prosperity most evident in London, the Home Counties and parts of the Midlands. This fed into the pro-Brexit vote in June 2016.

Indeed it has been argued that 'de-industrialisation' not 'decline' should be considered the most appropriate 'meta-narrative' for post-war British history – perhaps even comparable with the epic historical transition from an agricultural to an industrial economy, given its wide-ranging effects on 'income distribution, unemployment, the gendered distribution of work and the shape of the social security system'.[77] The new service economy is highly polarised between what have been called 'lovely' jobs and 'lousy' jobs, with the latter routine and poorly paid, so that 'in-work' poverty has to be quietly mitigated by state benefits. Precipitate de-industrialisation has brought with it sharp increases in social inequality and economic insecurity. And in understanding the human costs, concepts such as 'growth' and 'decline' are not merely irrelevant but obfuscatory. The root questions are political more than economic. What have governments done to promote new economic activities, retrain unemployed workers and educate younger generations into flexible work skills? This agenda takes us into the realm of national policies rather than structural processes – and 'policies' in a much more sophisticated sense than political rhetoric about reversing national decline by acts of Napoleonic willpower.[78]

Yet the ideology of decline still has visceral power. There seems to be a 'gut feeling that Britain, having once been top dog, ought always to be top dog'. In which case, the fact that other dogs are bigger is taken as evidence of the nation's 'decline', even though the British dog is now a lot fatter than a century ago.[79] Some seem to find it particularly galling that former enemies, notably Germany, now occupy an elevated place. The insistence on 'greatness' – that Thatcherite aspiration to put the 'Great' back into 'Britain' – suggests a rooted Tory unwillingness to bid farewell to the position and status that had been lost. Yet it is striking that when the Europhile Liberal Democrat politician Nick Clegg published his 2017 manifesto about how to reverse the verdict of the EU referendum, he felt it necessary to entitle the book *How to Stop Brexit (And Make Britain Great Again)*. The appeal of the 'G' word, it seems, is not confined to the political right.

Magnifying this sense of lost greatness is the visibility of the past in contemporary Britain. The era of 'decline' is not only an age of affluence but also the heyday of Heritage. Yet what the 'H' word actually means is elusive. 'We could no more define the national heritage than we could define, say, beauty or art,' stated the first annual report of the National Heritage Memorial Fund in 1980–1.

In its view the term obviously included 'the natural riches of Britain', threatened by 'thoughtless development', but 'heritage' was also 'a representation of the development of aesthetic expression and a testimony to the role played by the nation in world history'.[80]

The prodigious growth of the 'heritage industry' has spawned many forward-looking projects of urban and rural regeneration. But it can also foster nostalgia funded by affluence. At one end of the spectrum is the National Trust – despite its name a private charity whose membership has mushroomed from 1 million in 1981 to over 5 million in 2017. Now one of the largest landowners in Britain, the Trust describes its mission as preserving 'special places' not only 'for everyone' but also 'for ever'. It has been credited with largely ensuring the survival of the English country house, and with that an alluring evocation of past gentility. At the other end of the spectrum, local councils and museums have given new life to a multitude of derelict industrial sites.[81] Some of these – Ironbridge, for instance – can be infused with a gritty grandeur to match, in a different way, country houses like Stourhead or Cliveden.

The vogue since the 1980s for 'heritage films' has also enhanced the 'historical imaginary' of Britain. Many influential blockbusters feature famous monarchs, such as Henry VIII, Elizabeth I and George III, and country-house dramas have always been popular, from *Brideshead Revisited* to *Downton Abbey*. Often memorably acted and beautifully filmed, these films and TV programmes can insidiously suggest that the nation's past is more impressive and exciting than its present. That can also be the effect of the most dynamic area of recent history television, so-called 'Reality History'. Moving away from an academic, informational approach, TV channels adopted a more emotive, participatory format – encouraging the viewer to identify with historical figures and their experience by adopting their lifestyle (the *House* genre), wearing their clothes, or enduring their experiences (*Trench, Ship*, and so on).[82]

Particularly potent have been movies about Britain's Second World War produced by post-war British studios. The total number was remarkable: about one hundred in the two decades from 1946 to 1965. Some 30 million people went to the cinema every week in the late 1940s, when Britain's population totalled 51 million. Although attendance fell below 15 million in 1959, this figure still virtually matched the circulation of all national daily newspapers. War films – though despised by many critics – proved consistent box-office successes. *The Dam Busters* was the top-grossing British film in 1955; likewise *Reach for the Sky* in 1956 (about the wartime aviator Douglas Bader). *Sink the Bismarck* was another big success in 1960. Unlike movies of the 1920s and 1930s about the Great War, there was very little questioning of the conflict's rightness; nor were soldiers on both sides depicted as essentially ordinary men led as victims to the slaughter. The post-1945 films celebrated men and masculinity; their heroes – stars such as Jack Hawkins and Richard Todd – were generally tough but reserved, stereotypically English, and their German and Japanese foes usually classic 'baddies'. Apart from a few Australians, the contributions of the empire to victory rarely figured, nor those of allies such as the Americans – let alone the Russians. Complementing the message of the popular boys' weekly, *The Eagle*, these movies projected the war as 'a great game' and 'a good cause'. Of course, most audiences probably enjoyed them simply as action-packed entertainment – escapes from Nazi prisoner-of-war camps being particularly popular. But, at a subliminal level, the films served to reinforce the heroic narrative of Britain Alone.[83]

These movies were seen by much larger audiences from the 1970s through endless repeats on television. And, more recently, the heroic narrative has been sharpened down to the person of Churchill himself, through what is called a process of 're-mediation' – as one medium refashions the product of another: book, journalism, film, with multiple feedback loops – and in the process amplifies the Churchillian impact. Churchill started the process with six volumes of war memoirs published between 1948 and 1954. He intended to shape the verdict of history at an early stage by, as he liked to put it, being one of the historians. The most vivid parts of those books were purveyed to a much larger audience through serialisation across the world in major newspapers, including the *Daily Telegraph* in Britain and the *New York Times* and *Life* magazine in the USA. Film-makers also picked up the memoirs, for instance, the *Winston Churchill: The Valiant Year* series shown in America and Britain in 1960–1, and Churchill's immortality was then assured by a state funeral in 1965, broadcast on TV across the world. Meanwhile, historian Martin Gilbert was gradually constructing Churchill's literary mausoleum in what became an eight-volume 'official biography', on which he worked for twenty years before its completion in 1986. These volumes and the accompanying tomes of supporting documents in turn provided vast amounts of additional information for new movies and TV films. In *The Wilderness Years* – an eight-part television series of 1982 – Churchill in the 1930s was brought to life for a new generation by the actor Robert Hardy. In the twenty-first century, British-American co-productions hiked up the budgets and also the special effects. In quick succession came Albert Finney in *The Gathering Storm* (2002), Brendan Gleeson (*Into the Storm*, 2009) and Gary Oldman's Oscar-winning performance in *Darkest Hour* in 2017 – the same year as the movie *Dunkirk*, another box-office triumph about Britain in 1940. And so the process of Churchillian re-mediation has continued for some seventy years, with books, films and journalism feeding on each other.[84]

In the process, however, there has been a gradual narrowing of the Second World War in popular British imagination to the story of one country and one leader in one year, and this has distorted the magnitude and complexity of that global conflict. In June 1940,

Churchill urged his beleaguered countrymen to 'so bear ourselves that if the British Empire and its Commonwealth last for a thousand years, men will still say, "This was their finest hour."' In his memoirs, Churchill turned exhortation into description, entitling the second volume, about 1940, *Their Finest Hour*. Over time, 'theirs' and 'his' have become intertwined. And 'finest' implies that Britain's Churchillian moment cannot be bettered, in other words that it has been all downhill ever since.[85]

In various ways, therefore, heritage is in danger of becoming a substitute for history in public awareness of Britain's past. 'The nation', observed historian Patrick Wright, 'is not seen as a heterogeneous society that makes its own history as it moves forward, however chaotically, into the future. Instead it is portrayed as an *already achieved* and timeless historical entity which demands only appropriate reverence and protection in the present.'[86] In other words, history is understood as content not process: a proud inheritance to be cherished and preserved, rather than an ongoing project of making and remaking.

If you are sure what Britain is, or should be, this may not be the book for you. But if you can cope with the challenges of living in the future tense, rather than luxuriating in the past pluperfect,[87] then read on. What follows is an attempt to conceive of Britain and its history as work in progress.

2

Europe

Our links to the rest of Europe, the continent of Europe, have been the dominant *factor in our history.*

Margaret Thatcher, Bruges, 20 September 1988

The idea of Britain existing separately from Europe is a familiar feature of modern British culture. In daily speech, from football matches to weather forecasts, the two terms are often used to denote distinct entities. This has also been a trope of political rhetoric, from the long debate in the 1960s about whether Britain should 'join' Europe, via the 1975 referendum about whether to 'stay in', and on to the Brexit vote in 2016 to 'leave'. Of course, 'Europe' here signifies a specific political organisation – the EEC or the EU – but much of the political debate has drawn on a narrative about Britain's historic and special character compared with the Continent.

One of the most celebrated speeches about Britain's non-European identity was delivered by Hugh Gaitskell, the Labour leader, to the party's annual conference in Brighton in October 1962. He spoke at length about the conditions that would have to be fulfilled before Labour could agree to join the 'Common Market' – especially changes to the Common Agricultural Policy, which he denounced as 'one of the most devastating pieces of protectionism ever invented' – and he stressed Britain's obligations to the Commonwealth. Gaitskell's conclusion was that the arguments for British entry were 'evenly balanced' and that 'whether or not it is worth going in depends on the conditions of our entry'. He did not conceal his anger at the way Harold Macmillan's Tory Government seemed hell-bent on joining, despite the costs to the Commonwealth. Yet what caught the headlines was not Gaitskell's judicious weighing up of pros and cons but his emotional soundbites.[1]

For instance, he warned about a two-faced Europe, of which Britain had good historic reasons to be wary. 'For although, of course, Europe has had a great and glorious civilisation, although Europe can claim Goethe and Leonardo, Voltaire and Picasso, there have been evil features in European history, too – Hitler and Mussolini . . . You cannot say what this Europe will be: it has its two faces and we do not know as yet which is the one which will be dominant.' The 'ideal of Federal Europe' also stuck in the Labour leader's gullet. This meant that 'if we go into this we are no more than a state (as it were) in the United States of Europe, such as Texas and California . . . it would be the same as in Australia, where you have Western Australia, for example, and New South Wales. We should be like them. This is what it means; it does mean the end of Britain as an independent nation state.' And with that transformation would come, Gaitskell believed, a repudiation of Britain's historic identity: 'It means the end of a thousand years of history. You may say "Let it end" but, my goodness, it is a decision that needs a little care and thought . . . For we are not just a part of Europe – at least not yet. We have a different history. We have ties and links which run across the whole world.'[2]

A couple of months later this kind of British rhetoric about a thousand years of history and a global destiny was picked up by Dean Acheson – who had served as US Secretary of State of State in 1949–53 at height of the Cold War. Acheson's line about Britain losing an empire but not finding a role – quoted at the start of this book – has now become notorious, but the background story is important. In 1962, Acheson – now a crusty elder statesman – was asked to deliver the keynote address to a student conference at the US Military Academy at West Point on 5 December. He made his usual pitch about the importance of the Atlantic Alliance, and the speech attracted little attention in the United States. But embedded in a section about some of the problems facing Western Europe, was the single paragraph on Britain that proved incendiary:

> Great Britain has lost an empire and has not yet found a role. The attempt to play a separate power role – that is, a role apart from Europe, a role based on a 'special relationship' with the United States, a role based on being head of a 'commonwealth' which has no political structure, or unity, or strength, and enjoys a precarious economic relationship by means of the Sterling Area and prefer-ences in the British market – this role is about played out. Great Britain, attempting to be a broker between the United States and Russia, has seemed to conduct policy as weak as its military power. H.M.G. [Her Majesty's Government] is now attempting – wisely, in my opinion – to reenter Europe, from which it was banished at the time of the Plantagenets, and the battle seems to be about as hard-fought as were those of an earlier day.[3]

That whole paragraph is worth quoting both because of its contemp-tuous dismissal of the Commonwealth, the Sterling Area and Britain's Cold War diplomacy and also because of its (now rather uncanny) prediction that Britain's attempt to enter the EEC might presage another Hundred Years' War. Above all, however, it was the epigram about Britain losing an empire without finding a role that caught the eye in London and provoked an outcry in Tory circles. The *Express* denounced this American 'stab in the back' of its devoted ally; the *Telegraph* observed snidely that Acheson had always been 'more immaculate in dress than in judgement'.[4] And because the former Secretary of State was deemed to be close to President Kennedy, the Prime Minister himself felt it necessary to offer his own capsule narrative of British history, to placate his party and what he called 'the "patriotic" elements in the country'. Macmillan declared that 'Mr Acheson has fallen into an error which has been made by quite a lot of people in the course of the last four hundred years, including Philip of Spain, Louis XIV, Napoleon, the Kaiser and Hitler.'[5]

An Evening Standard *cartoon showing Prime Minister
Harold Macmillan begging President John F. Kennedy to let him
be the back legs of the American pantomime horse,
while Dean Acheson looks on from the wings.*

Acheson never retracted his argument but he did later express regret about how he had expressed it – albeit in a typically sardonic manner. 'The first requirement of a statesman is that he be dull,' he told an interviewer in 1970, adding that this was 'not always easy to achieve'. He admitted that the controversial sentence in his West Point speech suffered from being too epigrammatic and quotable. 'If I'd taken twice the number of words to express it, it would have been inoffensive and recognised as true at once. Since then it has been adopted by almost every British politician, though they have never given me credit for it at all.'[6]

Acheson was right: his one-liner about losing empire and not yet finding a role became almost a cliché of British commentary, especially for those who wanted Britain to join 'Europe'.[7] Yet the emotional invocations of national history by Gaitskell and Macmillan reflect an abiding counter-strain, which re-emerged, for instance, at the time of German unification in 1989–90. 'We beat the Germans twice, and now they're back,' Margaret Thatcher exclaimed during a European summit in December 1989, a month after the Berlin Wall was breached.[8] Her close friend Nicholas Ridley vented similar feelings splenetically to a *Spectator* journalist, calling the European monetary union 'a German racket, designed to take over the whole of Europe' and exclaiming that, as for handing over sovereignty to the EC, 'you might as well give it to Adolf Hitler, frankly.' The *Spectator* gleefully ran the interview as a cover story, graced by a poster of the West German chancellor Helmut Kohl daubed with a Hitler moustache, and Ridley was obliged to resign from the Cabinet. So Boris Johnson's battle cry in 2016 that the British must again be 'heroes of Europe' and stand up to German domination was more of the same. The *Telegraph* headlined that story: 'Boris Johnson: The EU wants a superstate, just as Hitler did'.[9]

To make some sense of these potted narratives we need to take in more than the Second World War and its aftermath, and look across the broad sweep of Gaitskell's 'thousand years'. An appropriate way to do so is by reflecting on the 'English Channel'. Although this figures much less in the narratives of Welsh or Scottish history (defined by the Marches or the Borders) and hardly at all for Ireland (across the Irish Sea), the Channel has come to symbolise the Britain–Europe divide: a maritime frontier etched out in the White Cliffs of Dover. But we need a more fluid understanding of the Channel within 'our island story' – a more nuanced perspective on Britain's changing interactions with a changing Continent.

The Channel – barrier and bridge

A millennium ago, what we British now call the English Channel was described as not so much a divide but a passageway between two land masses. Geoffrey of Monmouth, the twelfth-century chronicler, referred to it as 'the straits to the south' which 'allow one to sail to Gaul'.[10] His perspective was hardly surprising because, for several centuries after 1066, England was ruled by a political elite who spoke a version of French and who moved naturally between their domains on either side of the water. And in the age of sail, not rail, France could be reached from London far more quickly than Scotland. The result was 'a shared culture', ruled by an inter-married aristocracy and by the Roman Catholic Church, whose clerics constituted the administrative class (and also the historians).[11]

The sharing was, however, far from harmonious because of rival claims to territory and title. Armies from the French side of the Channel invaded England on several occasions, notably during the civil war of 1139–53 over the succession to Henry I and again in 1215–17 during the 'Barons' War' against King John about how to interpret and implement the Magna Carta. More common, however, were armies crossing in the opposite direction, from north to south.

After Henry I, the Anglo–Norman dynasty founded by William the Conqueror were succeeded by the descendants of Geoffrey of Anjou – Henry II and his sons Richard and John – whose 'Angevin empire' at its peak in the 1170s stretched in a great arc from Normandy west to encompass Brittany and then south down the coast to Bordeaux, Aquitaine and the Pyrenees, as well as east through the Massif Central to the Auvergne. Although covering about half of modern France, this 'empire' was a hodgepodge of separate possessions, plagued by disputes within Henry's fractious family. It fell apart during the Anglo–French wars in John's reign, with the loss of Normandy and all the other lands apart from Gascony, the southwest rump of the once vast duchy of Aquitaine.

Edward I and the Plantagenets struggled to hang on to what was left of their French lands. Their crucial claim was to the duchy of Aquitaine. The Capetian kings of France – engaged, like Edward I in Britain, in an aggressive programme of state building – claimed that, under the 1259 Treaty of Paris, the duchy could only be held in homage and fealty to the French crown. In 1286, Edward I did perform an act of homage to Philippe IV of France, using the words, 'I become your man for the lands which I hold from you on this side of the sea according to the form of peace made between our ancestors.'[12]

The implications of this vow became increasingly intolerable to his successors: a monarch who claimed to be sovereign on the English side of the sea was in a position of feudal inferiority to the Valois dynasty in respect of his continental inheritance. As the confrontation escalated, Edward III (the grandson of Edward I) took advantage of a French succession crisis in 1328 to assert his claim, via his mother, to rule France as well as England. The result was open warfare between the two monarchies on and off from 1337 – what became known as the Hundred Years' War. After Henry V's surprise victory at Agincourt in 1415, the English and their Burgundian allies did finally seem close to enforcing their claim. In the 1420s they controlled much of France from Brittany and the Channel to the Loire. But then the war turned against them, in part due to the inspirational leadership of Jeanne d'Arc, and by 1453 the English possessions were reduced to a small area around Calais. Despite new French wars under Henry VIII, Calais was eventually lost in 1558, though subsequent English monarchs did not stop reiterating their nominal claim to be rulers of France until the Napoleonic era.

Defeat in the Hundred Years' War therefore ended a period of almost four centuries when the Channel was a bridge as much as a barrier, linking two sides of an Anglo–French culture in which the English elite had roots and often lands in France. Over the next four centuries there slowly emerged a sense of contrasting and competing national identities, sharpened by the Reformation and the protracted struggle to establish a distinctively English form of Protestantism, which lasted till 1690, and then by another on-off Hundred Years' War with the French, this time against Louis XIV and later Napoleon. In this process, the Channel did assume the character of an iconic barrier, especially in official rhetoric. Yet it never ceased to function as a bridge because, as a Protestant nation, England could not be indifferent to the fate of the Reformation on the continent, now wracked by conflicts between Protestants and Catholics.[13]

Henry VIII's break with Rome began for very personal reasons: his desire for the Papacy to annul his barren marriage in the hope of producing a legitimate male heir with his latest infatuation, Anne Boleyn. When the Pope refused to grant him a divorce from his wife Catherine of Aragon, Henry set himself up as 'supreme head' of the English church and then, seizing on the convenient ideas of anti-clerical reformers, his regime attacked the institution of monasticism and dissolved all the religious houses, owners of about a third of the land in England. Instead of prudently managing those assets, however, Henry flogged them for ready cash to pay for an ego-trip bid to regain England's lost French empire. The war of 1544–6 was a costly disaster and England's incremental Protestant Reformation left the country increasingly exposed in Counter-Reformation Europe.

The 1550s proved a critical turning point, defined by the accidents of gender and mortality. Henry died in 1547. His young son Edward VI was an ardent Protestant, eager to promote his faith, but he died – probably of tuberculosis – in 1553, aged 15. Anticipating his death, Edward tried to ensure a Protestant succession by willing the Crown to his cousin, Lady Jane Grey. But her reign lasted only nine days before Mary, Catherine of Aragon's daughter, was installed on the throne. A staunch Catholic, committed to extirpating Protestantism, Mary married the heir to the Spanish throne, who became King Philip II in 1556. This placed England on the other side of Europe's wars of religion. But then in 1558, Mary died aged 42, possibly from cancer of the uterus. She was succeeded by her half-sister Elizabeth – the daughter of Anne Boleyn, who was then 25. Given the fate of her siblings, few would have predicted at her accession that Elizabeth would reign for nearly 45 years. In 1562, for instance, she contracted smallpox and seemed close to death. Her fortuitous longevity proved to be of huge historical significance.

Elizabeth was a firm but cautious Protestant. Both those adjectives mattered: she secured the Reformation but did not allow religion to divide the country as happened in France. Equally important, in 1559–60 Scotland's anti-Catholic nobles expelled the French and established a Protestant regime. What ensued has been described as 'the greatest transformation in England's foreign relations since the start of the Hundred Years' War' – making 'an ally of England's medieval enemies the Scots, and an enemy of its medieval allies the Burgundians' whose possessions in the

Netherlands had now passed to Philip of Spain.[14] What's more, France and Spain finally made peace in 1559 after nearly seven decades of periodic conflict, freeing Philip to concentrate on his mission of rolling back the Reformation.

In 1567 the Duke of Parma began a ruthless Spanish campaign to suppress the Protestant-led rebellion in the Low Countries; in 1572 thousands of French Protestants were killed in what became known as the Saint Bartholomew's Day Massacre. At home Elizabeth, pressed by her advisers, turned on recalcitrant Catholics as potential traitors; abroad she began to aid the Dutch revolt in the interests of national security. This escalating confrontation with Spain climaxed in Philip's abortive invasion in July 1588 – which was defeated not so much by English naval prowess as by the fabled 'Protestant wind' that prevented the Spanish Armada from linking up with Parma's army in Flanders and instead drove the sailing ships into the North Sea. A third of the original 130 vessels did not make it around Scotland and home to Spain.

From these years of fevered insecurity, when regime and religion both seemed to hang in the balance, there emerged a new national ideology. Rooted in providentialist interpretations of recent history, it depicted the English as a staunchly Protestant nation, blessed by God's protection. An intellectual landmark was John Foxe's *Actes and Monuments of these Latter and Perillous Days, Touching Matters of the Church* – popularly known *Foxe's Book of Martyrs* because it was a collection of stories – some true, others little more than rumour – about Christian martyrs, mostly anti-Catholic. Foxe had started compiling his work in Latin, while exiled on the Continent during Mary's reign. Returning to England in 1559, soon after Elizabeth acceded to the throne, he was quickly taken under the wing of her principal adviser, William Cecil, who put Foxe in touch with the printer John Day, persuaded him to publish in English and also helped finance what was a truly massive project – the biggest book printed in England to date. The first edition, which appeared in 1563, ran to 1,800 pages, lavishly illustrated with 60 woodcuts; the second, in 1570, filled 2,300 pages – more than two million words – in two volumes, with 150 illustrations. Over the course of Elizabeth's reign five editions were published; four more followed during the seventeenth century; and abridged versions, in cheap instalments, were printed throughout the eighteenth century – carrying Foxe's message to a new and much wider audience.[15]

'The Double Deliverance': Samuel Ward's print, published in Amsterdam in 1621 and widely distributed. In the centre the Pope and a Spanish grandee (King Philip II?), with advisers including the Devil, plot England's destruction. Left: the Armada of 1588 is blown away by the wind from Heaven. Right: Guy Fawkes prepares his deadly plot but the all-seeing Jehovah smiles on his chosen people in England.[16]

This providentialist sense of the English as a Chosen People – like the Israelites of old – became enshrined in the national calendar. Particularly significant in English national memory was what preacher Samuel Ward called in 1621 the nation's 'double deliverance' from 'the invincible navie' and 'the unmatcheable powder treason' – in other words, from the Armada of 1588 and the Catholic plot to blow up king and parliament in 1605. The failure of both were depicted as acts of divine intervention.

The Gunpowder Treason Plot became even more sacred to Protestant memory during the reign of the crypto-Catholic Charles I and the Wars of the Three Kingdoms. Charles' attempt to impose an Anglican prayer book on the Scottish Presbyterian church provoked the so-called Bishops' Wars of 1639–40. In an effort to put down the Scottish revolt, the King tried to raise an army of Irish Catholics, which deepened suspicions that he was a Papist. Finally obliged to call Parliament in London into session, after more than a decade, in order to obtain money for the Scottish war, Charles was confronted by a long list of civil and religious grievances from a legislature that voted itself into permanent session (the 'Long Parliament') until its demands were met. Deadlock turned into confrontation and then three English civil wars between 1642 and 1651, which were intertwined with the politico-religious struggles in Scotland and Ireland.

Charles was executed in 1649 and although his son regained the throne in the Restoration of 1660 as Charles II, he returned to a country permanently changed by the civil wars. England was now firmly established as a constitutional monarchy committed to a Protestant church. So much so that when Charles' brother and successor, James II, turned to Catholicism, he was displaced in 1688 in favour of his Protestant daughter, Mary, and her Dutch Calvinist husband William of Orange. After Mary died in 1694, 'King Billy' reigned alone until his death in 1702. The year before, a parliament dominated by Tory squires passed the Act of Settlement, prohibiting a Catholic (or anyone married to a Catholic) from acceding to the throne. This was no ritual act of piety. In 1707, ensuring the Protestant succession throughout Britain was a major reason for the Anglo–Scottish Treaty of Union, which established a new constitutional entity, Great Britain. And in 1714, when Queen Anne (Mary's younger sister) died without a living heir, Parliament passed over more than fifty individuals closer to her in blood yet Papist in faith. Instead they invited Georg Ludwig, Elector of Hanover – barely able to speak English but a staunch Lutheran – to be crowned King George I.[17] In other words, to preserve England as a constitutionally affirmed Protestant nation it was considered an acceptable price, both in 1688 and also 1714, to call in a continental monarch.

The Protestant succession also brought with it renewed engagement with the Continent. By the 1680s France, under Louis XIV, had replaced Spain as Europe's predominant Catholic power. Autocratic and aggressive, Louis and his successors sought to expand through enforced dynastic marriages and overt military conquest – a project seen by many in Britain as portending a 'universal monarchy'. The French directly supported the son and grandson of James II in their bids to put the Stuarts back on the throne through invasions in 1715 and 1745. This threat forced Britain into continental alliances in the wars of 1689–97, 1702–13 and 1743–8 – waged to restrain French power.

In any case, the Protestant succession meant that Britain was itself a continental monarchy. Except for the twelve years of Queen Anne (1702–14), 'from 1688 to 1837 the holder of the British thrones was simultaneously ruler of significant continental European territories' – the United Provinces under William III and the Electorate of Braunschweig-Lüneburg under the Hanoverian dynasty. Although generally known as Hanover after its capital city, the Electorate actually covered much of north-central Germany – from Brunswick to Bremen on the North Sea, and from Göttingen to the edge of Hamburg. George I and George II were rulers of two separated territories and – retaining deep German roots – they took their continental obligations seriously, spending at least one summer in three in Hanover, together with key ministers usually headed by the senior Secretary of State. This pattern was broken only in 1760 with the accession of George III – the first Hanoverian to be born in Britain and to speak English as his mother tongue. Indeed he never visited Hanover during his sixty-year reign.[18]

The Hanover connection and the experience of fighting continental wars gave the eighteenth-century British political elite a keen awareness of Europe as a whole, both geographically and politically. This also discouraged insular isolationism. In 1716 the Earl of Sunderland asserted that 'the old Tory notion that England can subsist by itself whatever becomes of the rest of Europe' had been 'justly exploded since the revolution' of 1688. In 1742 the MP John Perceval ridiculed the idea 'that this country is an island entrenched within its own natural boundaries, that it may stand secure and unconcerned in all the storms of the rest of the world'. The politician Lord Carteret insisted in 1744 that 'our own independence' was closely linked to 'the liberties of the continent'.[19] And setbacks against the French were often blamed on eighteenth-century equivalents of lack of willpower: luxury, selfishness, even an addiction to tea. 'Were they the sons of tea-sippers', asked the pamphleteer Jonas Hanway, 'who won the fields of Cressy and Agincourt, or dyed the Danube's streams with Gallic blood' at Blenheim?[20]

It became an explicit theme of Whig political rhetoric during the first half of the eighteenth century that the 'national interest' required Britain to maintain a 'balance of power' on the Continent, through judicious alliances and selective intervention. Yet there were many who disagreed. One critic claimed in 1742 that the idea of it 'being the Honour of England to hold the balance of Europe has been so ignorantly interpreted, so absurdly applied, and so perniciously put into practice, that it has cost this Nation more lives, and more money, than all the national Honour of that kind in the World is worth'.[21] The Tory politician and political philosopher Lord Bolingbroke offered an alternative strategy. 'Great Britain is an island,' he insisted. 'The sea is our barrier, ships are our fortresses, and the mariners that trade and commerce alone can furnish are the garrisons to defend them.' Bolingbroke did not totally rule out sending soldiers to the Continent. 'Like other amphibious animals, we must come occasionally on shore,' he admitted, 'but the water is more properly our element, and in it, like them, as we find our greatest strength, so we exert our greatest force.'[22]

Emerging here was what would prove to be a lasting tension in debates about British foreign policy between a 'continental' and a 'maritime' strategy. The latter became more plausible after 1760 under a monarch who did not share his predecessors' orientation towards Hanover, both personally and politically. What's more, Britain's trade had now shifted away from northwest Europe to the Mediterranean, East Indies, Caribbean and the American colonies, in an increasingly profitable nexus of goods, commodities and people-trafficking. The major wars against France in the second part of the 'long eighteenth century' – 1756–63, 1778–83, 1793–1802 and climacterically 1803–15 – were struggles for global empire, especially in North America and the Indian sub-continent. Indeed Britain was now, to quote historian Peter Marshall, 'a nation defined by Empire'.[23]

Yet also still defined by its relations with the rest of Europe: every one of these wars entailed threats to the security of the British homeland, above all the menace of invasion by Napoleon in 1803–5. But except for the crisis years of 1812–15, Britain did not deploy large armies on the continent – using instead its commercial wealth

and stable national debt to employ foreign mercenaries as its contribution to continental alliances. In 1760, for instance, at the height
of the Seven Years' War, there were 187,000 soldiers in Britain's pay
yet the contingent of British and Irish troops sent to Germany
numbered only 20,000.[24] In the seven wars against France from
1688 to 1815, the British were diplomatically isolated just once,
when Spain and the Dutch joined France in 1779–80. As a result,
Britain lost control of the seas and, with this, its American colonies.

These conflicts had a profound effect on national identity. 'Great
Britain' – the union of England and Wales with Scotland in 1707
– was an invented nation, forged and hardened through these
conflicts. 'A powerful and persistent threatening France became the
haunting embodiment of that Catholic Other which Britons had
been taught to fear since the Reformation,' historian Linda Colley
has observed. 'Confronting it encouraged them to bury their
internal differences in the struggle for survival, victory and booty.'[25]

The global struggle against France between 1793 and 1815 (over
twice as long as both of Britain's twentieth-century world wars
combined) revived a real threat of invasion. A small French force
landed in Wales in 1797, followed by more substantial invasions of
Ireland in 1796 and 1798 – one of the main reasons for incorpo-
rating Ireland into the United Kingdom in 1801. Indeed from 1798
to 1805 the invasion of England was Napoleon's main strategic aim.
'Eight hours of night in our favour would decide the fate of the
universe,' he blustered. 'We have six centuries of insult to avenge.'
Britain was mobilised as never before. In 1804–5, nearly a tenth of
the country's 10.5 million people were directly involved in national
defence. In these years, France became Britain's bogeyman, with
fears fanned by propagandists. 'That perfidious, blood-thirsty
nation, the French,' one pamphlet claimed in 1793, was 'the source
of every evil you have experienced for a century past.'[26]

Only when he lost control of the seas after the Battle of Trafalgar in 1805 did Napoleon turn east against Prussia and then Russia. But he posed a new challenge in the form of economic warfare. His 'Continental Blockade' of Britain from 1806 and British retaliation against any state that cooperated with him proved the climax of this battle to control the narrow seas. It also had wider implications. The refusal of Portugal to join the blockade allowed the British to open a vital second front from 1808 in the Peninsular War, fighting Napoleon in Spain. And the Tsar's refusal to maintain the blockade was a major factor in Napoleon's hubristic invasion of Russia in 1812, which marked the beginning of his end. In 1814 and again in 1815 Britain was able to subsidise a coalition of three major powers (Prussia, Russia and Austria) as well as its own now-substantial army and thereby twice defeat the Little Emperor – culminating in the British-Prussian victory at Waterloo in June 1815.

The French wars from 1793 to 1815 led to a sharper definition of national borders. For the British, the sea between the two countries became generally known as 'The English Channel' – reflecting their claim that 'the maritime frontier was defined by the French coast'. For the French, the waterway was known as 'La Manche' – the sleeve – indicating a looser conception of territorial waters. 'The sea became an external limit of the French territory, without belonging to it,' but the English claimed the sea as well.[27] Affirming Britain's security interest in the other side of the Channel coast, in 1839 the Foreign Secretary, Lord Palmerston, orchestrated an international agreement to guarantee the independence and neutrality of Belgium, which had broken away from the United Kingdom of the Netherlands. France and Prussia were among the signatories. This had fateful consequences seventy-five years later.

After Waterloo there was periodic friction with France and occasional invasion scares, but, to quote historian François Crouzet, the French 'never again picked up the gauntlet'. They 'understood that they would not have a chance, and so backed down when the risk of war was serious, for example in 1840 and again in 1898'.[28] Gradually relations between Britain and France moved haltingly towards co-existence, then entente and eventually alliance – redefining Britain's continental connection until 1940.

The Channel – transcended yet triumphant

During the century between 1815 and 1914, Britain tried to maintain its hybrid grand strategy – maritime and continental – by new means. Global expansion, often conducted by limited wars such as the conquest of Egypt in 1882, was combined with periodic bouts of calculating diplomacy to maintain a European balance. Throughout, large-scale wars such as the Crimea (1854–6) and South Africa (1899–1902) were the exception. But in the last decades of the nineteenth century – after the geopolitical turning points of American and German unification between 1861 and 1871 – the implications of Britain's relative decline began to kick in. During the long eighteenth century the British had battled against a single foe, France, for European stability and global hegemony. The struggle was immense, but the chess game was essentially simple. By 1900, however, the country faced simultaneous challenges on the continent and globally from a variety of powers, even though Germany was the most threatening because closest to home. The first German war (1914–18) was won by Britain and France, but only with massive American help; in the second France quickly became irrelevant geopolitically and America all-important. In the process the Channel lost much of its strategic significance – transcended by the bomber and then the nuclear missile. Yet its psychological importance for British identity was triumphantly re-asserted by the events of 1940. The era of the two world wars requires closer attention because it has become central to national debate.

In the late-nineteenth century, Britain's default response in the face of multiple challengers was a policy of selective 'appeasement' – in those days a perfectly respectable diplomatic term. It meant, according to historian Paul Kennedy, 'satisfying grievances through rational negotiation and compromise, thereby avoiding the resort to an armed conflict which would be expensive, bloody, and possibly very dangerous'.[29] But the rationality and acceptability of appeasement was more obvious to the British than to others. 'We are not a young people with *an innocent record and* a scanty inheritance,' Churchill privately admitted in 1914. 'We have got all we want in territory and our claim to be left in the unmolested enjoyment of vast and splendid possessions, *mainly acquired by violence, largely maintained by force*, often seems less reasonable to others than to us.'[30] He chose to omit the italicised phrases when quoting this memorandum in his war memoirs – a sign, presumably, of his awareness that they did not accord with what the British liked to present as their principled love of peace.

The United States, at least, could be managed around the turn of the century by calculated appeasement – backing down on points of friction, while playing up the economic and cultural ties between the two 'Anglo-Saxon' powers. The US was a force only in the Americas and the Pacific, with – at this stage – minimal political engagement in Europe. In Europe itself, Germany was not geographically a direct threat – unlike Napoleonic France had been. However, its aspirations under Kaiser Wilhelm II to become a 'world power' equal to the others did pose a serious challenge, especially in the 1900s when Germany built a large modern fleet to rival the Royal Navy. This prompted Britain to draw closer to France and Russia – colonial rivals in North Africa and the Indian subcontinent respectively but also European states that feared the growth of German military power. The Anglo–French entente of 1904 and the Anglo–Russian agreement of 1907 were intended to resolve, or at least reduce, imperial tensions in the interests of deterring Germany.

London did not join the formal Franco – Russian defensive alliance – successive British governments wished to maintain their freedom of action – but secret staff conversations with the French in 1912 led to a de facto entanglement because the French had deployed much of their navy in the Mediterranean (against any threat from Austria and Italy) on the understanding that the Royal Navy would be concentrated in the Channel against Germany. And this mattered in the crisis of July 1914, when Europe suddenly began to polarise. After Serbian nationalists assassinated the heir to the Habsburg throne, the government in Vienna decided, with German backing, to embark on war against Serbia, whereupon Russia threw its support behind the Serbs – with increasing encouragement from France.

For most of July, the British Foreign Secretary, Sir Edward Grey, kept both France and Germany guessing. His policy of calculated ambiguity was intended to retain Britain's 'free hand' for as long as possible while working to broker a negotiated agreement between the two armed camps.[31] But Grey ended up leaving both the French and the Germans confused about Britain's intentions: in particular he failed to send a clear deterrent signal to Berlin until it was too late.[32]

In any case, the ambiguity was false because the FO was sure the country could not afford to stand aside from a European war. Eyre Crowe, a senior diplomat, posed the alternatives starkly. If the Kaiser won, defeating Russia and France and leaving Germany 'in occupation of the Channel, with the willing or unwilling cooperation of Holland and Belgium', what, he asked, would be 'the position of friendless England?' And if France and Russia won alone, 'what would be their attitude towards England? What about India and the Mediterranean?' In other words, sitting out a great war would leave Britain vulnerable in Europe, or globally. That is why the British – as a truly global power – felt they could never make a stark choice between a continental and an imperial foreign policy.[33] And also why Britain, like an ageing lion, would ultimately have to fight in order to maintain its dominance. As Crowe told Grey, 'the theory that England cannot engage in a big war means her abdication as an independent state . . . A balance of power cannot be maintained by a State that is incapable of fighting and consequently carries no weight.'[34]

Grey's dilemma was eased by Germany's own folly. In an effort to knock France out of the war quickly before the Russian juggernaut could plough into East Prussia, the German army thrust towards Paris through Belgium. This violation of the 1839 Treaty of London – dismissed by the German Chancellor as just 'a scrap of paper'[35] – was a spectacular diplomatic own-goal, allowing Grey to head off a fundamental rift in the Cabinet and giving Britain a clear legal and geopolitical justification for war. But no one in London in August 1914, even those who dismissed glib talk of a war 'over by Christmas', imagined a conflict that would last more than four years and claim the lives of some 750,000 UK service personnel – the most costly war in British history.

This time, Britain's traditional strategy of deploying its naval strength and subsidising others to fight proved much less effective. After a frantic war of movement in 1914, the conflict on the Western Front bogged down in inconclusive but bloody trench war. And nothing came of the alternative 'peripheral' strategy of striking at Germany's weaker allies – the Ottomans in the Dardanelles campaign of 1915 or the Habsburgs via reinforcing the Italians in 1917. In terms of the old dualism, therefore, neither a continental nor a maritime strategy proved decisive. In 1916 the British were obliged to impose conscription, instead of relying on volunteers, and to embark on a major continental land offensive of their own in order to relieve the pressure on the French at Verdun. The four-and-a-half month battle of the Somme did not achieve a breakthrough

– the maximum advance was some six miles at the cost of nearly half-a-million British Empire casualties – and Passchendaele in 1917 was another futile bloodbath, costing at least a quarter of a million lives for minimal gains. By now Britain's own financial resources were running low because this was war on an utterly different scale. Not only had defence spending risen astronomically – from £91 million in 1913 to nearly £2 billion in 1918, over half of GDP[36] – Britain was also the principal banker of the Entente against Germany and the Central Powers, loaning the equivalent of more than $11 billion during the war, mostly to Russia, France and Italy. The British war effort became dependent on imports of food, raw materials and munitions from the USA and on loans from New York bankers. It required American finance and then, after the USA joined the war in April 1917, American manpower to help tip the balance in the Allies' favour, ultimately offsetting the collapse of the Eastern Front at the end of 1917 after the Bolshevik revolution.

The Armistice of 11 November 1918, the implosion of Imperial Germany and the punitive Treaty of Versailles the following June all conveyed the impression that Britain had won the war – and won big. Yet the crucial geopolitical questions posed in the 1860s about America and Germany had not been resolved. It was deeply unsettling in 1917, as the press baron Lord Northcliffe put it, to be 'down on our knees to the Americans', and many British policy-makers resolved that keeping on good terms with the United States should now be a guiding principle of the country's diplomacy. But the British intended to define that relationship as far as possible. 'There is undoubtedly a difference between the British and the Continental view in international matters,' Lord Robert Cecil told the War Cabinet in September 1917. 'I will not attempt to describe the difference, but I know that you will agree in thinking that, where it exists, we are right and the Continental nations are, speaking generally, wrong. If America accepts our point of view in these matters, it will mean the dominance of that view in all international affairs.' He felt confident that the USA could be induced to follow the British line because, 'though the American people are very largely foreign, both in origin and modes of thought, their rulers are almost exclusively Anglo-Saxons, and share our political ideals.' Here, in embryo, was the British notion of a 'special relationship'.[37]

Yet 1919–20 showed the risks of relying too closely on Cecil's politico-cultural assumptions. The US Senate refused to accept Wilson's League of Nations and, with it, the Versailles treaty. During the 1920s the United States pulled back from European commitments. One of the casualties was the Anglo-American guarantee of French security, which Paris had seen as essential because of not being allowed to shift France's border right up to the Rhine. The British did not intend to enforce that guarantee alone. Just like the Americans pulling back from their wartime alliance with Britain, so the British rapidly distanced themselves from France.

In 1921 Georges Clemenceau, the French Prime Minister, told Lloyd George that 'within an hour after the Armistice I had the impression that you had once again become the enemies of France.' Lloyd George responded, 'Has not that always been the traditional policy of my country?'[38] The two wartime allies rapidly resumed their colonial rivalries, this time in the Middle East, and they were at odds over policy towards Germany. Once the Kaiser's fleet had been eliminated, Britain did not feel threatened because of the Channel, whereas France had only a land border with Germany – a country which boasted 50 per cent more people and four times the heavy industry. They wanted to dismember Bismarckian Germany, or at least keep it down through punitive reparations and strict enforcement of the Versailles treaty – whereas most British policymakers looked for ways to bring Germany back into the community of nations and save it from Bolshevism. Austen

Chamberlain, Britain's Foreign Secretary in 1924–9, was a rare exception, insisting in 1924 that 'we should make the Entente with France the cardinal object of our policy.' But by 1932 even Sir Robert Vansittart, the Francophile permanent secretary of the Foreign Office, observed that 'France has of late virtually attained the very thing that we have traditionally sought to avoid in Europe, hegemony, if not dictatorship, political and military.'[39]

Given this mood, it is not surprising that the idea of building a Channel Tunnel to link Britain and France – debated on and off since the late nineteenth century – got short shrift in London after the war on grounds of national security. 'Providence has made us an island – I think for a great purpose in the history of Europe and the world,' declared Lloyd George in 1919. 'The fact that it is an island has been the means of saving the liberty of Europe many a time' and he did not want to lose that privileged geography without very good cause. Amid assorted fears of saboteurs, lightning enemy raids, Bolshevik infiltrators and hordes of refugees, only Churchill stood out as a firm Cabinet supporter of a tunnel, largely for its commercial benefits. There was majority agreement with the Foreign Office view, expressed in 1920, 'that our relations with France never have been, are not, and probably never will be sufficiently stable and friendly to justify the construction of a Channel tunnel, and the loss of security which our insular position, even in spite of the wonderful scientific and mechanical developments of recent years, still continues to bestow.'[40]

Yet those 'wonderful' technological developments were now literally overriding England's 'providential' insularity. The dawning era of airpower meant that the 'moat defensive' might soon prove irrelevant. 'The old frontiers are gone,' Tory leader Stanley Baldwin warned the Commons in 1934. 'When you think of the defence of England you no longer think of the chalk cliffs of Dover, you think of the Rhine.' Fear of the bomber came close to paranoia in the mid-1930s. Even Whitehall's Joint Planning Committee, representing the three armed services, predicted 20,000 casualties in the initial twenty-four hours of air attack, rising to perhaps 150,000 by the end of the first week. This was a gross exaggeration – Britain sustained fewer than 150,000 casualties from all forms of air attack in the whole Second World War – but the panic skewed British defence policy in the 1930s.[41]

Once Hitler gained power in 1933, determined to reverse the *Diktat* of Versailles by military means, the British government did not respond with a balanced programme of rearmament but concentrated on the threat from the new *Luftwaffe*. The rationale for doing so had been stated with chilling candour by Baldwin in 1932. 'I think it is well also for the man in the street to realise that there is no power on earth that can protect him from being bombed. Whatever people may tell him, the bomber will always get through.' The implication, Baldwin went on, was that 'the only defence is in offence, which means that you have to kill more women and children more quickly than the enemy if you want to save yourselves.'[42]

So, for most of the 1930s, the government concentrated on building up a bomber force of its own – hopefully as a deterrent, if necessary as a lethal weapon. Only in 1939 did it no longer seem inevitable that the bomber would get through. The development of fast monoplane fighters (Hurricanes and Spitfires), combined with an even more novel system of radar stations around England's southeast coast, offered the prospect of detecting and destroying enemy bombers before they got through. Defence budgets reflected the top priority given to airpower. The Navy came second in terms of spending; the Army a distant third. In the isolationist atmosphere of the times and with memories of the Somme and Passchendaele still raw, the idea of sending another great army to its death across the Channel was anathema. No nation would 'stand the losses we went through again for another 100 years,' warned General Sir

George Milne in 1927: 'civilisation itself would go to pieces if a war similar to the last one were fought.' The Army tried to insist that, in the age of airpower, Britain's traditional commitment to Belgian territorial integrity was more important than ever – so that 'Belgium would be available as an air base for ourselves and not as an air base for Germany' – but in early 1938 the Cabinet abandoned even contingency planning for sending another 'field force' to the Continent. In short, as far as 'Europe' was concerned, British policy was one of 'limited liability'.[43]

This policy had been shaped particularly by Neville Chamberlain – Prime Minister from May 1937, having controlled the purse strings since 1931 as Chancellor of the Exchequer. Chamberlain took a particularly sceptical view of potential allies: he resisted French attempts to entangle Britain in continental commitments and argued that it was 'always best and safest to count on *nothing* from the Americans except words'.[44] Drawing lessons from Grey's perilous fence-sitting in July 1914, Chamberlain took personal control of foreign affairs once in Number Ten, meeting Hitler on three occasions during the Czech crisis of September 1938. His aim was to avoid another Great War – this time involving Armageddon from the air – over a 'faraway country' that he deemed of no significant interest to British security. Hence his sacrifice of Czechoslovak territory and independence at Munich, which was when 'appeasement' developed its current connotations as a term of abuse. But then in the crisis of March 1939 he and a panicked Cabinet decided they must guarantee the territorial integrity of Poland in order to deter yet more German expansion. It was no longer plausible to claim that Hitler's aims were 'strictly limited' or that 'limited liability' made sense. Peacetime conscription was imposed (for the first time in British history) and staff talks began with the French. When Hitler – in league with Stalin – carved up Poland in September 1939, Britain and France declared war.

During the so-called 'Phoney War' of winter 1939–40, British policymakers reflected on what had gone wrong since 1918. Many admitted privately that they had been naïve in the 1920s and 1930s about the threat from Germany and were determined not to repeat such a mistake once the current conflict was over. Sir Orme Sargent, a senior official at the Foreign Office, suggested in a minute written in February 1940 that it would therefore be essential to construct 'such a system of close and permanent cooperation between France and Great Britain – political, military and economic – as will for all international purposes make of the two countries a single unit in post-war Europe'. By this remarkable phrase Sargent signified close cooperation between the two governments rather than any federal structure, but even that would require a revolution in British thinking. He therefore proposed a major propaganda and education campaign for the public at large. 'I entirely agree,' noted Chamberlain.[45] On 28 March 1940 the two countries issued a Joint Declaration pledging that 'after the conclusion of peace' they would maintain 'a community of action in all spheres for as long as may be necessary to safeguard their security and to effect the reconstruction, with the assistance of other nations, of an international order which will ensure the liberty of people, respect for law, and the maintenance of peace in Europe'. A Whitehall committee started to identify key areas for administrative cooperation; the Board of Education and the BBC began a special campaign to promote greater understanding of France in British schools.[46]

In public, Churchill proclaimed on 30 March that the unity of Britain and France was now 'indissoluble'; a *Times* leading article stated that the two countries were moving to 'ever closer union' – ironically a phrase later used in the Treaty of Rome in 1957.[47] Of course, there was also plenty of scepticism in private – both about the Union and also the French. But the Declaration was viewed as the start of a long learning process. Had the two countries fought together as allies against Germany for four years – as in the Great War – 1940 might today be seen as the moment when Britain turned permanently toward 'Europe'. Instead the second German war turned out very differently from the first: after France collapsed in June 1940, there was no Western Front until D-Day in June 1944.

Because their volte face on continental commitments came so late, the British had been able to commit only ten divisions to the Western Front in May 1940 – the Dutch managed eight and the French deployed more than 100. The paucity of Britain's military commitment probably made little difference to the Battle of France. The crucial factor was Hitler's change of strategy from a main thrust into Belgium – repeating the Schlieffen Plan of August 1914 – where the *Wehrmacht* would have crashed into the bulk of the French and British forces. Instead he mounted a surprise left hook around their southern flank, using most of his armoured divisions to drive through the Ardennes, across the Meuse river and then push northwest to the Channel. The Allied defeat was the result of intelligence failure compounded by paralysis in the French high command: a few more British divisions in Belgium would not have made much difference.

On the other hand, thanks to the persistent bias of 1930s rearmament, London had a superb system of air defence and this proved vital in the Battle of Britain that summer after France collapsed. Around the story of 1940 much of the subsequent debate about British history and identity has revolved.

The French collapse changed the whole direction of British foreign policy. May 1940 put an end to British plans for a new relationship with France – though the Cabinet did endorse a formal proposal for Anglo-French Union, including shared citizenship, on 16 June in a futile, last-ditch effort to head off France's capitulation next day. Britain now confronted a great power in command of the Channel coast without – for the first time in its history – the support of any continental allies. This was worse than the predicament of

Elizabeth I facing the Spanish Armada. And if the RAF lost control of the air, then a German invasion seemed inevitable. Had Britain also lost its army in France, then some kind of compromise peace would have been likely: this was, indeed, debated by the War Cabinet on 26–28 May when it initially seemed that only 20,000 to 30,000 troops could be brought home from the beaches around Dunkirk.[48] The eventual figure by 3 June, however, was 335,000 – two-thirds of them of them British and mostly regulars and territorials. This gave Churchill the core of an army with which to face invasion.

The Dunkirk evacuation also provided the country with its modern providentialist saga, composed in the heat of the moment. On 25 May *The Times* likened the struggle for control of the Channel ports to epics of English history such as Agincourt, the Armada and Waterloo. On 6 June, the paper was already enjoining readers to draw inspiration from 'the spirit of Dunkirk'. Most of the press, whatever its political hue, followed the same line: with the country venturing into an unknown future, it seemed that only 'history' could provide a script. 'Some nations are separated by a sad gulf from a heroic past,' declared *Picture Post*; 'but we are not.' And the 'miracle' of Dunkirk was widely extolled, like that of the Armada. Churchill also played a major part in the process of history-making. On 4 June, after Dunkirk, he declared himself fully confident that 'we shall prove ourselves once again able to defend our island home, to ride out the storm of war, and to outlive the menace of tyranny, if necessary for years, if necessary alone.' And on 18 June, he told the Commons and then the world that 'Hitler knows that he has to break in this island or lose the war' and urged the British people to 'so bear ourselves that if the British Empire and its Commonwealth last for a thousand years, men will still say, "This was their finest hour."' A millennium is a very long time, and none of us will be around in 2940 to check up but, thus far, Churchill's prediction has been borne out.[49]

"VERY WELL , ALONE"

*Echoing Churchill's defiant words in the House of Commons, Low's
cartoon in the* Evening Standard *on 18 June 1940 proved to be a
classic statement of heroic isolation.*

Churchill's 'alone' became a catchphrase in the summer of 1940.
David's Low's now celebrated cartoon, captioned 'Very Well, Alone',
depicted a Tommy, fist in the air, defying the storm-tossed seas and
the menace from the air. 'Now we know where we are!' shouted
the pugnacious skipper of a Thames tug-boat: 'No more bloody
allies!' King George VI made the same point more decorously,
telling his mother, 'Personally, I feel happier now that we have no
allies to be polite to & to pamper.' And the poet T. S. Eliot announced
that 'History is now and England' – capturing the incandescence
of the moment in his poem 'Little Gidding', drafted while

fire-watching in the Blitz. Eliot's line would have been inconceivable during the Great War: more likely in September 1914 'History is now and Belgium'.[50]

Dunkirk was of major importance in inscribing the 'White Cliffs of Dover' into the iconography of British identity. The chalky coast-line had started to assume this role during the nineteenth century, thanks to artists such as J. M. W. Turner, and also because cross-Channel ferries and the development of prints and then photo postcards made their seaward visage widely known. Around that image began to accrete stories of national defence and British distinctiveness – historical associations that helped 'picture the nation' so that this icon of landscape became 'storied'.[51] This construction was elevated further after Dunkirk and the Battle of Britain, through Alice Duer Miller's *The White Cliffs* – a bestselling verse-novel of 1940 which MGM turned into a movie in 1944 – and the 1941 song 'The White Cliffs of Dover' which Vera Lynn made into one of the top hits of the war. The chalk ramparts of the English coast became perhaps the most evocative symbol of Britain alone.

Yet 'alone' was a heroic fiction. What Churchill called 'our island home' could only survive because of its vast imperial supply chain. He declared in his memoirs that, even in 1940, he was never seri-ously afraid of invasion but that he did fear defeat in 1942 if the country's oceanic lifelines were cut, driving imports of food and raw materials below the acceptable minimum for national survival.[52] The empire/Commonwealth also proved an essential source of manpower. By late 1940, two Canadian divisions were deployed along the North Downs in Surrey to protect London, and in early 1941 two Australian divisions and one each from India and New Zealand fought the Axis in North Africa and the Mediterranean to protect the empire's main artery, the Suez Canal.[53]

Although the empire was vital for Britain's survival, its resources were not enough to defeat Germany. On 25 May 1940 the Chiefs of Staff submitted a memo entitled 'British Strategy in a Certain Eventuality' – euphemism for the likely fall of France. The Chiefs' central assumption was that the United States would be 'willing to give us full economic and financial support, *without which we do not think we could continue this war with any chance of success*.' This became the basic axiom of British foreign policy – for wartime and after. As early as July 1940 Lord Halifax, the Foreign Secretary, observed: 'It may well be that instead of studying closer union with France, we shall find ourselves contemplating some sort of special association with the USA.'[54]

This was a theme that the half-American Churchill made his own later in the war, dilating on the 'special relationship' between the two leading 'English-speaking peoples'. And after five years of war during which Britain's closest allies were the United States and the empire/Commonwealth, that orientation seemed almost inevitable. Yet it would not have happened but for the abrupt and total fall of France in little more than a month. Nor if President Franklin D. Roosevelt had been unable to persuade his countrymen to reject the isolationism of the 1930s and instead treat Britain as America's front line of defence. FDR contrived this with a mixture of oratorical skill and devious diplomacy until Pearl Harbor thrust the USA openly into the world war. Thereafter the British Isles became the indispensable base for bombing Hitler's Europe and for building up a British-American-Canadian army of liberation in preparation for the 'Overlord' landings in Normandy on 6 June 1944.

Until D-Day – as Churchill was at pains to show statistically in his memoirs – Britain and its empire/Commonwealth could be considered America's equal in the war effort. But in the last year of the conflict, as the reinvented Western Front gradually rolled across France and into Germany, Britain became increasingly the junior partner to a fully mobilised USA. 'Our armies are only about one-half the size of the American and will soon be little more than one-third,' Churchill lamented in December 1944, 'so it is not as easy as it used to be for me to get things done.'[55] Had the United States withdrawn into post-war isolationism again, as seemed possible in 1945–6, that imbalance might have proved temporary. But this time America's engagement with Europe proved permanent: the deepening Cold War with the Soviet Union led in 1949 to the North Atlantic Treaty – an unprecedented US peacetime commitment to Western European security, soon institutionalised in a full military alliance.

This was an alliance founded on American nuclear superiority. The advent of the nuclear age in 1945 left Britain even more vulnerable than in the era of airpower. The Channel and the White Cliffs – so potent symbolically – were totally irrelevant against atomic and thermonuclear weapons: identity was at odds with security. Admittedly, this outcome was not evident immediately. There were hopes in 1945–6 that wartime cooperation with the USSR – so important for Britain's wartime survival though later largely erased from national memory – might be sustained in some form. But the Sovietisation of Eastern Europe and Stalin's test of an atomic bomb in 1949 rendered such hopes illusory. Unlike the USA, Britain lay well within range of Soviet bombers and, as a highly urbanised country – more than 40 per cent of the population lived in cities of over 100,000 people – it was acutely vulnerable. The Chiefs of Staff warned in 1946 that thirty Soviet atomic bombs might be enough to 'produce collapse in this country' and that the USSR would have such a stockpile by the mid-1950s. As Churchill put it in 1951, the UK was now 'the target, and perhaps the bull's eye, of a Soviet attack.'[56]

If, then, the United Kingdom was almost indefensible in the event of a nuclear war and if alliance with the United States was the only conceivable deterrent, why did the British Government decide to develop its own nuclear capability at huge expense? The story reveals another facet of the country's complex matrix of identity and security. The foundational decision was taken in 1945–6 by the Labour government – led by Clement Attlee and Foreign Secretary Ernest Bevin. At this time the Cold War had not assumed its fully frozen shape: Britain was still negotiating with Moscow and Washington was distancing itself from London – especially with regard to wartime collaboration on nuclear weapons. When the Cabinet debated the issue at a crucial meeting in October 1946, the argument was framed in terms of cost versus credibility. On the one hand, concern was expressed about the diversion of resources away from post-war economic recovery at a time when, given present trends, 'we might find ourselves faced with an extremely serious economic and financial situation in two or three years.' Against that it was argued that 'we could not afford to be left behind in a field which was of such revolutionary importance from an industrial, no less than from a military point of view. Our prestige in the world, as well as our chances of securing American co-operation would both suffer if we did not exploit to the full a discovery in which we had played a leading part at the outset.' As Bevin, a no-nonsense former union leader, put it more pungently – having just been talked down to by his US counterpart Jimmy Byrnes – 'we have got to have this thing over here whatever it costs . . . We've got to have the bloody Union Jack on top of it.'[57]

As a result of the Cabinet's decision, in 1952 Britain became the third power, after the USA and the USSR, to test a nuclear device. But it became ever harder and more costly to keep the Union Jack on top of the Bomb in the era of thermonuclear weapons and long-range missiles. In 1962, with its V-bomber force obsolescent and unable to develop its own missile delivery system, Harold Macmillan's Tory government decided to purchase Polaris missiles from the USA for use on British submarines. This was depicted by Macmillan as one facet of the 'interdependence' of the two countries within their 'special relationship' but it was hardly a partnership of equals

– the US defence budget was now ten times larger than the UK's – and, as the Ministry of Defence privately observed, by 'having to rely on America for certain important and expensive weapons' that had 'proved beyond our resources to develop' Britain was actually in a situation of 'one-sided dependence'. Yet it was politically essential for a Tory Cabinet to represent the new arrangements as preserving Britain's 'independent' deterrent: this was done by insisting that, although normally under NATO control, Polaris could be used unilaterally if a British government decided that 'supreme national interests' were at stake'.[58]

This 'struggle to alchemise dependence and inferiority into partnership and equality' continued in 1981 when the Thatcher Cabinet had to decide whether to upgrade again by buying US Trident missiles. The Defence Secretary John Nott claimed that 'two-thirds of the party and two-thirds of the Cabinet were opposed to the procurement of Trident. Even the Chiefs of Staff were not unanimous.' But he and Thatcher were both determined to go ahead. The Foreign Secretary Lord Carrington remarked that failure to do so would leave the French as 'the only nuclear power in Europe. This would be intolerable.'[59] And again in 2016 a Tory government agreed to purchase a successor for Trident, even though it would consume about a quarter of the defence equipment budget over the next decade. This decision was endorsed in the Commons on 19 July by 472 votes to 117 – all Tory MPs but one being supported, less enthusiastically, by three-fifths of the parliamentary Labour party. This tacit cross-party consensus reflects the 'doctrine of unripe time' (this is not the moment to disarm) and the consequent pursuit of 'a set of rationales to clothe that gut decision', to quote defence intellectual and former civil servant Sir Michael Quinlan.[60] And, in a volatile and ever-changing world, it also reflects the fact that no city has been 'put to the Bomb' since Nagakasi on 9 August 1945. Unless and until another one is, it seemed imprudent to change British strategy in any way that might undermine the doctrine – or fiction – of nuclear deterrence. In any case, the status argument still had weight for many MPs: Great Britain needed to keep its place on the top table.

Paying the 'price of victory'

Between the 1930s and the 1960s the revolutions in military technology – from the bomber to the Bomb, from battleships to missiles – gradually rendered the Channel irrelevant to Britain's strategic security. What counted above all was the country's NATO alliance with the world's leading nuclear superpower across the Atlantic. Yet, at the same time, the twists and turns of the Second World War – especially in 1940 – had reinforced the place of the Channel in the country's distinctive sense of national identity, particularly for the English. 'Britain had not been conquered or invaded,' declared Jean Monnet, France's greatest European: 'She felt no need to exorcise history.'[61]

What, then, of 'Europe' in this challenging new age for those shaping British foreign policy? How did they deal with that great historic novelty – a European Community? This started with six founding West European states in 1958, led by France and West Germany, doubled to 12 by the mid-1980s, before spreading eastward after the end of the Cold War to embrace another 15 countries by 2007 – thus encompassing most of the European continent. Where did this New Europe fit within the long narrative of British history?

Despite 1940, the idea of an Anglo-French entente was not completely dead after the Second World War. In 1947 the two governments signed a treaty of alliance – aptly (or ironically) at Dunkirk. This was enlarged the following year into the Brussels pact with Belgium, Luxembourg and the Netherlands for mutual military, political and economic cooperation. But 1940 had left deep scars. 'We have a major interest in European recovery. Failure of Europe to recover spells communism,' senior Whitehall officials warned in January 1949. 'But the concept must be one of limited liability. In no circumstances must we assist them beyond the point at which the assistance leaves us too weak to be a worthwhile ally for USA if Europe collapses.' Churchill personified this ambivalence. In 1946, in a major speech in Zurich, he called for a 'United States of Europe', built on a historically novel 'partnership' between France and Germany – with Britain as one of the 'friends and sponsors'. But he envisaged this sponsorship being exercised mostly from the sidelines and viewed Britain's European connection as only one of 'three circles' – separate but overlapping – in which the country was involved. 'Our first object is the unity and consolidation of the British Commonwealth and what is left of the former British Empire,' he told his Cabinet after returning to power in 1951. 'Our second is the "fraternal association" of the English-speaking world; and third, United Europe, to which we are a separate, closely- and specially-related ally and friend.'[62]

This semi-detached policy was not entirely surprising. West Germany was one of two German states, split along the Cold War divide, and France was polarised between left and right. Both were still struggling to recover from the war. In 1951–2, Britain's exports and its industrial production were both comparable to those of France and West Germany combined.[63] During the 1950s, however, the balance of power – or at least of potential – shifted dramatically, leaving British leaders flat-footed. Their failure to play a decisive part in the formative years of European integration proved one of the most costly mistakes of post-war British history. And it was a mistake made by both main political parties. The cardinal error was not engaging in these formative discussions and trying to shape them in a direction more suited to British interests. Instead it was assumed that the 'Continentals' would never get their act together. This complacency, even arrogance, about countries that had so recently been either wartime enemies or feeble allies has been called 'the price of victory'.[64]

In 1950 the Labour Cabinet declined involvement in the Schuman Plan to create a European Coal and Steel Community (ECSC). Though welcoming the Plan as a device to reconcile France and Germany, they doubted its economic benefits for the UK, given that only 5 per cent of Britain's steel exports went to Western Europe, and they distrusted its 'federalist' overtones. 'If you open that Pandora's box', declared Bevin, 'you never know what Trojan 'orses will jump out'. He told American advocates of European integration heatedly that 'Great Britain was not part of Europe; she was not simply a Luxembourg'. In any case, British policymakers assumed that the Schuman Plan would fail to get off the ground, allowing London then to make a counter-proposal on its own terms. In fact, the ECSC came into existence in 1952.[65]

This miscalculation was repeated in 1955 when the six members of the ECSC invited Britain's Tory government, now led by Anthony Eden, to join in discussions about further integration – in the areas of atomic energy or a possible common market. At this stage the proposals were vague and Harold Macmillan, the Foreign Secretary, argued that Britain could exert 'a greater influence' on the talks if it were a full participant, 'on the same footing as the other countries concerned and not in the capacity of an observer'. But Rab Butler, the Chancellor of the Exchequer and Macmillan's great political rival – claimed that the proposals were 'fraught with special difficulties' given Britain's diverse global interests. In the end the government sent only an observer, a senior civil servant from the Board of Trade who was to sit in on the talks without commitment. Most other governments were represented by their foreign ministers.[66]

This set a pattern for the subsequent negotiations in Brussels. It did not help, from Britain's perspective, that their pace was largely set by the Benelux nations – keen to promote European integration having so often in the past been trapped in the jaws of Franco-German antagonism. The main lobbyist was the Dutch foreign minister Johan Beyen, whom Butler later described as 'very pushing' and 'always telling you what to do'. Butler did not take him too seriously: 'I was sort of looking rather to the bigger nations.' An interdepartmental committee, chaired and managed by the Treasury, investigated the idea of the common market during 1955 and concluded that 'on the whole' it would be bad for Britain both economically and politically – mainly because the country was a truly global power whose interests should not be trapped within some narrow European box. Most of Whitehall favoured playing things long; it was widely believed that the Brussels negotiations would collapse of their own accord given the febrile volatility of French politics. Strikingly, the issue was hardly discussed in Cabinet. According to Butler, 'Eden was bored with this . . . even more bored than I was.'[67]

The complacent British failed to anticipate two crucial developments.

First, the unlikely alliance forged by Guy Mollet, French Prime Minister from January 1956, and West Germany's Chancellor, Konrad Adenauer. Mollet was a socialist and Adenauer a Catholic Christian Democrat. But both shared a commitment to Franco-German rapprochement, and Mollet's determination was reinforced when Eden lost his nerve during the Anglo-French operation to topple Nasser in the autumn of 1956. 'Europe will be your revenge,' Adenauer reputedly told Mollet. The French premier managed to win over (the many) French critics of a common market with concessions made and paid for by the German chancellor, desperate to bring his country back into the European family of nations. Among the sweeteners offered were membership not only for France but also all its overseas territories, and preferential terms for France's inefficient but politically potent farm sector.

Second, Adenauer achieved this despite the opposition of his economics minister Ludwig Erhard – lauded by many Germans as architect of their 'economic miracle' after 1945. Erhard favoured a wider and looser free-trade area, opening out to the rest of the world, which suited West Germany's diverse commercial links with Scandinavia, Britain and the USA. But Adenauer insisted that politics trumped economics: what mattered above all was to get a deal with France. So Erhard was effectively ordered to pay whatever price was needed. That's why the French were able to call the shots.[68]

And so the Treaty of Rome was signed without the British in March 1957. Little more than a decade since the end of Hitler's war, and after three centuries of chronic war-making, the French and the Germans had finally made peace. If Britain, as Erhard wanted, had been involved in the negotiations, the dynamics would have been very different and the result less protectionist, more like a free-trade area. Alternatively, had the British been willing to accept a customs union, suggested historian Miriam Camps, 'they would have had little difficulty, at this period, in negotiating the kind of sweeping exceptions for agriculture and the Commonwealth that, later, it became impossible for them to do.'[69] Although the sticking point for Britain is often described as the principle of national sovereignty, it was more exactly – given the centrality of NATO for Macmillan's defence policy – British unwillingness to abridge that sovereignty through *European* as well as *transatlantic* interdependence.

Compounding these strategic errors, the British also failed to anticipate the pace at which the Six deepened their cooperation after the European Economic Community came into existence on

1 January 1958. After only a few years, agreement was reached on a high tariff wall against the rest of the world and a common agricultural policy which protected the agricultural sector and absorbed most of the EEC's budget. Once again the French had been able in large measure to dictate their own terms. So Britain was faced once more with its historical bugaboo – a continental bloc on the other side of the Channel, dominated moreover by France. And by 1960, even though the economic case for going 'in' remained evenly balanced, the geopolitical implications of staying 'out' could no longer be ignored. 'If the Community succeeds in becoming a really effective political and economic force', a special interdepartmental committee advised, 'it will become the dominant influence in Europe and the only Western bloc approaching the importance of the big Two – the USSR and the United States. The influence of the United Kingdom in Europe, if left outside, will correspondingly decline.' Given that 'this will be happening simultaneously with the contraction of our overseas possessions', the Committee warned, Britain risked 'ceasing to exercise any claim to be a world Power'.[70]

At this point, too late, the British perceived the consequences of not being present at the creation. The hurried fabrication of a rival European Free Trade Area (EFTA) of seven countries in an attempt to rival the Six was too little, too late – leaving Europe, it was joked, 'at sixes and sevens'. British fears about the EEC were not just economic, as often claimed, but power-political. In September 1961 the Macmillan government opened negotiations for British membership of the EEC, only to have its application vetoed in January 1963 by the French president Charles de Gaulle – who had still not forgiven *les Anglo-Saxons* for treating his Free French as minor allies after the debacle of 1940. The veto's rationale was explained with chauvinistic elegance by de Gaulle's agriculture minister to his British counterpart: 'My dear chap. It's very simple. At the moment, with the Six, there are five hens and one cock. If you join (with the other countries), there will be perhaps seven or eight hens. But there will be *two* cocks. Well, that's not so pleasant.'[71]

Afterwards, the British were happy to blame France completely for their exclusion – this fitted with old historical stereotypes. And not without reason: it's clear that the other five were not willing to stand up to de Gaulle, especially Adenauer, given the importance he attached to the new Franco-German entente. But the Macmillan government had made it much easier for the French president because London had consistently overestimated its bargaining position: applying to join the EEC with a long list of conditions, being slow to reduce these when the talks bogged down and, above all, failing to recognise that the Six would insist that Britain accepted the EEC's existing rules in their entirety – what was called the *acquis communautaire*. In other words, the British failed to see that the onus for adaptation lay with an applicant not with the EEC. Continental critics of Britain's tactics again detected the hubris of a wartime victor.[72]

De Gaulle repeated his veto in November 1967 against the application by Harold Wilson's Labour Government – who belatedly, like the Tories, had concluded that Britain had to be in, not out. It was not until the General finally retired in 1969 that the Parisian door was unbarred and unlocked. Britain's case was helped by the fact that its leader was now Edward Heath, the only unequivocally Europhile premier in post-war history. Heath knew he would have to accept the *acquis*, which had vastly expanded since the first set of negotiations in 1961–3, when the 1957 Treaty was 'the decisive sector of European law' which Britain was being asked to accept. Since 1963 'an almost inconceivable flood of European law' had been enacted which had to be accepted by Britain and the other candidates for membership in 1970.[73] The *acquis* included the unpalatable fact that two-thirds of spending went on the Common Agricultural Policy (CAP). The UK was now paying a high price for trying to join late. Heath hoped to get around all this by expanding the Community's budget and by creating a large regional development fund from which Britain's industrial rustbelt could be rejuvenated. But the complex business of completing successful negotiations, wriggling out of trade obligations to the Commonwealth, and winning over his own party took several years. It was not until January 1973 that the UK (with Ireland and Denmark) joined the European Community.

Timing mattered in another way, because 1973 happened to be the year in which the bottom dropped out of the world economy with the Middle Eastern oil crisis and the ensuing mixture of economic stagnation and rampant inflation ('stagflation'). This brought to an end a quarter-century of growth on whose high tide the new Europe had been launched. The 1970s economic crisis scuppered Heath's hopes of growing the EC out of the CAP. By the end of the decade Britain was contributing 20 per cent of the EC's income – roughly equivalent to its share of the EC's GDP – while receiving less than 9 per cent of EC spending. John Bull had joined the European train late, and found himself stuck in the second-class carriage.[74]

In the 1980s Margaret Thatcher tried a different form of catch-up – demanding a rebate on some of Britain's disproportionate budget contributions: 'We want our money.' On this issue she was a zealot, going far beyond what the Foreign Office felt diplomatically prudent: the total EC budget in 1983 was only £15 billion, equivalent to that of a large UK government department such as Education. But she ended up after five years with a rebate far greater than they believed possible, as well as the political kudos of being seen triumphantly battling for Britain. Yet the row hardened the continental image of Britain as the uniquely 'bad European', always making trouble. The Foreign Office therefore persuaded Thatcher to follow the others in dressing up the pursuit of national interest in Euro-rhetoric – a game that Britain had been slow to play. The aim was to show that the Thatcher government had 'ideas as good, and as *communautaire*, as anyone else'.[75]

And so, after the budget deal, Britain took the initiative in a major way for the first time, proposing closer European political cooperation and the completion of the free market by removing residual barriers to the movement of goods, capital and labour. The 'Single European Act' in December 1985, whereby the EC agreed to bring about the single market by 1992, was hailed in London as a British victory. What's more, in January 1986 Thatcher and French president François Mitterrand announced a deal, at last, to build a Channel tunnel. Thatcher had wanted a road link – the motor car incarnated her concept of mobile individualism – but the French collectivist preference for high-speed train travel proved much more viable. She did, however, successfully insist that it would all be paid for by private investment, rather than being an inter-governmental *grand projet* of the sort beloved by the socialist Mitterrand.

Thatcher's commitment to Europe, on *her* terms, was powerfully articulated in her Bruges speech on 20 September 1988. This is now remembered mainly for the line that 'we have not successfully rolled back the frontiers of the state in Britain, only to see them re-imposed at a European level, with a European super-state exercising a new dominance from Brussels.' Yet Thatcher began the Bruges speech with a long narrative of 'Britain and Europe' from the Romans and Saxons through the Norman and Angevin kings to Britain's role in two world wars. She even declared that 'our links to the rest of Europe, the continent of Europe, have been the *dominant* factor in our history.' A single market, as part of 'willing and active co-operation between independent and sovereign states,' was her ideal of a European Community.[76]

Yet the single market came at a double price. First of all, Thatcher conceded the principle of qualified majority voting (QMV) on some issues. In her memoirs she insisted that she had 'surrendered no important British interest', but as early as 1990 the Commons Foreign Affairs Committee concluded that the Single European Act was having 'much greater institutional impact than anyone predicted' when it was signed.[77] QMV did indeed prove the thin end of a very big wedge, making it far harder for a single national government such as Britain to block Community decisions it disliked. And, secondly, Thatcher's success in advancing 'market Europe' provoked Jacques Delors, the French socialist head of the European Commission, into balancing action, as he saw it – to promote 'social Europe' through enhanced workers' rights and welfare provision. He also wanted to create full economic and monetary union, including a single European currency. Although EMU was rejected by both main British political parties, Delors' social vision captivated many in the Labour Party, especially after *Frère Jacques* earned a standing ovation for his address to the Trades Union Congress in September 1988.

Hitherto, Labour had been largely Eurosceptic, if not Europhobe, advocating an insular socialism. In 1975, Wilson, during his second premiership, held a referendum on British membership – which he won – in order to placate his left-wing MPs, and the party's 1983 election manifesto pledged that a Labour government would leave the EC. But Delors' 'Social Chapter' seemed to offer Labour an acceptable international dimension to British socialism. At the same time Delors' policies strengthened antagonism to Europe among Tory backbenchers, who treated the negative passages in Thatcher's Bruges speech – largely a riposte to Delors – as their bible. So 1988 was something of a tipping point in British political attitudes towards 'Europe', with the Tories becoming more sceptical while Labour found something to cheer about.

After Thatcher's brief 'single market' moment in the mid-1980s, the initiative slipped rapidly out of Britain's hands. German

The European threat to British sovereignty – as seen by Cummings for
the Daily Express, *28 June 1989. The dastardly duo – Helmut Kohl*
(West Germany) and François Mitterrand (France) – are about to
violate Margaret Thatcher in her island sanctuary.

unification in 1989–90 suddenly made Delors' plan for monetary
union diplomatically viable. Like Thatcher, Mitterrand was worried
about the prospect of a strong united Germany at the heart of
Europe. In the weeks after the Berlin Wall was breached, he spoke
to her darkly of Britain and France being back in the same predicament as in 1913 or the late 1930s.[78] But, unlike the British Prime
Minister, the French president saw closer European integration as
the answer to this new German question. He persuaded Chancellor
Kohl that monetary union – including the sacrifice of West
Germans' cherished *Deutschmark* – was the necessary condition
for fast-track German unification, in order to reassure the rest of
the Continent still less than half a century after Hitler's war. The

Mitterrand – Kohl deal was a double setback for Thatcher: it meant that she had thereby simultaneously lost the support of the only ally likely to oppose German unification and of the only ally capable of blocking France's EMU project.

In the course of 1990 the Iron Lady became an isolated figure. When the EC leaders' summit in October set a timetable for a central bank by 1994 and a single currency by 1997, she told them they were living in 'cloud cuckoo land'. Letting rip in the Commons, she fumed that Delors and the Commission were 'striving to extinguish democracy', that this was 'the back door to a federal Europe' and that 'we have surrendered enough'. Her performance was certainly enough for Geoffrey Howe, already sacked as Foreign Secretary over differences about Europe. He now resigned completely from her Cabinet – and justified this in the most effective speech of his career, which opened the way to a decisive leadership challenge. On 28 November 1990 Thatcher's long premiership came to an end. One of Howe's 'commonsense' principles was 'the need to work imaginatively in and through Europe if we were to maximise our position in international affairs'. He believed that Thatcher's go-it-alone mentality reflected a hubristic tendency to 'overrate our international weight'. Here was a fundamental faultline within the Tory party, which would gradually become a chasm.[79]

From this moment, too, British leaders increasingly lost any control over the direction and pace of European integration. Thatcher's successor John Major shared few of her hang-ups about the Germans – initially developing a warm relationship with Kohl – and he agreed with Howe and the FCO that 'Britain needed to raise its voice from within the charmed circle' rather than railing from the sidelines. 'I want us to be where we belong,' he declared in March 1991. 'At the very heart of Europe. Working with our partners in building the future.' He also negotiated an arrangement whereby his Tory Members of the European Parliament (MEP) could sit with the main centre political bloc – the European People's Party (EPP) Group. This ensured that Tory MEPs could join and chair key committees and generally engage in the backroom deal-making through which most parliamentary business is conducted. In other words, Britain was learning to play the Euro-game, like all its partners.[80]

Yet Major could not slow the momentum of further integration. The Maastricht Treaty, concluded in December 1991, fleshed out the Franco-German deal on monetary union, and also satisfied some of Kohl's demands for a stronger European parliament and closer coordination of foreign and security policy. Delors also got his plans for greater workers' rights enshrined in the so-called 'social chapter' of the agreement. In addition, Maastricht enlarged the principle of 'freedom of movement' from 'workers' to 'persons' – part of a more expansive concept of 'European citizenship' that would have significant implications for migration. And, as a further step towards 'an ever-closer union between the peoples of Europe', the EC would now become the European Union. Britain's opposition to most of this was unequivocal and so, in order to avoid a veto, Britain (with Denmark) was allowed to 'opt out' from both monetary union and the social chapter. Major's aides trumpeted this as famous victory, another Waterloo.[81] In fact, Dunkirk was a more apt historical analogy – a skilful retreat, leaving the British free but alone. And this time, there would be no 'Overlord'.

Until Maastricht, the EC had decided plans for further integration on the principle of unanimity, which enabled the most reluctant member to set the pace. But now the opt-outs for Britain and Denmark allowed the other ten members to put their foot on the accelerator. As the implications of the Treaty became clear, Major faced an uphill task getting it ratified in Parliament, even with the British opt-outs. After the 1992 election, he enjoyed only a narrow Commons majority, and many of the new Tory MPs were

Eurosceptic. Thatcher, bitter at being evicted from Number Ten, was happy to stir up trouble by egging on the critics. There were 61 debates and 70 votes; in the end Major prevailed only by making it an issue of confidence. Even so, his opponents did not relent. For them, to quote the subtitle of a book by Tory MP Michael Spicer, Maastricht was 'a treaty too far'. This allusion to *A Bridge Too Far*, the classic book/film about the abortive Arnhem airborne operation in 1944, illustrates again the British propensity to see European politics through a wartime (movie) lens. Thatcher provided an endorsement of the book, enjoining opponents of the Treaty to ignore assertions that Maastricht was 'inevitable' because 'that's what they said about Communism'.[82]

Despite Major's private anger at 'the bastards' in his own party, he was forced to adopt a more Eurosceptic tone, announcing that he was 'a European more in my head than in my heart' and predicting, after the failure of the European Exchange Rate Mechanism in 1992, that the 'mantra of full economic and monetary union' had 'all the quaintness of a rain dance and about the same potency'. Here was the same tone of derision from the sidelines voiced by British leaders in the 1950s.[83] By the end of Major's beleaguered premiership, Britain was hardly 'the heart of Europe' – more like its grumbling appendix.

On a larger canvas, the British press had been moving steadily from what has been called 'permissive consensus' about European membership to 'destructive dissent'. In the vanguard was Rupert Murdoch who revolutionised the newspaper industry in the 1980s: under his ownership *The Times* and the *Sun* charted an increasingly anti-EU neoliberal line, which was emulated by other proprietors such as Richard Desmond at the *Express* and the Barclay brothers at the *Telegraph*. The years 1989–91 accelerated the process, with a surge of 'don't-forget-the-war' Germanophobia in the tabloids after the Berlin Wall came down and the post-Maastricht reaction against the 'treaty too far'. The 'Murdoch effect' was unabashedly political: giving evidence to the Leveson inquiry into media ethics John Major stated that Murdoch said he 'wished me to change our European policies. If we couldn't change our European policies, his papers would not and could not support the Conservative government.'[84]

Major's Labour successor, Tony Blair, who won a landslide victory in 1997, was in many ways the British premier best suited to Europolitics. His charm, easy manner, and fluent tongue – not to mention very passable French – made him a natural networker in Brussels. His substantial Commons majority left him much less vulnerable than Major in the Commons and he also believed firmly in the European project, as long as British concerns were protected. 'The drift towards isolation in Europe must stop,' he told his party and the nation; it should be 'replaced by a policy of constructive engagement'.[85] Blair certainly supported the widening of the EU to welcome in from the Cold (War) the former Soviet satellite states. That 'big bang' enlargement in 2004, with ten new members, required massive adaptations by the EU, in institutions, budgets and immigration policies.

In the process, however, Blair made what proved in retrospect two serious mistakes. First, he gave up some of the rebate that Thatcher had dragged out of her partners in 1984, not least because the sum involved would actually have increased as a consequence of eastward enlargement, which seemed improper. But the rebate had totemic importance for the Tory right: they and their backers in the press laid into Blair. Second, the Labour government agreed that 'freedom of movement' into Britain should begin as soon as the Eastern European states joined in May 2004. Blair decided not invoke the seven-year transitional period for gradually phasing in full freedom of movement. At a time when the economy was booming, and unemployment under 5 per cent, his government believed the country needed more workers. They were advised to expect 13,000 net newcomers a year with freedom of movement. But after Germany and all the other existing members except Ireland and Sweden opted for the full transition period, the actual figure was over 400,000 a year.[86]

When David Cameron entered 10 Downing Street in 2010, he inherited these problems: a Eurosceptic, even Europhobic, hardcore within his own party; the evident popularity of the far-right UK Independence Party (UKIP) led by the demagogic Nigel Farage; growing resentment about immigration; and mounting demands for some kind of referendum on 'Europe'. He also faced a political situation where, once again, a Tory PM was particularly vulnerable to Eurosceptic pressure because of the parliamentary arithmetic. In 2010 a hung parliament obliged him to form a coalition with the Europhile Liberal Democrats, which infuriated many of his Europhobe backbenchers, but then, to general surprise, he won a narrow Tory majority in the election of May 2015.

Cameron's former communications director claimed that the issue of whether to 'remain in or leave the EU had been a slow train coming for years': 'it just happened to arrive in the station on David Cameron's watch.'[87] While there is truth in this statement, many of Cameron's problems over Europe were of his own making. He reverted to a more Thatcherite style in relations with the rest of the EU, pulling the Tories out of the EPP group and trying to get his way through confrontation rather than quiet politicking. His attempt to derail the election of Jean-Claude Juncker as head of the European Commission was a textbook example of how not to do it. To relieve the mounting pressure from the right, Cameron also decided – against the advice of George Osborne, his closest colleague – to promise in 2013 that, if the Tories won the next election, he would seek to reform the EU, then renegotiate the terms of British membership and finally hold a referendum on whether the UK should remain in the EU. These became known as his 'three Rs'.

At the time, Cameron was a coalition premier and the chances of an outright Tory victory seemed remote. But when the Tories did gain power in their own right in May 2015 and Cameron had to deliver, he fumbled all three Rs. His thin list of proposed reforms was totally insufficient to satisfy his critics: 'Are EU kidding?' asked the *Sun* scornfully. The chances of meaningful renegotiation by 1 against 27 were remote, especially given Cameron's reluctance or inability to do the serious work of hard bargaining until late on. In the referendum debate, his case for Remain was damaged by the relentlessly scaremongering tone of his 'Project Fact' campaign ('Project Fear' as Leavers more plausibly called it) and, even more, by the decision of the charismatic opportunist, Boris Johnson (after 'veering around like a shopping trolley'), to oppose his fellow Old Etonian – on principle, if you believe Johnson; to boost his own leadership prospects among the party faithful, if you don't.[88]

Cameron's biggest mistake was complacency about the result. Assuming most of the British people would do what they were told (as in 1975), he deliberately made no contingency plans for a Leave vote. Although determined to control the Remain campaign, he and his aides were no match for the social media skills of Leave's ruthless strategist, Dominic Cummings. And Cameron chose not to exacerbate the divisions in his own party by taking the gloves off against Johnson – the heaviest hitter among the Leavers but notoriously stronger on soundbites than substance – or by going out of his way to highlight the positive features of the EU. Cameron's Churchillian outburst on BBC's *Question Time* on the last Sunday of the campaign – about not being able to fight for what you believe in 'if you're not on the pitch' – was a rare moment of passion, perhaps provoked by a questioner's claim that he was a Chamberlain-like appeaser.[89]

And so on in the early hours of 24 June 2016 Cameron and Johnson faced up to a reality that neither had expected: a narrow but clear 4 per cent majority for Leave. The slogan would now have to be turned into a policy. Cameron had no stomach for such a task – announcing that very day he would not continue as Prime Minister and quickly signing a lucrative deal for his memoirs. This gave Johnson his chance but he was then stabbed in the back by fellow front man of the Leave campaign, Michael Gove, who – having regularly denied prime ministerial ambitions – suddenly declared that he had 'come, reluctantly, to the conclusion that Boris cannot provide the leadership or build the team for the task ahead' and announced that he was the man for the job. With this act of what seemed breathtaking treachery, Gove succeeded in knifing Johnson but also killed his own credibility. In the ensuing chaos Theresa May – who had long harboured prime ministerial ambitions and who seemed a 'safe pair of hands' – eagerly picked up the poisoned chalice. As we shall see in the final chapter, May proved a totally ineffectual leader. But she would never have been in that position but for Cameron.[90]

* * *

It is easy to highlight Cameron's personal mistakes in what has been called 'one of the most dramatic cases of self-inflicted prime ministerial damage ever seen in the United Kingdom'.[91] His referendum is up there (or down there) with Anthony Eden's 'Suezide' in 1956 and Neville Chamberlain's 'peace for our time' in 1938. His justifications hardly convince. 'Obviously I regret the personal consequences for me,' he told an audience in Bangkok in April 2017. 'But I think it was the right thing. The lack of a referendum was poisoning British politics and so I put that right.' He even claimed that the Tory party had 'accepted the referendum result and got on with the process of responsibly delivering it', which showed, he said, that 'it is probably the most healthy mainstream political party anywhere in western Europe.'[92] Hmm.

Yet many of Cameron's failings mirrored those of his predecessors when dealing with 'Europe'. A preference for grand rhetoric, often aimed at the domestic audience, rather than coalition-building in the corridors of Brussels. And an assumption that Britain would be heeded simply because of the grandeur of its Churchillian past rather than on the merits of what it now proposed. In any case, no Prime Minister could really redeem Britain's original sin – failing to engage with the European project at conception in the 1950s and to shape the embryo into a form more suited to British interests, as the French managed to do so successfully. Instead, the British jumped on the European train late, and then found it running away in a direction they disliked but could not control.

Of course, on the other side, the failings of the EC and EU were also manifold. The Six, and the Nine after Britain joined, were largely developed Western European economies, with a coherence of their own. But successive enlargements, mainly for political reasons, brought in countries at totally different levels of economic development. Yet, instead of envisaging a multi-speed Europe in the future – with different degrees of integration – the original vision was not abandoned. This commitment to closer integration at the same time as enlarging the membership created more dysfunctionality. The heady atmosphere at the end of the Cold War was particularly intoxicating, fostering the grandiose but messy Maastricht treaty. At root, the EU never really addressed two underlying problems – its 'democratic deficit', which helped fuel the anger behind Brexit, and its leadership vacuum, with authority being dispersed between the heads of government, the Commission and the Parliament. Even a 'passionate' Europhile like Nick Clegg argued that 'the EU must look and feel different, if we are to stay a part of it' – it must 'reshape itself for the twenty-first century'.[93]

So was Britain's referendum result the logical response to an increasingly dysfunctional union by an increasingly awkward partner? Allowing the British to go it alone again and negotiate free trade deals across the world without being vassals of Brussels. To seize 'the opportunity to break free of the EU's petty rules and redefine Britain as economically liberal and open to the world'. To regain its destiny as a global power after losing its nerve following Suez – a bout of declinism which prompted the 'escapist' bid to join the EEC. Requiring above all an act of will to overcome such 'dismal lack of self-confidence', to believe that 'this country will succeed in our new national enterprise' of Brexit, 'and will succeed mightily'.[94]

Or was the Brexiters' free-trade fervour the relic of an outdated Cobdenite philosophy – a belief that trade would bring peace rather than peace fostering trade? Wasn't the larger lesson of Britain's long history that the country could not be indifferent to shifting power blocs on the other side of the Channel? That Britain had repeatedly needed to play a full part in continental politics – for reasons of prosperity *and* security, because the two were linked. That, since the glory days of the Second World War, it had proved essential to temper independence with interdependence – as in the case of security issues within the transatlantic nuclear alliance. If so, was interdependence within Europe's often problematic union a better option than trying to go it alone in a global economy dominated by America and China?

Only time will tell what kind of relationships the UK manages to construct with the EU – and whether these can deliver the benefits that Brexiters had promised. But the future trajectory of Britain's continental connection will also have to interlock with two other 'island stories' – the growing disunity of the 'United Kingdom' and the changing nature of Britain itself as the empire came home.

3

Britain

Instead of histories of Britain, we have, first of all, histories of England, in which Welsh, Scots, Irish, and in the reign of George III Americans, appear as peripheral peoples when, and only when, their doings assume the power to disturb the tenor of English politics.

J. G. A. Pocock, 1974[1]

'What is it to be British?' asked Gordon Brown on 14 January 2006. Tony Blair's Chancellor of the Exchequer devoted an entire speech to answering his question.[2] After more than a decade playing second fiddle to Blair, Brown could not wait to move into Number Ten. And, as a man with a history PhD – though this was unmentionable, being almost as politically embarrassing as a police record – Dr Brown had views of his own about the *longue durée*.

'What has emerged', he told the Fabian Society, 'from the long tidal flows of British history – from the 2,000 years of successive waves of invasion, immigration, assimilation and trading partnerships; from the uniquely rich, open and outward looking culture – is a distinctive set of values which influence British institutions.' And these, said Brown, could be summed up as: 'liberty for all, responsibility from all and fairness to all.'

On the first theme, Brown discerned what he called 'a golden thread which runs through British history – that runs from that long ago day in Runnymede in 1215; on to the Bill of Rights in 1689 where Britain became the first country to successfully assert the power of Parliament over the King; to not just one, but four great Reform Acts in less than a hundred years – of the individual standing firm against tyranny and then – an even more generous, expansive view of liberty – the idea of government accountable to the people, evolving into the exciting idea of empowering citizens to control their own lives. Just as it was in the name of liberty that in the 1800s Britain led the world in abolishing the slave trade . . . so too in the 1940s in the name of liberty Britain stood firm against fascism.'

But, secondly, according to this veteran Scottish socialist, 'woven also into that golden thread of liberty are countless strands of common, continuing endeavour in our villages, towns and cities – the efforts and popular achievements of ordinary men and women, with one sentiment in common – a strong sense of duty and responsibility.' This too, he asserted, was 'the Britain we admire', made up of voluntary associations, mutual societies, and cooperatives, of churches and faith groups, of public service and civic associations. 'The British way' had always been more than 'self-interested individualism' because 'at the core of British history' are to be found the ideas of 'active citizenship', the 'good neighbour', 'civic pride' and 'the public realm'.

Moving to his third theme, Brown argued that 'the twentieth century has given special place' also to the idea that 'liberty and responsibility can only fully come alive if there is a Britain not just of liberty for all, and responsibility from all, but fairness to all.' Of course, he claimed, 'the appeal to fairness runs through British history', from early opposition to the first poll tax in 1381 and the Civil War Leveller Thomas Rainsborough asserting that 'the poorest he that is in England hath a life to live as the greatest he', until it became 'the whole battle of 20th century politics' – about whether fairness would simply mean 'formal equality before the law' or 'a richer equality of opportunity'. The latter was seen notably in the principal achievement of the 1945 Labour government, the National Health Service which, Brown declared, 'like the monarchy, the army, the BBC' was 'one of the great British institutions'.

Here was the British saga spun for a Labour audience: as a story of social progress, not geopolitical decline. But this narrative also had its own problems. Not just its silent slide from English history – 1215 and all that – to British history, but also Brown's assertion of British exceptionalism. He defined Britain's 'distinctive' values as liberty, responsibility, fairness. An echo of *liberté, égalité, fraternité*, but without the Gallic resonance. And, arguably, pretty much the same set of values to which most Western liberal politicians at the turn of the millennium would have subscribed.

Underlying Gordon Brown's rather contrived explanation of Britishness were several aims. One was to offer a revivalist narrative to confront declinism. He was addressing a country which, as he put it, 'faced with relative economic decline as well as the end of empire' after 1945, had 'lost confidence in itself and its role in the world and became so unsure about what a confident post-imperial Britain could be'. What's more, Brown – a Scot with a chip on his shoulder about the London Establishment yet who aspired to run a United Kingdom that was largely English – had to present himself as a truly national figure. And he was attempting to do so at a time when – in the decade after Scotland and Wales had regained their own parliaments and the Good Friday agreement had opened up the prospect of new relationships between Northern Ireland and the Irish Republic – the United Kingdom looked more disunited than it had been for a century. Brown's attempt to conceptualise national values showed that the identity of Britain had become a serious political, and historical, problem.

This is perhaps not surprising because, on closer inspection, the unity of the United Kingdom has always been problematic. In the early modern era, much of its coherence derived from the expansionary thrust of English empire-building and the embattled nature of the Protestant Reformation, complicated by the vicissitudes of sixteenth-century 'dynastic roulette'.[3] Since the 1700s the globalist energies of what had become the 'British Empire' and then the extended crisis of the two world wars served to mask the absence of a unified 'British nation'. But since 1945 decolonisation and devolution have opened up the British problem in an acute form – which the simple slogan of 'Brexit' not merely evades but exacerbates. In fact, the 'British' problem might more accurately be described as the English problem, because England has never really come to terms with the United Kingdom – its union with Wales, Scotland and Ireland (whole or part) – let alone with the European Union.

Constitutionally, the country is the 'United Kingdom of Great Britain and Northern Ireland' – 'and Ireland' between 1801 and 1922. But nobody calls themselves a 'UKanian', and the acronym 'UK' only seems to have caught on from the 1970s.[4] Yet talking of 'Britain' and 'British' ignores the Irish dimension, which the English have been happy to do for most of the time. And the still frequent use in England of 'English' as a synonym for 'British' hints at the underlying English sense of ownership of the UK – also evident in the Brexit debate. Of course, that is not surprising given the population imbalance between England and the rest, and the dominant position of London within the whole polity and economy, but it glides over the fact that, although England's empire-building made the Union, it never created a unitary UK state or fostered a strong and coherent sense of British identity. To write a book about 'English history' begs most of the important questions.[5]

THE UNITED KINGDOM

Uniting kingdoms

What is a nation? The French intellectual Ernest Renan posed that question back in 1882, and the debate still rumbles on.[6] People's sense of identity can take many forms, all of them defined and refined by gender or class or religion. In the past, identity was often local and concrete, expressed through friendship groups, churches or clubs. For a person to feel part of a nation requires a considerable leap of the imagination, which is why national consciousness has often been sharpened, or even generated, by fear of a hostile 'other' against which to counterpose one's own nation and its values. Yet nationalism also needs expression in a political structure – a nation *state* – in order to gain the legal and emotional leverage over people that is required to firm up the sense of identity. In 1800, Europe comprised some five hundred political units, varying hugely in size and viability; by 1900, there were only about twenty.[7] During the nineteenth century states were forged largely by people's wars, fought in the name of the nation and involving mass armies raised by conscription, for which the prototype was France during the era of Revolution and the Napoleonic Empire. France's wars in turn stimulated national self-consciousness elsewhere, especially in the lands that became Italy and Germany. To quote Thomas Nipperdey's history of modern Germany, 'in the beginning was Napoleon'.[8]

From these nineteenth-century struggles, scholars developed a distinction between a *civic* nation and an *ethnic* nation. The former signified a community of laws, institutions and citizenship within a defined territory, whereas an ethnic nation was characterised as a community of shared descent, rooted in language, ethnicity and culture. France was seen as the embodiment of civic nationalism, inspired by the ideology of the Revolution (*liberté, égalité, fraternité*), Germany as the classic example of ethnic nationalism, steeped in Romantic conceptions of the *Volk*. This stark contrast between civic and ethnic nations has been questioned by many recent historians. For instance, Germany before Bismarck had a powerful sense of civic identity at the municipal and regional level – part of a rich tradition of 'urban citizenship across pre-1789 Europe' – while even in France the project of nation-building in the nineteenth century revolved around the imposition of cultural uniformity by rooting out separate languages such as Breton, Basque and German. Yet the civic–ethnic distinction remains useful, not as a clear binary but to indicate points at different ends of the spectrum.[9]

Recent scholarship on the concept of nationalism has helped clarify the British case. Using a wide array of sources – governmental and legal as well as traditional texts such as the medieval chroniclers

– it seems clear that by the late thirteenth century there already existed 'a deep-rooted concept in English literary culture of "England" not only as a tangible, measurable place, but also as a source of pride to those who lived in it, and a powerful symbol of the English people and their collective interests'. This was sharpened by a sense of superior 'otherness' towards the rest of the archipelago – underlined by the distinction in official terminology between the 'kingdom of England' (*regnum Anglie*) and the other 'lands' (*terrae*). A partial exception was Scotland, acknowledged as a separate *regnum* in its own right, particularly as the residual power of Norway was eliminated from the Orkneys, Hebrides and Western Isles during the thirteenth century. English nationality was defined in law primarily by birth within the kingdom of England, and thus within the English people – a sort of double-helix combination of birthplace and parentage. To use legal terminology, 'definitions of nationality in medieval England combined elements of *ius soli* and *ius sanguinis*'.[10]

By 1400 it is possible to discern a clear divide between the four countries in the archipelago. In each of them there existed a keen sense, at least among the political and literate classes, of their distinctive identity as a people (*gens*). This identity was formulated both negatively, in a sense of differences from the other peoples, and also by reference to certain distinguishing features – even if these could not easily be defined. 'The Welsh', declared one weary English official in 1296, 'are Welsh'. But there was also a perceived divide between the four peoples. In England and in Scotland 'people and kingship had become formally unitary – the kingdoms of the English and the Scots; and once they were unitary they could be territorialised as the kingdoms of England and Scotland'. This was not the case, however, in Wales and Ireland. These were still fragmented polities and they remained 'patently, even painfully, countries of two peoples': Welsh and English; Irish and English. In other words, there was a fault line between 'natives and settlers, vanquished and victors'. The congruence between people and polity – *gens* and *regnum* – was distinctive to Scotland and especially England.[11]

Yet the clear concept of medieval 'England' lay in tension with the residual idea of ancient 'Britain' – derived from the foundation myth of Brutus whose kingdom was divided in three after his death. The word 'Britain' was used to signify the whole island by many chroniclers who wrote about early history, but accounts of the later medieval period often used 'England' in the same way. And the problem of definition was exacerbated by the fluidity of frontiers to the west and north – the Welsh marches and the Scottish borders – though not on the south, where Dover was usually cited as the southernmost extremity of the kingdom. So, by the fourteenth century there existed a definite sense of English identity, which was 'inextricably tied up with inhabiting "England" – even if the precise location of "England" remained the site of unresolved tensions'.[12]

The medieval power balance in the 'British Isles' ebbed and flowed with the vicissitudes of the English monarchy. Strong kings such as Henry I (1100–35), Henry II (1154–89) and Edward I (1272–1307) progressively extended royal power into Wales, Ireland and Scotland. At other times of royal weakness or civil war – as in reigns of Stephen (1135–54), John (1199–1216) and Edward II (1307–27) the English tide ebbed. Yet a broad trajectory of English imperialism was clear. The relentless expansionary appetite of the English state has been defined as an 'imperial nationalism', characterised by a powerful sense of a 'civilising' mission. 'As with the Germans in the Habsburg Empire and the Russians in the Russian Empire, the English identified themselves with larger entities and larger causes in which they found their role and purpose'.[13]

The scope of England's shifting *imperium* was defined by the two poles of the English monarchy and the (generally subordinate)

Scottish monarchy. Yet its centre of gravity had been established by the Anglo-Norman configuration of the English crown, which 'confirmed lowland England as the main location of power within Britain'. The central axis of royal authority 'lay between London and Winchester on the one side and Rouen and Caen on the other'.[14] Thus, even in the medieval period, 'England' was defining Britain, but so too was 'Europe'.

The Hundred Years' War (1337–1453) kept the locus of English power and the focus of English policy firmly on that southern axis. And then the ensuing civil conflict of the Wars of the Roses (1455–85) preoccupied and weakened both Crown and aristocracy. It was not until the reign of Henry VIII that English expansion within the islands was resumed in earnest. The prime catalyst was the King's 'Great Matter' – his obsessional drive for a divorce from Catherine of Aragon so he could marry Anne Boleyn and, hopefully, secure a male heir. With the divorce blocked by Pope Clement VII, Henry's chief minister, Thomas Cromwell, concocted a Statute in Restraint of Appeals to Rome, passed in 1533. This prepared the ground for legislation to make Henry the 'Supreme Head' of the Church, and thus set in motion the whole English Reformation. But the Statute also had momentous territorial implications because the claim in its preamble to 'plenary, whole, and entire power' was rooted in the bold yet undocumented assertion that 'by divers sundry old authentic histories and chronicles, it is manifestly declared and expressed that this realm of England is an empire, and so hath been accepted in the world, governed by one supreme head and king'.[15]

Extending that 'empire' within the islands was the King's main foreign-policy project after his territorial ambitions in France had been blocked. Two pieces of legislation by the English parliament in 1536 – usually known now as 'Acts of Union' – imposed English law and local government on Wales, and gave the Welsh seats in the Westminster Parliament. By the end of Henry's reign, Ireland was effectively under English control. Building on the 1533 Act of Appeals, in 1542 a new law was passed to declare that the King of England was also King of Ireland, rather than exercising his authority as a feudal 'Lord of Ireland' beholden to the Pope. And when the Scots wars resumed in the 1540s, propagandists of the English Crown laid claim to the Crown of Scotland as well, invoking the old story of Brutus' united kingdom to justify their bid to create anew 'Great Britain'. During the brief reign of Henry's fervently Protestant son Edward VI (1547–53), this would-be union was also intended to advance the cause of the Reformation – a civilising mission that attracted support from some Scottish Protestants who wanted to 'bring ordour and civilitie' to the 'rude and barbarous' Highlanders and to root out 'the papistical, curside spirituality of Scotland'.[16] This equation of civilisation and Protestantism was a recurrent thread in the British imperial project, both in the islands and across the seas.

The 'Edwardian moment' was brief – the young king died before reaching the age of sixteen – and the succession of his Catholic half-sister Mary signalled a return to 'Rome' and a continental foreign policy tied to Spain. But Mary, in turn, was soon stricken, dying childless in 1558, and the game of 'dynastic roulette' now spun England decisively back into the British Protestant groove. The forty-five-year reign of Elizabeth I (1558–1603) not only confirmed the English Reformation, it also coincided with Scotland's own fiercely Calvinist Reformation from 1559, which severed the 'Auld Alliance' with Catholic France. This Anglo-Scottish convergence strengthened those advocating a Protestant island under a British Crown – such as the scholar Sir Thomas Smith, who wrote approvingly of 'great Brittaine, which is nowe called England', and especially William Cecil, Elizabeth's closest adviser. Fascinated all his life by maps, Cecil developed an almost unique cartographic sense of the shape and interconnectivity of the archipelago, and of the need to see it as strategic whole. An integral part of his British strategy was solidifying the Protestant Reformation in Scotland and imposing it on Ireland – to ensure the religious unity of the kingdoms.[17]

But Cecil's queen was harder to persuade. Cautious and pragmatic, she did not buy into what has been called his 'ideological commitment to a Protestant and imperial British kingdom', and, notorious for trying to keep her options open, she deflected all attempts to marry her off or to confirm a successor. This frustrated Cecil's son, Robert – who followed his father as the Queen's principal counsellor – in his efforts to ensure a Protestant and British succession in the person of James VI of Scotland, with whom he maintained a secret correspondence for two years before Elizabeth's death. By the time she breathed her last, at Richmond Palace, Surrey, on 24 March 1603, Cecil had arranged a series of post-horses all along the road north to Edinburgh to carry the news to James.

As a polity, therefore, Britain originated as a union of the crowns. It has been likened to the 'composite monarchy' created in Spain after the dynastic union of Aragon and Castile in 1469 – with two crowns worn by one person.[18] In retrospect, the process may look logical, even inevitable, so it is worth underlining how much depended on the contingencies of the moment. In the last years of Elizabeth's reign, commentators identified between twelve and sixteen plausible heirs. So 'this crown is not like to fall to the ground for want of heads that claim to wear it', wrote the lawyer Thomas Wilson, 'but upon whose head it will fall is by many doubted.'[19] As for James' prospects, he had been waiting for years. Indeed, when Elizabeth, after endless dithering, executed his deposed Catholic mother, Mary, Queen of Scots, in 1587, he and the outraged Scottish lords seriously contemplated avenging her death by an invasion of England. But after due consideration, James decided to bide his

time on the grounds that Elizabeth was 'of good years and not like
to live long'. After all, she was then nearly 44; her father Henry
VIII had died at the age of 52 and her half-sister Mary at 42, whereas
James had just turned 21. In fact, Elizabeth defied the actuarial
odds and James had to cool his heels for another decade and a half,
during which he might easily have expired before her.[20]

And even when the welcome news from Robert Cecil finally
arrived, an easy political transition seemed far from certain. Since
no successor had been officially named while Elizabeth was alive,
the Privy Council was anxious for 'the peace and welfare of the
State'. Rumours swirled around about treasonous plots and there
were fears about how a foreign king would be received, especially
one from England's most ancient foe: it was widely said that the
result would be 'too great an increase of ye Scotts upon us'.[21] To a
considerable extent this did prove the case. The Scottish nobility
invaded in large numbers – but peacefully: many took English wives
and established themselves as substantial landowners on both sides
of the border. On the other hand, no English peer married a Scottish
heiress, and none of them acquired land in Scotland at any point
before 1688. 'This is surely a direct consequence of James VI inheriting England and not a descendant of Edward VI inheriting
Scotland.'[22]

In 1603, the dynastic dynamic was reversed: instead of an English
monarch taking over the kingdom of Ireland, as in 1542, it was a
king of Scotland who also became king of England. And James I
totally bought into the concept of a British *imperium*, proclaiming
his new realm to be 'Great Britain' and seeking to 'civilise' its Gaelic
extremities. An abiding target, before and after 1603, were the
Highland Scots – 'these unhallowed people, with that unchristian
language', but the more important project was the colonisation of
Ulster with Protestant 'planters'. The most substantial and expensive
military effort of Elizabeth's reign had not been her support of the

Dutch Revolt against Spain but the 'Nine Years' War' (1594–1603) against an alliance of Irish Catholic lords, led by Hugh O'Neill of Tyrone – who were backed by Spain. Although Tyrone and his allies got surprisingly generous terms from London after their defeat, in 1607 several of them fled from Ulster to the Continent, hoping to raise support for a new war. The 'Flight of the Earls' has become celebrated in Irish historical mythology as the end of the old Gaelic order, because it gave the British Crown the opportunity for whole-sale transformation of Ulster. Nearly 4 million acres of land were confiscated and then redistributed to English and Lowland Scottish 'undertakers', also to Trinity College Dublin, the Irish church and a few 'deserving natives'. By 'planting' loyal Protestants in the soil of Ulster, it was intended to spread true religion and strengthen the security of the new British kingdom.[23]

In some ways, therefore, the union of the crowns represents a Scottish takeover of the 'British' project. The accession medal depicted James as 'Emperor of the Whole Island of Britain' and a new unity coinage was introduced with appropriate inscriptions such as *Quae Deus coniunxit nemo separet* ('Those God has joined let no one separate'), together with a new 'Union Jack' flag of 1606 superimposing the Cross of St George on the Cross of St Andrew. Yet what is also striking is the profound sense of 'Englishness' that James encountered. Elizabeth had always made much of being 'borne mere Englishe here among us', and the length and intensity of her reign – including the Reformation and the Armada – helped to forge what has been called 'a peculiarly Elizabethan synthesis of international Protestantism, vehement anti-Popery, xenophobia and adulation of the monarch' which by the 1600s had become 'entrenched in the dominant public discourse'. The failure of James to recreate what he believed to be the ancient realm of Britain and achieve a full parliamentary union was further evidence of 'the continuing strength of a pre-existing "English" identity'.[24]

In any case, his 'Britishness' was perhaps as much propaganda as principle. Such rhetoric was a way to justify and sustain the new Scottish presence at the heart of a regime that had not only murdered his mother but was also responsible for the deaths of his great-grandfather and grandfather, James IV and James V, after each of them had mounted catastrophically foolish invasions of England in 1513 and 1542 respectively. Faced with a stronger neighbour that could mobilise punitive force, though without ever being able to conquer his country, James saw diplomacy and ideology as more effectual than warfare when trying to deal with Scotland's English problem.[25] From the English perspective, Great Britain made sense as a response to England's chronic Scottish problem: it has been calculated that in the seven centuries between 1040 and 1746 every monarch in London except three either had to repel an invasion from the north or chose to invade Scotland – in some cases doing both.[26]

So 1603 did not constitute a union of laws, let alone of hearts, but what has been dubbed a 'dynastic agglomerate' of three kingdoms: England and Wales, Ireland and Scotland. These were separate entities – each with its own complex polity, society and culture – but over subsequent centuries they 'have not only acted to create the conditions of their several existences but have also interacted so as to modify the conditions of one another's existence'. This observation by historian John Pocock is crucial to understanding the British problem right down to the Brexit era. England has shaped its neighbours in the archipelago, but they have also shaped the history of England. And at no time was the Pocock principle of modifying interactions more evident than in the 1640s and 1650s during what was once known as 'the English civil war' – now often called 'the War of the Three Kingdoms'.[27]

Charles I (1625–49) lacked his father James' skill and restraint. Far more openly he asserted his belief in the divine right of kings

– for eleven years finding dubious and unpopular ways to raise money without convening a parliament. What's more, his High Anglicanism was seen by many Puritans, acutely aware of the religious wars raging on the Continent, as presaging a return to Roman Catholicism. The threat he was perceived to pose both to private property and Protestant identity reached crisis point at the end of the 1630s – an escalating crisis in which one kingdom, England, crashed into the others.

The King's attempt to impose the Anglican Prayer Book on the Church of Scotland provoked widespread resistance north of the border: a National Covenant abolished the episcopacy and established a Presbyterian church order. Unable to put down the rebellion, Charles was forced finally to call a parliament in London in order to raise the money for an army. But Commons and Lords refused to provide any funds until their grievances were satisfied. When the King tried to raise an army of Irish Catholics to suppress the Scots, this exacerbated fears in Edinburgh and London of Counter-Reformation tyranny. A failed coup by Irish Catholic gentry in October 1641 escalated into a more general Irish revolt, which capitalised on local hatred of the plantations and spawned bouts of ethnic cleansing on both sides. By the autumn of 1642 an Irish Catholic Confederation had been formed, nominally loyal to the King but now in control of much of Ireland.

Even more significant was the impact of the Irish revolt in Britain itself. News of the rising reached London on 1 November 1641, feeding the annual ferment of Gunpowder Treason Day. It is now estimated that during the killings, perhaps 3,000 or 4,000 Protestants were killed but sensationalised atrocity stories were pedalled in Puritan tracts – modelled on Foxe's *Book of Martyrs* – and connected with similar reports from continental Europe to convince many of another monstrous Popish Plot against the Protestant faith. In this way, 'the Irish Revolt generated the Civil War in England'.[28]

Woodcut from James Cranford, The Teares of Ireland *(1642) depicting atrocities against Protestants during the 1641 Irish rebellion and seen as another example of Popish perfidy. These atrocity stories were used to justify Cromwell's subsequent campaign against Irish Catholics.*

Convinced of the perfidy of the monarch and his advisers, English Parliamentarians and Scottish Covenanters joined forces against him. The Parliamentarians wanted only a military alliance, the Scots still hoped for a religious union on Presbyterian terms within some kind of British confederation. But royalist success in the fighting of 1642–3 forced them into a compromise 'Solemn League and Covenant', coordinated from London by a 'Committee of Both Kingdoms'. When a Covenanter Army crossed the border into England in January 1644, it made a decisive impact – tying down the royalists in the north and preventing the King's separate forces converging together on London. Two major defeats – at Marston Moor in 1644 and Naseby in 1645 – turned the tide overwhelmingly against Charles and in May 1646 he surrendered to the Scots at Newark, hoping to exploit the growing tensions between the Scottish Covenanters, who favoured a Presbyterian form of church government, and English Parliamentarians, most of whom did not. Although the Scots handed Charles over to Parliament in January 1647, he tried to bargain with them behind the scenes about a Presbyterian polity, while also negotiating with the Parliamentarians. Now the victors fell out among themselves.

Oliver Cromwell and the Army, backed by a purged parliament, 'the Rump', eventually tried Charles I for treasonously levying war against Parliament and people. They executed him in January 1649 and declared England a republican Commonwealth. The Scottish Covenanters, on the other hand, appalled that a Stuart had been so treated, adhered to a 'British' and monarchical polity. They, and the Confederate government in Ireland, recognised the dead king's son as Charles II, ruler of Great Britain and Ireland. The Scottish executive even committed itself to introduce its Presbyterian Covenant into all three kingdoms – so intense was its belief that there could be no security for Scotland except through the union of both the three kingdoms *and* their three churches.[29]

The English Commonwealth however – viewing the Union of 1603 to have been purely monarchical – was now treating the other two kingdoms as enemies. Cromwell and his army were dispatched to sort them out. First, he brutally subdued Ireland in 1649–50. The massacres after taking Drogheda and Wexford were a fusion of religious animosity, ethnic prejudice and military indiscipline

– justified by Cromwell as the judgments of Providence – but they indelibly blackened his name in Ireland. In the summer of 1650, Cromwell turned his attention to Scotland. While he was defeating the Covenanters at Dunbar in 1650, Charles and his Scottish royalist army seized the chance to invade England, but Cromwell pursued him south and routed the royalist forces at Worcester on 3 September 1651 – exactly a year after his victory at Dunbar.

The London pamphleteer Thomas Jenner proudly noted that the 'Commonwealth of England' was 'now almost absolute commander of the British Isles'. The Rump enforced a parliamentary union on

Massacre at Drogheda.

The Irish Catholic image of Cromwell, the murderer of women and children: 'Massacre at Drogheda, 1649', from Mary Frances Cusack, An Illustrated History of Ireland *(1868)*

Scotland, removing feudal tenures though not imposing English law, and obliging the Kirk to end religious coercion of non-Presbyterian Protestants. Even so, the new order required a large and costly English garrison to maintain some kind of stability. In Ireland there ensued the biggest ever programme of Anglicisation. The country was rigorously mapped and then its acreage redistributed by confiscation and reallocation. Some 40,000 new Scottish and English families were settled in Ulster. The 1652 'Act for the Settlement of Ireland' contained the chilling statement that it was 'not the intention of the Parliament to extirpate that whole nation' – promising 'mercy and pardon, both as to life and estate' for 'the inferior sort' – but the Cromwellian conquest and its aftermath was a major act of ethnic cleansing. In 1641 two-thirds of Irish land had been owned by Roman Catholics; by the mid-1650s this was reduced to 6 per cent, and even after the Restoration rebound the figure was less than 30 per cent.[30]

Yet the imperial 'Commonwealth of England, Scotland and Ireland' that had emerged by 1654 was based on force and became impossible to sustain financially. And the experiment of republican government was doomed after the death in 1658 of Cromwell, its Lord Protector, when the regime fell apart. A coup in Dublin by conservative army leaders in league with Protestant landowners neutralised support there for the Commonwealth, and prompted the decision of General George Monck, the Army commander in Scotland, to march south in January 1660. In London he effected the return of Charles II as ruler of all the kingdoms. Fittingly, an English experiment triggered by events in Ireland and Scotland was finally brought to an end by politics in Dublin and Edinburgh.

Psychologically, the cascade of wars from 1639 to 1660 served as an enduring and terrible reminder of what could happen when the three kingdoms collided rather than converged, especially if England imposed itself on its neighbours by force like a billiard-ball. During the extended bloodletting of the 1640s and 1650s, the Irish populace had been reduced by perhaps a third, and in England 'a larger percentage of the population may have died than in the First World War'.[31]

Yet the result of all that was the return of the Stuarts to the British throne, and then the attempt by Charles II's Catholic brother James II (1685–8) to subvert the rights of Parliament, create a standing army and apparently turn the country back to Rome. It was only with James's flight and what quickly became known as the 'Glorious Revolution' that the issues of constitutional monarchy, parliamentary government and a Protestant succession were definitively settled in England. North of the border, 'Jacobite' supporters of James staged a rising – interlinked with clan rivalries and support for an episcopal church – but this was suppressed in 1690. As in England, the supremacy of Parliament over monarch was confirmed but the Scottish settlement also abolished episcopacy and reinstated a Presbyterian church. In Ireland, the Glorious Revolution was accomplished only through a two-year war between forces loyal to William III and a Catholic rising in support of James, backed by Louis XIV's France. This bitter struggle etched the Siege of Derry and the Battle of the Boyne indelibly into Protestant loyalist memory.

Given the carnage and instability caused by these conflicts, a closer framework of union between the three kingdoms might seem only natural. But its creation – first through the Anglo–Scottish Treaty of Union and then the Act of Union between 'Great Britain' and Ireland – was neither inevitable nor definitive. Understanding the historical circumstances surrounding the constitutional agreements in 1707 and 1801 makes it easier to understand why those 'settlements' became so unsettled and unsettling when circumstances changed.

Union for Empire

From Westminster's perspective, full legislative union with either Scotland or Ireland was never an end in itself. It was 'an expedient to which ministers resorted in order to overcome difficulties in political management' at particular times.[32] Such difficulties increased markedly after 1688 as parliaments in all three kingdoms – not just at Westminster – met more frequently and became more assertive, with the Scots being particularly truculent. But the outcome, Anglo – Scottish union, was not – as some have suggested – a special case of 'British' genius. Other significant composite monarchies across Europe in the early modern period, including the Habsburgs, the Bourbons and the Vasas in Sweden, made similar responses to the challenge of running domains which they held under various titles. So the deal of 1707 was the 'British variant' of a wider European pattern.[33]

In terms of specifics, the Anglo–Scottish Treaty of Union was both a legislative union and a common market – the commercial aspects being as important as the political. It reflected both the precocity of Scotland and also the country's weakness compared with England. Crucially, it was the product of another European war that endangered the Protestant succession.

By 1700, Scottish traders posed a serious threat to England's attempt to run a tight trading empire through its mercantilist Navigation Acts. Not just through smuggling ventures and canny engagement in the carrying trade, but by mounting a full-scale challenge to England's dominance of American colonisation through establishing its own colony of 'Caledonia' at Darien, on the Isthmus of Panama – which might then become a pivotal trans-shipment point between the Atlantic and Pacific for global trade. The Darien scheme became a Scottish speculative mania, fuelled by dreams not only of personal profit but also of national status. It sounded a wake-up call in London about Scotland's ambitions as an empire. In the event, however, the Darien project failed catastrophically in 1699–1700 – a victim of disease, Spanish aggression and English obstruction – bankrupting its sponsors, the Company of Scotland, and bringing financial disaster to the country as a whole. It had been subscribed to the tune of £400,000 – nearly two and a half times the estimated value of Scottish exports, and worth well over £100 billion today – of which 40 per cent came from Glasgow and Edinburgh. The Darien fiasco persuaded much of the landed and commercial interest in Scotland that they could not go it alone in colonial ventures, but had to work with England.[34]

With regard to the political aspect of the Scottish problem, the catalyst was Britain's 1701 Act of Settlement, legislating that the Crown would pass to the House of Hanover in the increasingly probable event that Queen Anne would die without any surviving children. (Victim of a rare disease of the immune system which turned the body against itself, she had eighteen pregnancies but just five live births, and the only child to live beyond infancy died at the age of eleven.) A century and a half earlier, English parliaments had tried in vain to persuade Queen Elizabeth to marry or to identify her heir. By 1701, it was not just that Parliament had more authority but also that the monarch was more obliging: Anne took the lead in affirming the Hanoverian succession.

Yet the Act of Settlement was a unilateral move by the English Parliament, without consulting its counterpart in Edinburgh, and they retaliated by passing a bill in 1703 stating that, if Anne died without issue, they would appoint a Protestant successor but from their ancient House of Stuart – in other words from a different branch than James II and his descendants. When this bill was denied royal assent, the Scots forced the London government to back down by refusing taxes and troops for the war against France. Their 'Act for the Security of the Kingdom' became law in 1704, whereupon the English ministry upped the ante with 'An Act for the effectual securing the kingdom of England from the apparent dangers that may arise from several acts lately passed by the parliament of Scotland'. Known in short as the 'Alien Act', this threatened a selective trade embargo and a tariff war by Christmas 1705 unless the Scottish Parliament agreed to open negotiations for a legislative union and a free-trade area. Faced with what has been called this 'naked piece of economic blackmail', the Scots agreed to talk.[35]

From the English perspective, therefore, the union negotiations were a response to what, in modern terminology, might be termed a neighbouring 'rogue state'. Scotland was impeding England's commerce, undermining its politics and even challenging the royal prerogative. None of this would have been so urgent, however, but for the war with France, which resumed in 1702. Geopolitically, this was a power struggle to prevent Louis XIV establishing a 'Universal Monarchy' in Europe and specifically gaining control of the Netherlands. But it was also dynastic and existential: because England had opted for the Hanoverian succession and France had thrown its support behind the Jacobite cause, the 'War of the Spanish Succession' could easily become 'the War of the British Succession'. For London, dealing with the Scottish problem and confirming the succession was now imperative, and legislative union seemed the least unsatisfactory answer.[36]

The English ministry expended considerable funds and patronage to cement the support of a majority of Scottish MPs. They also despatched spies and spin-doctors to Edinburgh to monitor and influence the course of events, including a man now known mostly for authoring the children's classic, *Robinson Crusoe* – the multi-talented Daniel Defoe. Not surprisingly, to vehement Scottish nationalists, 1707 was – and still is – a dirty deal, a kind of *Anschluss*. And some of the terms were indeed disadvantageous, even humiliating. The Scots gave up their Parliament, and were granted only 16 seats in the House of Lords and 45 in the Commons – fewer than Devon and Cornwall combined. English concepts of parliamentary sovereignty and the common law would continue to take precedence over Scottish demands for Britain to have a written constitution. The Company of Scotland was wound up, yet the London East India Company retained its lucrative monopoly. Not surprisingly, the Treaty of Union was greeted on 1 May 1707 with bonfires, bell-ringing and services of thanksgiving south of the border, but the response in Scotland was muted: no protests but no celebrations.

Yet the Treaty also brought real advantages for Scotland, or more precisely for Scottish landed and commercial interests. They received the sum of £232,000 in compensation for the Darien fiasco. There was also the change of name. England's project of incorporation was masked by the statement in Article I of the Treaty that the two kingdoms would henceforth, 'and forever after, be United into One Kingdom by the Name of Great Britain'. Most important, Article IV of the Treaty affirmed freedom of trade within the new united kingdom and in 'the Dominions and Plantations thereunto belonging'. In other words, English capital could flow across the border into a country still recovering from the depression of the 1690s, including a series of harvest failures that caused 'probably the most severe mortality crisis in the nation's history'. Scottish traders were now also guaranteed access to England's lucrative colonies on the American seaboard and in the Caribbean. As a result, Glasgow merchants quickly secured dominance in the tobacco trade, squeezing out English ports like Whitehaven (previously third in the Atlantic trade after Bristol and Liverpool) – so much so that in 1710 the Cumbrian town petitioned for repeal of the Treaty of Union. By the mid-eighteenth century tobacco accounted for nearly half Scotland's imports from outside Britain.[37]

Through the incorporative union, in short, 'Scottish manpower, Scottish enterprise and ultimately Scottish intellectual endeavour were harnessed in service of empire. The Union gave Scotland free access to the largest commercial market then on offer. The unrestricted movement of capital and skilled labour within that market stimulated and fructified native entrepreneurship both domestically and imperially.'[38] And although Scottish interests were hard to promote in the Westminster Parliament, given the preponderance of English MPs, they were maintained and advanced north of the border by the continued autonomy of Scottish legal and religious institutions, notably the courts of Session and Justiciary and the General Assembly of the Kirk. Union did not mean uniformity: the Scots were left to run their own affairs, except on issues of security and order – notably during the two abortive Jacobite risings of 1715 and 1745.[39] On both sides, therefore, union was not an end in itself, but the means to an end: the advancement of what was now the 'British Empire'. This was the strength of the 1707 Treaty of Union, but also – over a much longer historical span – its weakness.

Legislative union was not, however, the English solution in the early eighteenth century for the problems of managing Ireland. The success of the Anglo–Scottish negotiations in 1706–7 did prompt the Irish Parliament to petition Queen Anne for 'a yet more comprehensive union', but English ministers were not interested. According to Sidney Godolphin, the Lord Treasurer, London's aims were simply that there should be no 'trouble' in Ireland and that the Irish Parliament would 'give the necessary supplys and make a short session'. As long as its parliament raised the money for domestic administration and was not a charge on the Treasury, London wanted neither to intervene vigorously in Ireland nor have another bloc of non-English MPs at Westminster. Just to be sure the Irish knew their place, the Declaratory Act of 1720 reaffirmed the supremacy of the Westminster Parliament over that of Dublin, as the official title made clear: 'An Act for the better securing the dependency of the Kingdom of Ireland on the Crown of Great Britain'.[40]

Another, more notorious Declaratory Act was imposed in 1766 on Britain's unruly American colonies, which is a reminder that the Anglo–Irish relationship was much more 'colonial' than the Anglo–Scottish. Indeed Ireland was governed by a Viceroy, appointed by the Crown and usually an English grandee. But the colonial analogy must not be pushed too far: Ireland was far closer to home for Westminster politicians and the Viceroy was subject to persistent meddling by the Prime Minister and Home Secretary. What's more, the Irish Parliament was boisterous and highly factional, becoming increasingly difficult to manage. By the end of the Seven Years' War in 1763 – just when historians usually focus on the problems of governing British America – 'Ireland was causing more trouble than the thirteen colonies,' as far as London was concerned. Simmering beneath the surface of Dublin politics was the exclusion of both Catholics and Presbyterians from public life by an Anglo-Irish landed elite who belonged to the Anglican Church of Ireland. Within the Irish Parliament itself the core issue was finance, with demands for greater powers over expenditure and taxation. Ireland's underlying constitutional dependence on Britain highlighted parallels with the American colonies and encouraged Irish radicals to adopt a similar rhetoric of 'Patriot' opposition to governmental 'corruption'. Yet in their case the goal was not 'independence' but a demand for the restoration of 'lost rights' and the wish to 'engage more profitably in imperial trade'.[41]

The War of American Independence proved invaluable for the cause of Irish 'Patriotism', whose chief spokesman was the charismatic politician Henry Grattan. From 1778 Britain was engaged in a conflict not only against the American colonists but also France – a combination that challenged the Royal Navy's command of the seas and eventually forced the surrender of Lord Cornwallis' army at Yorktown. The redeployment of some British regiments from Ireland for war service gave Patriots a pretext for raising self-constituted militias (the Volunteers), outside the control of the Viceroy, in order to protect Ireland from possible French invasion. Not only did the Volunteers admit Presbyterians and sometimes Catholics, they also developed a political agenda – agitating for free trade between Ireland and England and for repeal of the 1720 Declaratory Act. This buttressed the politicking of Grattan and an economic boycott of English goods: the 'Buy Irish' campaign. The conjunction of all this pressure with the Yorktown debacle, the fall of Lord North's Tory government and its replacement by the Whigs in 1782 led not only to negotiations for American independence but also the concession of full legislative independence for Dublin.

'Grattan's Parliament', as it became known, saw a marked increase in legislative activity – with annual sessions, rather than one every other year – and also a readiness to challenge London politically. One issue was the extension of the franchise to Catholics – not least because wider representation was the way to break the hold of the Protestant elite and its patronage politics. Another, during George III's mental incapacity in 1788–9, was the support by the Irish opposition for his son, the Prince of Wales, to assume full royal powers rather than acting as a carefully circumscribed Regent. These were both areas of particular sensitivity because they affected the powers of the King and the sanctity of his coronation oath as defender of the Protestant faith. The unruliness of Ireland's 'independent' parliament was making the idea of formal union seem more attractive in London.

The real catalyst, however, was national security. As in the 1700s, so in the 1790s. The British polity was reshaped within the European crucible – by war with France. From 1789, Irish radicalism was invigorated and transformed by the spectacular upheavals in Paris, with their highly combustible mix of revolution and republicanism. By the mid-1790s the Society of United Irishmen, founded in 1791 as 'a middle-class club dedicated to achieving parliamentary reform and Catholic emancipation', had become 'a mass-based, secret revolutionary organisation determined to establish a non-sectarian republic in Ireland'.[42] The United Irish 'catechism' captured the international dynamics of its inspiration:

> *What have you got in your hand?*
> *A green bough.*
> *Where did it first grow?*
> *In America.*
> *Where did it bud?*
> *In France.*
> *Where are you going to plant it?*
> *In the crown of Great Britain.*

France, at war with Britain from 1792, supported the Irish cause with an invasion in 1796. Although abortive, this provoked a harsh British crackdown during which many of the United Irish leaders were captured. So the rest decided to act before it was too late. In May 1798 they started a rebellion in Dublin which spread across much of the country and took particular hold in County Wexford. But it was put down by Government forces in a couple of months, using often brutal repression. And French landings in August and October, although this time in greater strength than two years before, proved too little, too late. They were soon crushed. That summer Napoleon had concentrated his energies and forces on gaining Egypt – only to be humiliated and left stranded by Nelson's destruction of the French fleet in Aboukir Bay on 1 August. Two decades later, in exile after Waterloo, the erstwhile emperor lamented, 'If, instead of the expedition to Egypt, I had undertaken that against Ireland, what could England have done now?'[43]

The French-backed rising proved the last straw in London. In December 1798, William Pitt, the British Prime Minister, secured the support of the Cabinet for union with Ireland on the argument that this would guarantee the security of Britain and enhance the commerce of Ireland, thereby increasing 'the power and strength of both'. That, of course, was essentially the same justification as offered for Anglo–Scottish Union nearly a century before, but the crisis of 1798 finally made its application to Ireland seem unavoidable. The object, Pitt told the Commons, was to 'counteract the restless machinations of an inveterate enemy, who has uniformly and anxiously endeavoured to effect a separation' between Britain and Ireland.[44] He pushed the measure through both national legislatures, using the full weight of government patronage, and the Acts of Union by the British and Irish parliaments came into effect on 1 January 1801, creating the 'United Kingdom of Great Britain and Ireland'. And so, ironically, the republicans and their rebellion, instead of 'fostering the union of all Irishmen' actually 'precipitated the very unwanted union of Ireland with Great Britain'.[45]

In reality, the United Irish movement was deeply fractured – being an unstable mix of 'Catholic disaffection, Presbyterian radicalism, anti-English patriotism, agrarian discontent, loyalist anxiety and plebeian sectarianism' – with acute tensions between Dublin Catholics and Belfast Presbyterians belying the non-sectarian image.[46] In nationalist memory, however, the French connection has been played down and the Rising of '98 romanticised. Catholic Defenders morphed into a kind of peasant underground while the Volunteer movement established what became a rooted Irish tradition of paramilitary politics.

Pitt intended that the Union would lead to the political emancipation of Catholics and thus, through their enfranchisement, to a dilution of the power of the Protestant landowners. As Lord Cornwallis, now Viceroy of Ireland, put it: 'Until the Catholics are admitted into a general participation of rights (which, when incorporated with the British Government, they cannot abuse) there will be no peace or safety in Ireland.'[47] Wise words. In the event, however, the opposition of George III and the Protestant elite blocked further progress; it was not until 1829, during the reign of his son George IV, that passage of the Catholic Emancipation Act allowed Roman Catholics throughout the UK to enter Parliament and hold civil and military office. In Ireland that hardly addressed the broader issues of Catholic 'rights'.

Aside from Catholic emancipation, a more immediate legacy of the Union was its effect on the Westminster Parliament. A total of 100 Irish MPs were added to the Commons, as well as 28 temporal peers and four Irish bishops to the House of Lords. This was a far larger increase than the 45 Scottish MPs and 16 peers admitted under the Treaty of Union in 1707. Even so, in 1801 English MPs outnumbered Irish by five to one and Scots by ten to one (even though the population of England was only double that of Ireland and five times that of Scotland). This became a perennial source of resentment in Dublin and Edinburgh.[48]

For the moment, however, the creation of the United Kingdom seemed to London a signal achievement. And it both coincided and connected with another force for unity – the reinvention of the monarchy as a focus of national identity. The Restoration of 1660 had failed to restore the Crown to its earlier dignity. Not only was royal power and wealth trimmed back after the 1688 Revolution, but the Jacobites cast a shadow of illegitimacy over the Hanoverian succession. It did not help royal authority that in the century between the accession of Charles I in 1625 and the death of George I in 1727, Britain had no fewer than seven monarchs, five of whom reigned for less than thirteen years – often in very turbulent times. Neither of the first two Georges was particularly interested in Britain – their hearts remained in Hanover – nor were they bothered about creating a personality cult. And after 1760 the desire of the young

George III to rule as well as reign made him first controversial and then pitiable after his descent into madness in 1788.

But 1789 changed all that. To quote lawyer and diarist Samuel Romilly, what 'added tenfold strength to every motive of endearment to the King' were 'the horrors of the French Revolution'. As Europe descended into anarchy and war, the monarchy became '*the* uncontentious point of national union', observes historian Linda Colley. Royal residences such as Windsor Castle were upgraded; royal thanksgivings and parades sought to match the French revolutionary festivals; and 'God Save the King' became the national anthem. Between George III's accession in 1760 and 1781 that song received only four formal performances at London theatres, compared with more than ninety over the next two decades. And the start of the King's Jubilee year, 1810, was marked by celebrations in some 650 places in England, throughout Scotland and Wales and in outposts of the British Empire.

> A People, happy, great, and free;
> That People with one common voice,
> From Thames' to Ganges' common shores rejoice,
> In universal Jubilee.

George III's longevity also helped. He reigned for sixty years – longer even than Elizabeth's forty-five and, like her, at a time of European conflict and national insecurity. By the end, familiarity had bred affection as well as reverence towards a king now mostly noted for his probity and domesticity. 'Most of the qualities which George III possessed,' declared *The Times* on the day of his funeral in 1820, 'were imitable and attainable by *all classes* of mankind.'[49]

From the Thames to the Ganges: this was an imperial monarchy, and the empire a truly British project. Foreign trade, colonial administration and the Army (one of the few truly British institutions) all depended disproportionately on non-English manpower, especially from Scotland. Between 1850 and 1939, for instance, a third of the empire's colonial governors-general came from Scotland. The British Empire had a special allure for Scottish adventurers who felt excluded from the London establishment. It is not much of an exaggeration to say that 'England made the Union, but Scotland made it work.'[50]

Post-1707 Scotland had benefited hugely from being within the British commercial network. Not only did Glasgow merchants dominate the Atlantic tobacco and slave trade in the early eighteenth century, the subsequent rapid urbanisation of the Forth-Clyde valley, combined with low wage costs and access to English technology, fostered the Scottish textile industry – which also plugged into world trade. And by the time textiles began to decline in the later nineteenth century, Clydeside had become one of Britain's leading regions for shipbuilding and engineering, again for the world market. Scotland's global reach was not confined to manufacturing. The firm of Jardine, Matheson – founded in 1832 – became the greatest of the India and China brokerage and banking houses. James Matheson tried to quell Presbyterian qualms about selling opium to China by arguing that this was 'morally equivalent to the sale of brandy and champagne in Britain'.[51] Overall, the advanced state of the Scots educational system and the inheritance of the Scottish Enlightenment, combined with access to key natural resources such as water and coal, enabled Scotland to exploit the English connection for national advantage. Of course, most of the population did not enjoy the benefits – Scotland was a profoundly unequal society – but union had not meant absorption.

While the Scots more than held their own in the British world, that could not be said for the Irish. Scotland's precocious industrialisation allowed it to exploit English capital and commerce; whereas, given Ireland's heavily agrarian society outside Belfast, union served to accentuate the country's colonial status. The potato blight and famine of 1846–51 cost perhaps a million lives, and decimated smallholders over much of Ireland. Landlords, mainly Protestant, were widely blamed; more generally, the crisis exacerbated Anglophobia. And London's belated response in 1850 highlighted the double-standard of Union talk: the rate-in-aid of 1850 to alleviate Irish suffering was levied on Ireland alone, not the United Kingdom as a whole. For many Irish people, emigration was the only answer. Seasonal migration across the Irish Sea became commonplace, to earn money in the flourishing industrial areas of northern England and Lowland Scotland, and many workers eventually stayed, bringing over their families. The 1841 census recorded the presence of 419,000 Irish-born in Britain; the 1851 figure was 734,000. Between 1845 and 1870 more than 3 million people left Ireland, with the United States increasingly the preferred destination. By 1911, the population of Ireland was only 4.4 million – nearly half the figure of 8.2 million in the early 1840s.[52]

The politicisation of Irish antagonism to the Union developed slowly but inexorably. A succession of bad harvests precipitated the Land War of 1879–82. Tenant protest and gang violence escalated, as did the landlords' programme of rural evictions. The charismatic politician Charles Stewart Parnell used the furore to put 'Home Rule' firmly on the political agenda at Westminster. Gladstone's Liberal governments responded with Home Rule bills in 1886 and 1893, but this drove Liberal unionists who wanted to preserve the UK into alliance with the Tories. Tory opposition, and that of largely Protestant Ulster, ensured the defeat of the Home Rule bills in Gladstone's time but the battle lines were being drawn for the future.

Blocked politically, Irish self-consciousness – especially among a younger generation – found expression in the cultural revival of the 1890s. The Gaelic League, founded in 1893, sought to rekindle a sense of Irish identity through national sports such as hurling and Gaelic football and also through language and literature. One of the League's founders, Douglas Hyde, spoke of 'De-Anglicising' Ireland: he deplored the way Irish sentiment 'continues to apparently hate the English and at the same time continues to imitate them'.[53] Hyde's campaign for a cultural renaissance was taken up by the Irish avant-garde writing in English: W. B. Yeats and J. M. Synge were among the pioneers of an Irish National Theatre in Dublin. The political expression of this cultural nationalism was the *Sinn Féin* movement ('We Ourselves'), founded in 1905, under the leadership of Arthur Griffith.

This backlash against Britishness spread to Britain itself. In the 1880s the Welsh revitalised the annual arts festival (*eisteddfod*); new University Colleges at Aberystwyth, Cardiff and Bangor were fused in 1893 into the National University of Wales. In Scotland the tartan-clad Highlanders – once derided as primitives not just by the English but also by Lowland Scots – were now extolled and romanticised, while the poet Robert Burns and the medieval patriot William Wallace became cult figures. This Pan-Celtic revivalism was part of a Europe-wide celebration around 1900 of rural traditions against urbanised modernity – evident even in England in the 'Wessex' novels of Thomas Hardy and the folk tunes woven into the music of Ralph Vaughan Williams. But in those areas where the Celtic and Gaelic languages were still strong, cultural pride developed a political edge, sharpened by enlargements of the franchise in 1867 and 1884–5 which made politics less easy for London to control. And in Ireland the fusion of nationalist feeling and democratic politics created a constitutional crisis that shook the United Kingdom to its foundations.

Challenging the Union

Irish nationalism had a decisive impact on UK politics in the early 1900s for two main reasons. One was a legacy of the 1801 and 1707 unions: the more generous allocation of Irish seats in the House Commons than had been conceded to Scotland. This inequity had only been exacerbated by the halving of Ireland's population and the doubling of Scotland's during the nineteenth century and was not corrected by Victorian parliamentary reforms. In 1910, Ireland accounted for 103 of the 670 MPs at Westminster, compared with Scotland's 70. The second issue was that by the 1900s most of the Irish seats were being won by nationalists. In the election of December 1910 – the last, as it turned out, before the Great War – the ruling Liberals secured 57 of the Scottish seats whereas 73 Irish seats were won by the Irish Parliamentary Party (IPP), a tightly disciplined caucus bent on regaining Ireland's self-governing parliament. In other words, Irish nationalism possessed both numerical weight and political unity at Westminster. Indeed, after 1910 the Liberals had only one more MP than the Conservatives (272 to 271) and they were reliant on the IPP for their working Commons majority. As a result, Herbert Asquith's Liberal government introduced a third Home Rule Bill in 1912. This sparked a political crisis between Liberals and Conservatives – the latter now formally renamed the Conservative and Unionist Party to reflect Tory claims that the unity and identity of the kingdom were at stake.[54]

The bill of 1912 also rekindled the Home Rule movement in Scotland, championed by the Young Scots: a group of social reformers within the Liberal party. Blaming English reactionaries and the packed parliamentary timetable for blocking their reform agenda, they argued that there was 'not one single item in the whole programme of Radicalism and social reform today, which, if Scotland had powers to pass laws, would not have been carried out a quarter of a century ago'.[55] Scottish radicals introduced their Home Rule bill in the Commons and in May 1913 it passed its second reading with Government support. In Wales, calls for a national parliament were less clamorous: the Young Wales movement (*Cymru Fydd*) had collapsed in the mid-1890s. Instead, passions were directed against the established Anglican Church in Wales, whose endowments reinforced the power of largely English landlords. A bill to disestablish the Church and take away its endowments was introduced in the spring of 1912.

Ardent devolutionists advocated what was then called 'federalism', or 'Home Rule All Round', envisaging parliaments in Wales and England. They even predicted that from this 'federation of the United Kingdom' would spring 'a truly Imperial Parliament where representatives of the 'Overseas Dominions' would sit 'on terms of absolute equality'.[56] Enthusiasts for this idea – including Winston Churchill, whose elaborate scheme envisaged seven parliaments for the English regions – believed that devolution was essential in the modern world to preserve Union and empire, whereas diehard Unionists regarded it as the first step to destroying both.

The stakes therefore seemed huge. What's more, after a bitter political struggle in 1909–11, the Asquith government had pushed through the Parliament Act which removed the House of Lords' veto over legislation. Bills passed by the Commons in three successive sessions would now become law whether the Lords approved or not. Home Rule for Ireland seemed inevitable. So Unionists in Ireland and England turned to extra-legal means of opposition. Ulster Protestants, asserting that Home Rule meant 'Rome Rule', organised the paramilitary Ulster Volunteer Force (UVF) to oppose it; nationalists responded in kind with the Irish Volunteers. In March 1914, British officers at the Curragh Camp threatened to resign their commissions in order to block government plans to use force against the UVF. Politics became bitterly polarised, its language ever more extreme. The Unionist leader Andrew Bonar Law warned ominously, 'I can imagine no length of resistance to which Ulster can go in which I should not be prepared to support them.' From the opposite side, Churchill accused the Unionists of upholding the law only when this suited their 'appetite or ambition'. The 'veto of violence', he thundered, 'has replaced the veto of privilege.'[57]

A possible way out was to exempt Ulster, home to most of Ireland's Protestants, from Home Rule, but both the IPP and the Irish Unionists rejected partition – the first demanding independence for the whole of Ireland, the other committed to keeping the entire country within the UK. In any case, in Ulster no neat dividing line could be drawn on the ground. Catholics constituted a majority in the counties of Fermanagh and Tyrone, while in working-class areas of Belfast and Londonderry the two communities often lived in adjacent streets. On 25 May 1914 the Irish Home Rule bill passed the Commons for the third and, constitutionally, final time. Asquith offered Ulster a six-year opt-out but this was dismissed by Ulster Unionists: 'We do not want a sentence of death with a stay of execution for six years,' declared their leader Sir Edward Carson. In late July cross-party talks hosted by the King at Buckingham Palace broke up without agreement and jumpy British troops fired on a hostile crowd in Dublin, killing three people. The stage seemed set for civil war.[58]

But then, out of the blue, came the assassination in Sarajevo, the escalating July crisis between the great powers and Britain's declaration of war on Germany. Despite this, the Liberal Government still forced the Irish Home Rule onto the statute book in September 1914, together with disestablishment of the Anglican Church in Wales. But implementation of both pieces of legislation was suspended for the duration of the war, and the Scottish Home Rule bill failed to get a third reading through pressure of wartime business.

The general crisis of Britishness receded into the background as attention shifted across the Channel. Churchill and other hardliners in the Liberal Cabinet had no doubt that Britain must enter the continental conflict. Germany's support for Austria-Hungary, which escalated rapidly into a pre-emptive war against the Franco–Russian alliance, could easily threaten the Channel ports and upset the balance of power. For Churchill and his ilk, 1914 was an echo of earlier struggles against Louis XIV and Napoleon. But the Liberal party as a whole was split, and what tipped the balance for most of its MPs on 4 August, the day Britain declared war, was the German invasion of France via Belgium.

'Little Belgium' became the defining ideological marker. The Kaiser's armies had flagrantly invaded a neutral nation and then flouted conventional distinctions between soldiers and non-combatants, burning the university town of Louvain, and shelling the cathedral at Reims. Some 6,500 Belgian and French civilians were killed, often brutally and without provocation, by invading German troops during 1914. Such evidence of 'Hunnish barbarism' generated a broad feeling that the British stood for freedom and civilisation. In the UK, therefore, the war was presented as essentially an issue of morality rather than self-interest – 'The Great War for Civilisation', to quote the inscription on soldiers' victory medals.[59]

David Lloyd George, the Chancellor of the Exchequer, provides an instructive example of this moral nationalism. Brought up as a Welsh speaker in rural Caernarvonshire, he had initially applied his sharp mind and supple tongue to the cause of Welsh noncon-formists, attacking the privileges of the Anglican Church and asserting that the Welsh were treated like 'the niggers of the Saxon household'. As a radical Liberal MP in the 1890s, he supported Home Rule All Round and won national notoriety in 1900 as a critic of the Boer War in South Africa, denouncing 'this infamy which is perpetuated in the name of Great Britain' and proposing that after the war the Dutch settlers should be given 'full local autonomy'. But in September 1914, after a few weeks of inner turmoil, Lloyd George spoke out in fervent support of the war with Germany, lauding the resistance of Belgium and Serbia – like Wales 'little 5 foot 5 nations' who were 'fighting for their freedom' against the great big 'Prussian Junker' storming along like 'the road-hog of Europe'. This, he told a cheering London audience, was 'a great war for the emancipation of Europe from the thraldom of a military caste' which was 'now plunging the world into a welter of bloodshed and death'.[60]

Lloyd George expressed in typically colourful rhetoric the feelings of millions across the country. Patriotic fervour was a consequence of the war rather than a cause but, as it swelled in the first months of fighting, so political debate was refocused. The national question – which, unusually in Great War Europe, had exploded in the UK *before* the conflict broke out – now seemed to fizzle out. Or rather, ethnic nationalisms were increasingly subsumed in a rejuvenated civic nationalism as the conflict pitted British values against a new and menacing 'other' – militaristic Germany rather than Catholic France.

In Wales, the concession of disestablishment and disendowment of the Anglican Church satisfied the main demand of nationalists, and Lloyd George's elevation to the premiership at the end of 1916 showed that Welshmen as well as Scots could scale the summit of the British state. Welsh-language newspapers were overwhelmingly pro-war, many peddling what historian Kenneth Morgan has described as 'a crude anti-Teutonic racism'. Munitions orders fuelled an economic revival in the mines, factories and ports of South Wales.[61]

In Scotland, too, coal, steel and shipbuilding all boomed. By 1916, Dundee, home of the British jute industry, was producing 6 million sacks a month for sandbags in trenches along the Western Front: the war, crowed one manufacturer, had turned jute fibres into 'strands of gold'.[62] For such profits, Scotland paid a big price. Proportionate to its population the country had the highest rate of army volunteering in the whole of the UK – one in six of the British soldiers of the war were Scottish – and also the highest death rate among those who enlisted. The city of Glasgow boasted the record for war loans, contributing £14 million in one 'Tank Week' in January 1918, which eclipsed the previous weekly record (£3.5 million) set by London. Scotland's distinctive fervour for the Great War is not easily explained – possibly a reflection of the country's warrior past and competing martial traditions (Highland and Lowland) – but it showed that *Scottish* pride could be incorporated and displayed within the *British* war effort.[63]

In both Scotland and Wales, war boom was followed by post-war recession, which created real social and political tensions, but these were seen as issues of class not nation. Although the National Party of Scotland, precursor to the SNP, was founded in 1928, three years after Plaid Cymru in Wales, neither had much impact. It is reasonable to suppose that, 'had there been no war, some measure of Home Rule would have been on the statute book by 1920' for Scotland. Instead, participation in the struggle against Germany had revitalised the sense of Britishness in both Scotland and Wales.[64]

In Ireland, however, the post-1914 era turned out very differently from mainland Britain. The Great War has been called 'the single most central experience of twentieth-century Ireland' – generating a war for independence that succeeded only by fracturing the unity of Ireland that both Nationalists and Unionists, in their different ways, had desperately wanted to preserve.[65]

In 1914 the omens had looked favourable: Britain's declaration of war on Germany did have a pacifying effect in Ireland. The Catholic leader of the Irish Parliamentary Party, John Redmond, was a committed federalist, aspiring to an eventual place, rather like Australia or Canada, as a Dominion within the British Empire.

In his view, the passing of Home Rule and the decision to fight for Belgium showed that the British leopard had now changed its spots – standing up for the liberty of small nations, rather than stamping on them as in the Boer War. In September 1914, he offered the British Government the manpower of the Irish Volunteers – 'not only in Ireland itself, but wherever the firing line extends'. This was not just a tactical device to strengthen the IPP's position in London; Redmond genuinely hoped that if Irish Catholics and Irish Protestants fought alongside each other, rather than against each other, 'their union in the field may lead to a union in their home', so that 'their blood may be the seal that will bring Ireland together in one nation'. Dissident Irish Volunteers who opposed the war effort were dismissed by him as a bunch of 'isolated cranks' with 'no policy and no leader' who 'don't count to a row of pins as far as the future of Ireland is concerned.'[66]

Redmond might have been vindicated if the war had been won quickly: Irish volunteering rates in the autumn of 1914 were better than in some parts of England. But as the conflict dragged on and the carnage mounted, recruitment among Irish Catholics fell away and Redmond's gamble seemed increasingly like a sell-out. 'We've Home Rule now the statute book adorning,' ran one nationalist ditty. 'We brush the cobwebs off it every morning.'[67] In April 1916, the 'isolated cranks' cut the ground from under Redmond's feet. Their Easter Rising was intended as almost a suicide mission to keep the flame of Irish nationalism alive. Its principal leader, Padraig Pearse – a fervent apostle of the Gaelic revival – was described by Yeats as 'a man made dangerous by the Vertigo of Self-Sacrifice'. Their quixotic gesture was botched from start to finish. Vital heavy weapons from Germany were intercepted by the British, and the rebels failed to seize key points such as Dublin Castle, establishing their HQ instead in the General Post Office, from where they proclaimed an Irish Republic. Their movement attracted scant support outside the city and by the following weekend British troops had regained full control. Some 60 insurgents were killed, plus 130 troops and police and 300 civilians, many of them caught in crossfire.[68]

The immediate reaction among the bulk of Irish Catholics was admiration for the courage of the 'poor foolish young fellows' who had put up 'a clean and gallant fight', to quote one Redmondite clergyman in Kilkenny.[69] But the mood turned to patriotic fury after the ineptly brutal handling of the prisoners by British military commanders, who were left to do as they wanted for several weeks. During that time martial law was imposed, 3,000 people were arrested, 90 sentenced to death and 15 executed, some of them minor figures in the rising. One of the leaders, James Connolly, was too badly wounded to stand before the firing squad, so he was tied to a chair and then shot. The executions turned foolish youngsters into national martyrs, iconised in photographs and mourning badges, while the shattered buildings of central Dublin were often likened in words and pictures to the ruins of Ypres. Pearse's suicidal gesture had paid off. 'All changed, changed utterly', Yeats marvelled in his poem 'Easter 1916': 'A terrible beauty is born.'

Finally grasping the enormity of the disaster, Asquith tried to implement the 1914 Home Rule Act. With Britain increasingly dependent on US supplies and loans, there were fears that Irish-Americans in the United States could 'force an ignominious peace on us', unless the issue of 'Irish freedom' was settled. But pulling even more strongly in the other direction were fears that some diehard Unionists would resign from Asquith's coalition Cabinet. As a result, in July 1916 largely Protestant Ulster was excluded from the provisions of Home Rule. Asquith was not willing to face down the diehards, further weakening Redmond's position in Ireland.[70]

A major reason for this circumspection was that the summer of 1916 coincided with the start of Britain's great offensive on the

Somme. There, on the slopes of Thiepval Ridge, another Irish tragedy unfolded – very different from the Easter Rising but equally fateful. On 1 July the 36th (Ulster) Division lost a third of its 15,000 men killed, wounded or missing in courageous charges against the German lines. Many of the dead had been Protestant paramilitaries in the Ulster Volunteers in 1914. By the old calendar, 1 July was the anniversary of the Battle of the Boyne in 1690, which Ulster loyalists still commemorated as a God-given victory over Papist power, and the 36th went into battle pumped up by prayers, hymns and liquor. Many officers proudly wore sashes of the Orange Order. Back in Belfast, Unionists contrasted the Ulster Division's self-sacrifice for civilisation (including four Victoria Crosses) with the Judas-like betrayal perpetrated at Easter in Dublin. For both Nationalists and Unionists, therefore, 1916 was a year of blood sacrifice but, despite Redmond's hopes, the bloodletting drove them further apart. The Easter Rising and the First Day of the Somme would become markers for the rival ideologies.

For many Irish Catholics, the suppression of the Dublin Rising proved, contrary to Redmond, that the British Empire would still stamp on small nations. During 1917 Sinn Féin thrashed the IPP in a series of bye-elections. One of the victors was Éamon de Valera, the senior surviving commander from Easter Week, who was elected the party's president. Gone was the old IPP talk about separate parliaments and the same monarch: Sinn Féin had now pledged full independence as an Irish republic. The crisis escalated in March 1918 when the Lloyd George coalition, panicked by the great German spring offensive, announced that conscription, imposed in Britain in 1916, should now be extended to Ireland. This provoked strikes and protests across the whole county. Although the crisis on the Western Front abated and conscription was never enforced on Ireland, the political damage was irreparable. When the UK went to the polls in December 1918, Sinn Féin won 73 of Ireland's

105 seats but declined to take them up. Instead it convened as a revolutionary assembly in Dublin (*Dáil Éireann*), which proclaimed an independent Irish republic in January 1919.

Actually winning independence took two-and-a-half years of savage guerrilla war against the British, with mounting atrocities on both sides. In November 1920 the Lloyd George coalition imposed martial law across much of the country. This failed to stop the fighting but proved another propaganda own-goal comparable to the executions after the Easter Rising. By violence and intimidation the Irish Republican Army (IRA) gradually undermined British administration in rural areas: tax collection, the jury system and the Royal Irish Constabulary, the country's largely Protestant police force. In response, London bolstered the army and the RIC with its own paramilitary units, mostly English and Scots: the Black and Tans and the Auxiliary Division. Many of the paramilitaries on both sides were British army veterans brutalised by war service.

Britain's policy of reprisals was sanctioned by Churchill, now Secretary of State for War, even though his wife, a staunch Liberal, deplored resorting to what she called 'the rough, iron-fisted "Hunnish" way'.[71] It was well-chosen phrase: the British authorities were using methods inconceivable on the mainland, including paramilitary mercenaries reminiscent of the German *Freikorps* in the Baltic States. Martial law was never applied in modern Britain, but it was in Ireland on several occasions (1798, 1803, 1916 and 1920) and also in the colonies – another sign of the underlying British approach to the Irish question.[72]

The damage this policy was inflicting on Britain's international image as well as its transparent failure in Ireland eventually forced Lloyd George into a dramatic volte face. He agreed to a ceasefire and entered into negotiations. The Anglo–Irish Treaty of December 1921 conceded Dominion status to the 26 counties, making them comparable with the white elite of the empire – Canada, Australia,

New Zealand and South Africa – who remained subordinate to Britain only in foreign and defence policy. Irish supporters of the Treaty argued defensively that this was the first step towards full independence but many IRA men were irreconcilable, not because the Treaty 'failed to provide a united Ireland, but because it failed to deliver the "Republic"' and obliged them to swear allegiance to the hated British Crown. The rift over the Treaty proved impossible to bridge and this led to a ten-month civil war from June 1922 during which more Irish died than in the conflict with Britain.[73]

Six of the nine counties of Ulster were partitioned from the Irish Free State and, uniquely within the UK, given their own Home Rule parliament. London hoped that partition would be a cooling-off device to pave the way for an all-Ireland Parliament but nationalists remained committed to independence for the whole of Ireland. So, temporary expedient hardened into enduring reality. The new Northern Ireland government was financed by Britain, receiving four-fifths of its income direct from the UK Treasury. A temporary border had been imposed in the Government of Ireland Act of 1920, and in 1925 Dublin caved in and accepted the existing line, even though this left the largely Catholic counties of Fermanagh and Tyrone in Northern Ireland. In fact, the border was a complete nonsense. It followed the county boundaries of the seventeenth and eighteenth centuries, which often ran along rivers which later became the centre of urban areas. No fewer than 180 roads crossed the border and in nearly 40 cases they defined it, with the frontier running along the middle. In one case there was intense debate about whether to disenfranchise four people in a house in Fermanagh because they slept in a room that was part of the Irish Free State, even though the kitchen and sitting room were in Northern Ireland. But the Ulster Unionist view was 'what we have, we hold' and, after a decade of chaos and conflict, London wanted to forget Ireland. To quote Lord Salisbury, a senior Tory politician, the average English voter had 'little interest in, and less under-standing of, Irish affairs'.[74]

Nationalists within Ulster now had to come to terms with the fact of partition, and to try to live within a new statelet of Northern Ireland that was deliberately structured against them. The Government of Ireland Act had imposed proportional representa-tion, in the hope of protecting minority interests, but Unionists soon managed to abolish it and London acquiesced for fear of bringing down the Ulster government and provoking a new crisis. Unionists also had the constituency boundaries redrawn to suit their interests. In Belfast, for instance, the Unionist constituencies each comprised fewer than 20,000 voters, whereas Nationalists were piled into one mega-constituency of over 30,000. Catholics were also largely excluded from the police and civil service, under the beady eye of Prime Minister Sir James Craig, Ulster's bull-necked political boss. As the South became a 'Catholic state', with the church's special position enshrined in the constitution, Craig boasted that 'we are a Protestant Parliament and a Protestant State'.[75]

In some ways, the partition of Ireland had an air of historical inevitability about it, rooted in the early seventeenth-century 'plan-tation' of Scottish Protestants in Ulster and the ethnic cleansings of the 1650s. Across the rest of the island 'Britishness' had never taken hold and partition was being discussed well before 1914. Nevertheless the Easter Rising and the conscription crisis transformed a political argument about Home Rule into a bloody war for independence. The British state lost the war, but it did manage to salvage a rump territory for Protestant Unionists – though thereby storing up huge problems for the future. So the United Kingdom of Great Britain and Ireland was renamed the United Kingdom of Great Britain and Northern Ireland. Britain was more united than before 1914, while Ulster became an embattled outpost of ultra-Britishness in what was now a viscerally anti-British island of Ireland.

Towards a disunited kingdom

The events of 1914–18 redefined both Britain and Ireland for most of the twentieth century; it was only in the 1990s that what we might call the Great War settlement finally came apart.

In Scotland and Wales the patriotic sense of Britishness generated by that conflict was reinvigorated by the Second World War. Scots and Welsh shared in the national narrative about Britain's 'finest hour' – perpetuated in the 1950s by the string of war movies. This was a period of vigorous economic growth, in contrast to the interwar slump which had hit Scotland and Wales especially hard. The interventionist economics of both Labour and Conservative governments for a quarter-century after 1945 also made the Union seem directly beneficial through a nexus of state subsidies, welfare benefits and public housing – not to mention employment in 'nationalised industries' such as British Railways, British Steel, the National Coal Board and the National Health Service. Even rural areas benefited: by the 1950s the Forestry Commission had become Scotland's largest landowner.[76]

Not until the 1960s and 1970s, when Britain's defeated rivals Germany and Japan bounced back economically, did the war dividend run out both economically and psychologically. The Scottish and Welsh economies – built on coal, steel, shipbuilding and other heavy industries – became seriously uncompetitive. In this harsher climate, nationalist politics had more appeal: in 1970 the SNP finally won a seat at Westminster in a UK general election, while Plaid Cymru dramatically cut Labour majorities in hitherto safe constituencies.

The nationalist resurgence took different forms in the two countries, however. In Wales the dominant note was cultural, especially the survival of the Welsh language. In 1900 over half the population spoke Welsh, by the 1960s barely a quarter, but the Language Act of 1967 gave Welsh equal official status with English. Nationalist feeling in Wales was mainly concerned with 'the preservation of a disappearing way of life', whereas Scottish nationalism was more aggressively about 'building onto recognised institutions new ways of asserting distinctiveness from England'. Scotland's separate systems of law and education that had survived from 1707 were important platforms for this project.[77]

It was in Scotland that pressures for devolution became particularly insistent, aided by the rapid demise of the British Empire in which the Scottish contribution in manpower, finance and trade had been hugely disproportionate to the country's size and population. The tartan-clad Scottish regiments were now being steadily disbanded but they had enjoyed 'unchallenged prominence in Scottish society as symbols of national self-image'.[78] Also important was the decline of Scottish support for the Conservative Party, which in Scotland titled itself 'Unionist' until 1964. Anxious to undermine the growing appeal of the SNP, in 1979 a weak Labour government arranged a referendum on devolution in Scotland and Wales, which failed to win the necessary majorities.

During the 1980s, however, the Thatcher Government's aggressive privatisation of nationalised industries and drastic spending cuts hit especially hard in Scotland – where a third of the employed population still worked in some way for central or local government. Despite her rhetorical enthusiasm for the Union, Thatcher managed almost to kill off Scottish Conservatism (in 1979 the party had 22 MPs in Westminster but none in 1997) and she convinced many Scots that the Union was no longer working to their advantage. The changing international scene also influenced public attitudes. With not only two world wars but now the Cold War receding into history, there was no longer a clear external enemy, an 'other', to help sustain a sense of British identity.[79]

When the Labour government of Tony Blair offered new referenda in 1997, Scots voted decisively in favour. Welsh nationalists also won but with a much narrower majority. The new executives and elected assemblies established in Edinburgh and Cardiff in 1999 gradually acquired more and more devolved powers from Westminster. In Scotland the SNP – which formed a majority government from 2011 – manoeuvred its way to holding a full-scale referendum on independence in 2014. This was a year with special resonance for Scottish nationalists, being exactly seven centuries since the fabled victory over the English at Bannockburn. It was also the centenary of the outbreak of the Great War – a reminder of how 1914 had frozen British constitutional development for much of the twentieth century. The referendum result proved a lot closer than David Cameron's government in London expected. Asked 'should Scotland be an independent country?' nearly 45 per cent of those voting said 'Yes' and 55 per cent said 'No'. The turnout of almost 85 per cent was the highest for a UK election or referendum since the introduction of universal suffrage in 1928. Whether Scotland was viable as an independent state was an open question, especially at a time of declining oil revenues, but the fact that nearly half the country's voters wanted to leave the UK represented a damning commentary on Scottish enthusiasm for the Union. In the 2016 EU referendum the nearly two-thirds majority for Remain in Scotland sharpened the tensions with the Tory government in London.

The progress of Scottish and Welsh devolution showed that Britain was revisiting debates from before the Great War. This was also true in Ireland, and proved particularly painful because of the great divide of 1916, which had become more deeply entrenched in 1966 by rival fiftieth-anniversary commemorations of the Easter Rising and the First Day of the Somme in 1966. Indeed, this conflicted history moment was one of the catalysts for 'The Troubles', when a civil rights movement against Unionist discrimination against Catholics escalated into paramilitary violence from both sides of the sectarian divide. British troops were introduced in an effort to keep the peace but they became part of the problem, especially after the 'Bloody Sunday' shootings in January 1972. The crisis led to the suspension of the Northern Ireland Parliament and the imposition of direct rule from Westminster. During the Troubles 3,500 people died: 60 per cent of them were killed by the IRA or its allies, 30 per cent by loyalist paramilitaries and the rest by British security forces.[80]

Thousands of Catholic refugees fled south into the Republic and there were periodic IRA bombings in Britain itself – most notoriously at the Tory party conference hotel in Brighton in 1984 – but the Northern Ireland conflict remained surprisingly self-contained. Even though the British Embassy in Dublin was burnt to the ground by protestors with petrol bombs after Bloody Sunday, the Irish government showed no interest in advancing the old nationalist demands for a united Ireland. The Dublin politician and public intellectual Conor Cruise O'Brien criticised the 'colonial claim' on the north still enshrined in the Republic's constitution and claimed that the Irish Catholic community had 'an infatuation with its own mythology'. In London, senior Tories and civil servants mused about eventual British disengagement, but that would be unacceptable under the threat of force and without the consent of the majority. In any case, Dublin had no desire to pick up the tab for a statelet that only survived thanks to complex and grubby subventions from London, described by one Treasury official in 1939 as a system of 'fudges, dodges and wangles', under which public expenditure in Northern Ireland has steadily risen to what is now nearly 25 per cent above the UK average. And traditional English stereotypes still exerted their hold among politicians. During one heated debate with her advisers, Margaret Thatcher declared that if northern Catholics wanted to be part of the Republic, why didn't they move there? 'After all, there was a big movement of population in Ireland, wasn't there?' There was a puzzled silence. Then one civil servant asked if she was talking about the Cromwellian period. 'That's right,' she said briskly, 'Cromwell.'[81]

It was not until the 1990s that attitudes began to change, with both sides in Ulster wearying of the bloody deadlock. Intense efforts by John Major, Tony Blair and their civil servants to promote the peace process in Northern Ireland, in tandem with a more cooperative relationship with the Irish government, culminated in the 'Good Friday' agreement of 1998. As a result, London restored devolved government to a new Northern Ireland Assembly in 1999 and pulled British troops off the streets of Ulster. It now became possible to commemorate the past involvement of Irishmen of all persuasions in Britain's wars. The most dramatic expression of this was the dedication of the Island of Ireland Peace Tower near Mesen in Belgium, where the 36th (Ulster) Division and the 16th (Irish) Division went into battle almost alongside each other in June 1917. The Tower was dedicated after a Remembrance service on 11 November 1998 by President Mary McAleese and Queen Elizabeth II – the first time the heads of state of the Republic of Ireland and the United Kingdom had appeared together in a public ceremony.

The new atmosphere was most apparent in Anglo–Irish cooperation and in North–South relations on the island of Ireland. Implementing the Good Friday agreement within Northern Ireland was, however, much more difficult. Communal violence continued to simmer and it took years for the IRA to complete the 'decommissioning' of its weapons. Indeed, devolved government had to be suspended between 2002 and 2007. During this protracted process, power shifted from more centrist parties – notably the Ulster Unionists and the Social Democratic and Labour Party – to the extremes, but in 2007 the agreement seemed to come of age, when Ian Paisley became First Minister and Martin McGuinness his deputy. Paisley, an evangelical Protestant minister who had been the voice of diehard Ulster unionism during the Troubles, was the founder and leader of the Democratic Unionist Party (DUP), which had opposed the Good Friday agreement. McGuinness, a Provisional

IRA paramilitary in the 1970s, was now Sinn Féin's political leader in the north. That two men who were once mortal enemies could not only work together but become good friends (nicknamed the 'Chuckle Brothers') suggested that the old scars were finally healing.

Appearances deceived, however. Paisley soon retired, and the grassroots of his party had little sympathy for the Good Friday agreement. For many members, the scars of the past were still traumatic. Arlene Foster never forgot the moment as an eight-year-old when her father crawled into the kitchen on all fours, head covered in blood, after being shot up by the IRA. As a teenager she herself was nearly killed by a bomb on a school bus.[82] The DUP was not only diehard unionist but also socially conservative (opposed to abortion and gay rights) and fiercely Eurosceptic. During the 2010s its leadership was tarnished by a series of financial scandals. The culminating example – a renewable energy scheme in which Foster, by then the DUP's leader, was accused of gross incompetence and even fraud ('Cash-for-Ash') – prompted McGuinness to resign from the power-sharing arrangements on 9 January 2017, leading to another suspension of Northern Ireland's devolved government. But a few months later, in May, the DUP won ten seats in the UK parliament after Theresa May's ill-judged election. In order to ensure some kind of working Commons majority, May concluded a pact with them, loaded with pork-barrel. This gave Foster immense leverage over the Brexit deal that May was trying to strike with the EU.

Brexit called into question the whole process of constitutional change that had occurred within the UK since the 1990s. In Wales there was a clear majority for 'Leave', but 56 per cent of those voting in Northern Ireland opted for 'Remain' and an even larger 62 per cent in Scotland. Yet May, intent on 'delivering Brexit', insisted that the only majority that mattered was the UK-wide one for 'Leave'. Although constitutionally true, this was politically obtuse and reflected the lack of attention paid to the UK as a whole by English Leavers. With regard to Ireland, many English Tories were just plain ignorant. Karen Bradley, May's Northern Ireland Secretary from January 2018, said nine months later, 'I freely admit when I started this job, I didn't understand some of the deep-seated and deep-rooted issues that there are in Northern Ireland. I didn't understand things like when elections are fought for example in Northern Ireland – people who are nationalists don't vote for unionist parties and vice-versa.' And Boris Johnson, then Foreign Secretary, fumed in June 2018 about the time being spent on the issue of the Irish border. 'It's so small and there are so few firms that use that border regularly, it's just beyond belief that we're allowing the tail to wag the dog in this way. We're allowing the whole of the agenda to be dictated by this folly.'[83]

In fact, as a result of the peace process, Northern Ireland had become much more open to the Republic. The most striking sign of this was the dismantling of any formal border controls, but it was also evident in less visible ways such as the creation of a single electricity market for the whole of the island of Ireland and a sophisticated system of cross-border healthcare backed by EU funding. Furthermore, Northern Ireland also maintained distinctive border controls of its own in relations with Britain, such as extensive checks on imported livestock and special rules about the transport of hazardous waste. None of these pragmatic arrangements were contentious while the UK and Ireland were both members of the EU but, in the era of Brexit, the DUP and its backers at Westminster argued that any deal with the EU that singled out Northern Ireland alone threatened the integrity of the Union. Conversely, those committed to the peace process feared that any 'hard border' with the Republic might presage a return to the Troubles. With the Irish Republic a totally committed member of the EU, its border with Northern Ireland threatened to become the UK's new frontline facing Europe – less iconic than the White Cliffs of Dover but in its own way equally important.

* * *

Throughout her stumbling premiership, Theresa May frequently professed the 'absolute priority' she gave to 'protecting and strengthening our own precious Union', as she put it in Belfast in July 2018 – 'a union not just of nations, but of peoples bound by a common purpose, whoever we are and wherever we are from'.[84] Yet this, like much of her speechifying, rang hollow. As historian Linda Colley has observed, 'in terms of its borders and organisation, the UK, as it exists now, is substantially the result of luck, accident and, above all, multiple wars.'[85] Aggressive English expansion, especially under strong monarchs such as Edward I and Henry VIII, extended the reach of the English state into Wales, Scotland and more patchily Ireland. The formal incorporation of Wales had been completed early and easily – in the 1530s – but it took the extended security crises of two great wars against imperial France to accomplish union with Scotland in 1707 and Ireland in 1801. The shared project of extending, defending, enriching and administering the 'British Empire' provided a unifying force for the United Kingdom during the nineteenth century and the first half of the twentieth, but the process of decolonisation and the end of continental wars weakened the ties that bound.

In any case, the ideology of Britishness never had much hold in Ireland. The Union with Ireland as a whole lasted little more than a century, and Anglo–Irish relations retained their essentially colonial character. So-called Ulster 'loyalists' were playing the British card for their own embattled ends, to preserve their discriminatory, corrupt and heavily subsided province. It is ironic that during two of the UK's greatest constitutional crises of the last century – Home Rule and Brexit – Westminster politics were effectively held hostage by fortuitously powerful Irish lobbies: the IPP in 1912–14 and the DUP in 2017–19.

One of the many blindspots of Tory Brexiters was their Anglo-centric neglect of the Pocock principle, namely that the four countries of the UK have not only acted individually to create the conditions of their separate existences but, by their interactions, have also modified the conditions of each other's existence. Whatever Brexit 'means', it is unlikely to alter the trends within the UK that have been described in this chapter. Despite the damage done by the referendum and the DUP to the peace process, Northern Ireland will continue to develop closer functional relations with the Republic of Ireland. Even if Scotland does not gain independence, there is likely to be a continuing devolution of powers from Westminster to the Scottish and Welsh governments. Brexit alone will ensure that, because Brussels will return a whole range of powers that otherwise belong to the devolved administrations – notably in agriculture, fisheries and the environment, but also relating to energy, transport, health and justice. Despite Whitehall's efforts to agree 'common frameworks' with Edinburgh, Cardiff and Belfast, there will be much greater potential for friction especially with a nationalist government in Scotland. What's more, the creation of 'combined authorities' across the main conurbations of England, starting with Greater Manchester in 2011, may presage a larger and deeper process of regional autonomy within England. This harks back to the advocacy of 'Home Rule All Round' enthusiasts before the Great War and to current talk of 'urban citizenship' as a response to the modern challenges of globalism and populism.[86]

It will be interesting to see whether the English separatists who embarked on Brexit to escape from the 'vassalage' of European 'federalism' end up adopting a federal solution to the challenges of governing their own disunited kingdom.

4

Empire

Of course, we should teach history with warts and all. But we should be proud of what Britain has done to defend freedom and develop these institutions – Parliamentary democracy, a free press, the rule of law – that are so essential for people all over the world. This is the country that helped fight fascism, topple communism and abolish slavery; we invented the steam engine, the light bulb, the internet; and we also gave so much of the world the way of life that they hold so dear. As President Obama put it when he addressed MPs and peers in Parliament, 'What began on this island would inspire millions throughout the continent of Europe and across the world.'

David Cameron, 15 June 2014[1]

One of the most celebrated British imperial narratives was John Seeley's *The Expansion of England*, published in 1883. Despite being essentially the text of a rather arid set of Cambridge University lectures, the book became an international bestseller. It was read by several generations of British policy-makers and opinion-formers and only went out of print in 1956 – rather appropriately the year of Suez. Seeley traced a story of grandly soaring Britishness – relating how the English had expanded

across the British Isles, bringing first Wales and then Scotland
into 'Great Britain' and finally pulling Ireland into the 'United
Kingdom'. He went on to narrate how 'the British' expanded across
the sea to create 'Greater Britain' – concentrating on the 'empire
of settlement' populated by British settlers in what became known
as the 'White Dominions' of Canada, Australia, New Zealand and
South Africa. Greater Britain, Seeley argued, was 'not in the ordinary sense an Empire at all. Looking at the colonial part of it
alone, we see a natural growth, a mere normal extension of the
English race into other lands, which for the most part were so
thinly populated that our settlers took possession of them without
conquest.' The ties that united Greater Britain, he asserted, were
not those of other empires: 'Its union is of the more vital kind.
It is united by blood and religion.'[2]

Seeley chastised Whig historians for fixating on the flowering of
liberty and democracy in Britain while taking little account of 'the
extension of the English name into other countries of the globe'.
This, he suggested, was because imperial expansion attracted less
opposition at home than did political reform. 'We seem, as it were,
to have conquered and peopled half the world in a fit of absence
of mind.' Nor, he added, despite this spectacular British global
diaspora, 'have we even now ceased to think of ourselves as simply
a race inhabiting an island off the northern coast of the Continent
of Europe'.[3]

Seeley's expansionary narrative contained numerous problems.
His book was, for instance, characterised by an often slippery elision
between 'English' and 'British', based on his premise that Greater
Britain was 'an extension of the English nationality'. For him, the
core of 'Britishness' was 'Englishness' – even though the empire
depended for its running to a large extent on the Scots and Irish:
as governors and traders, soldiers and sailors. Globally, Seeley
dismissed most of Britain's possessions as an 'empire of conquest',

in contrast with the exported and energised Britishness of the settler colonies. He reserved some of his harshest comments for India which he said was 'really an Empire, and an oriental Empire' – meaning by 'oriental' one always on the edge of anarchy and corruption. 'It is doubtful', he claimed, 'whether we reap any balance of advantage from our Indian Empire' – a statement at odds with the massive contribution made by India in terms of finance, trade and military manpower. And Seeley ignored the enforced subservience of the indigenous populations of the Dominions, who would increasingly challenge white settler supremacy as the twentieth century progressed, especially in southern Africa but also in Australasia. In fact, he never acknowledged the degree to which the 'empire of settlement' originated as an 'empire of conquest'.[4]

Mr Punch reviews the fleet off Spithead (near Portsmouth) on the occasion of Queen Victoria's Diamond Jubilee in June 1897, at the peak of Britain's imperial pride.

In any case, writing in 1883, Seeley was able to narrate only an unfinished story. A century later, in an essay aptly entitled 'The Contraction of England', historian Antony Low provided an update, seeking to show how the 'Britishness' of the once 'British World' faded after 1945.[5] This chapter will develop Low's approach, discussing some of the ways in which 'the empire made us' – in values and identity, as much as in wealth and power (chapter two). The 'Anglosphere' and the 'Special Relationship' are integral parts of this story; so, too, are the legacies of the slave trade and the impact of mass immigration as the empire literally 'came home' in the second half of the twentieth century.

A contrary approach, flatly denying that the empire had shaped Britain, was strikingly articulated by the Tory politician Enoch Powell in a speech to the Royal Society of St George, England's patron saint, on 22 April 1961 – the eve of St George's Day. Although Powell's oration naturally extolled Englishness, it did so with remarkable extravagance. His starting point was Seeley and the explosive expansion of England, made possible by what Powell called 'the strange and brief conjuncture of cheap and invincible seapower with industrial potential'. By the 1960s 'that phase was ended' – as it was for other colonial states – but Powell insisted that there existed a 'deep' and 'providential' difference between Britain's empire and the rest because 'the nationhood of the Mother country remained unaffected through it all, almost unconscious of the strange fantastic structure built around her' – so that England had somehow remained 'uninvolved' in the enterprise. He described his generation as 'like one which comes home again from years of distant wandering' to a country that, as the 'looser connections which had linked her with distant continents and strange races fell away', discovers the 'continuity of her existence' to be 'unbroken'. This was because the 'unique' institutions of 'the Crown in Parliament' had managed to preserve the 'homogeneity of England'.

And so, Powell told his St George's Day audience with mystic reverence, 'We today at the heart of a vanished empire, amid the fragments of demolished glory, seem to find, like one of her own oak trees, standing and growing, the sap still rising from her ancient roots to meet the spring, England itself.'[6]

The contraction of England – and the rediscovery of England, in its unsullied purity: Powell's romanticised argument was both fanciful and fallacious. The 'strange races' had not 'fallen away': they were still in Britain and indeed arriving in greater numbers. 'They are here', observed the Jamaica-born sociologist Stuart Hall, 'because you were there.' As historian David Olusoga points out, Powell's speech in effect called for 'the denial and disavowal of four hundred years of history', because the 'amputation' of Britain's imperial history was essential to realise his vision of England 'as an ethnic and racial state'.[7] But – with regard to empire, just as with Europe and Britain – a country cannot simply throw off its past as if it were a garment that no longer fitted well and now looked out of date. The Seeleyesque narrative about how Britain made the empire neglects the inescapable fact that the empire also made Britain.[8] That is another of our island stories.

Slavepower: the Atlantic World and the Industrial Revolution

The 'empire' was never a possession, more a project always in process – improvised and incomplete. It was, in fact, a variety of imperial projects, with little command and control, which were pursued by a network of competing lobbies in London and with the geographical focus changing over time. Coexisting in what historian John Darwin calls 'uneasy and often quarrelsome partnership as the "objects" of empire', were 'colonising (with British settlers), civilising (with British officials), converting (with British missionaries) and commerce (preferably without migrants, officials or missionaries)'.[9] These various projects left lasting legacies.

The commercial imperatives were always the most compelling. And they grew out of the failure of empire-building on the continent of Europe, with the disastrous end of the Hundred Years' War in 1453 and loss of all England's profitable possessions in south-western France. The search for new opportunities gradually drew merchants from Bristol (the country's second port after London) into Atlantic seafaring, already pioneered by the Spanish and Portuguese. At the same time, the consolidation of the French and Spanish monarchies, combined with England's break with Rome, posed a security crisis. Facing the threat of invasion by the Counter-Reformation great powers, the Tudor state invested in the 'Navy Royal' and invoked the doctrine of the 'freedom of the seas' (*mare liberum*) to justify piratical ventures against Spanish and Portuguese colonies and trade. The Iberian silver convoys provided easy pickings but the English were unable to break into Spain's well-established domains in Central America. So they latched onto the Caribbean islands, and then gradually crept up the Atlantic seaboard of North America during the seventeenth century to create their own colonies of trade and settlement.

By the mid-eighteenth century the 'English Atlantic'[10] (in which Scottish merchants participated vigorously after 1707) had proved exceptionally lucrative, thanks to energetic and precocious settler colonies producing for Britain's booming consumer market. Although this 'first British Empire' is now less well remembered because the American colonies broke away in 1783 after the War of Independence, its long-term effects were profound – both through the intertwining of the empire with slavery and racism and Britain's shifting but symbiotic relationship with the United States.

It is impossible to establish precise figures for the extent of Britain's slave trade over the whole period up to its abolition in 1807, but considered estimates suggest that about 470,000 slaves were exported on British vessels from Africa up to 1700, a further 3.3 million transported from Africa via England after that date, and another 426,000 shipped elsewhere from British America during the eighteenth and nineteenth centuries. Amounting to some 4.2 million people in the course of a century and a half, human trafficking was clearly a profitable business.[11] Initially the trade was dominated by the Royal Africa Company, chartered by Charles II in 1660 with the aim of finding gold along the Gambia River, but the 'black gold' of slaves soon proved more alluring. In fact, the Company was not able to hang on to its monopoly against 'interlopers' because of the voracious demand for slave labour on the eastern Caribbean island of Barbados and on much larger Jamaica. The supply of white 'indentured servants' – who paid for their passage from Britain by contracting themselves to a master for a term of years – was simply insufficient.

Whereas the Caribbean colonists 'plunged' into the slaveholding business, those on the American seaboard 'inched' into it.[12] Slaves had been imported to the settlement of Jamestown, Virginia, as early as 1619 but they were not exploited industrially until later in the century. In 1670, Barbados provided the initial settlers to found the city of Charleston and also the slaveholding model for the whole royal colony of Carolina. This was split in two in 1712. In South Carolina, by 1740, black slaves outnumbered free whites by two to one, making this the only British colony in mainland America to have an African majority.[13]

What fuelled the demand for slaves across the Atlantic was Britain's sustained consumer revolution – its apparently insatiable appetite for commodities like sugar, tobacco and later cotton. In the early modern period, sugar (sucrose) was mostly used by the wealthy as a medicine, a spice or as food decoration. After the Restoration it was added as a sweetener to tea or coffee – the new dietary fashions for the rich – and imports to Britain escalated dramatically. Some critics damned such indulgence, but the writer and politician Horace Walpole would have none of this. In a letter in 1779 he wittily mocked such attempts at 'reducing us to our islandhood and bringing us back to the simplicity of ancient times, when we were the frugal, temperate virtuous old England'. To those who asked 'how we did before tea and sugar were known', Walpole replied: 'Better, no doubt; but as I did not happen to be born two or three hundred years ago, I cannot recall precisely whether diluted acorns, and barley bread spread with honey, made a very luxurious breakfast.'[14]

'A rarity in 1650, a luxury in 1750, sugar had been transformed into a virtual necessity by 1850,' according to the historical anthropologist Samuel Mintz. Each person in England and Wales consumed on average four pounds of sugar in 1700, twelve pounds in 1789, eighteen pounds by 1809 and over 90 pounds in 1901. During the Industrial Revolution sweetened tea became a staple for women and children, to help boost their calorie intake at a time when all the family were often working but the men got most of the meat and potatoes. By the mid-nineteenth century sugar literally came home – in the institution of 'high tea' – a late-afternoon meal for the lower classes featuring heavily sweetened tea, bread covered with fruit jams that used sugar as the preservative, and cakes made of sweetened pastry. For weary working wives and their families, sugar had become essential both as a calorific supplement and as a psychological comfort – connecting the 'will to work with the will to consume'. Of course, this gradual 'proleterianisation of sugar' spans a period much longer than the slave trade itself, but it was during the days of slave labour that the nation's sweet tooth grew long and addictive.[15]

Sugar production flourished in the Caribbean colonies. On the American mainland, however, the climate was better for tobacco. That became the most profitable crop in the seventeenth century – catering, like sugar, to growing consumer demand on the other side of the Atlantic. In Virginia it proved possible, in the words of one contemporary, to 'found an empire upon smoke'.[16] Over time, tobacco proved another luxury that was proleterianised by 'the downward spiral of fashion and social emulation' during Britain's consumer revolution.[17] But demand was never on the scale of sugar, which was the country's most valuable import until the 1820s. After that, sugar was overtaken by cotton – another commodity that relied overwhelmingly on slave labour. By this time, Britain had not only abolished the slave trade (1807) but also the institution of slavery itself (1833), yet slave labour remained basic to the economy and society of the American South – whose main crop, cotton, was sustained by British demand.

The English cotton industry took off in Lancashire from the 1790s. A series of crucial mechanical innovations in the business of spinning and weaving, combined with the development of factories ('mills') on the fast-flowing streams from the Pennines, created an industry of truly global reach. In 1770 cotton manufacturing made up just 2.6 per cent of the value added in the economy; in 1831 the figure was 22.4 per cent – by which time one British worker in six laboured in the cotton industry. At mid-century Britain accounted for around 25 per cent of global exports, of which some 40 per cent by value were cotton goods from around Manchester, known as 'Cottonopolis', with the other northern boom city of Liverpool acting as conduit for the global trade. Most of Lancashire's raw cotton came from the American South – at least 75 per cent in the years 1840 to 1858 – and nearly half of the USA's 4 million slaves were engaged in cotton production, which accounted for about half of American exports. For Karl Marx, this transatlantic synergy proved that 'bourgeois civilisation' depended on 'barbarity'. According to the British colonial administrator Herman Merivale, the 'opulence' of Liverpool and Manchester was 'as really owing to the toil and suffering of the negro, as if his hands had excavated their docks and fabricated their steam-engines'.[18]

The conclusion drawn from all this by many Southern slave-owners was that they had England in their pockets. If there was any serious threat from abolitionists on either side of the Atlantic to slavery and thus to cotton, then 'England would topple headlong and carry the whole civilised world with her, save the South', declared Senator James Hammond of South Carolina in March 1858. 'No, you dare not make war on cotton. No power on earth dares to make war against it. Cotton *is* king.' The long-awaited Civil War broke out just over three years later and, for a while, Hammond's boast seemed warranted. In 1862 British imports of American cotton were a mere 4 per cent of pre-war levels, and by the end of that year the so-called 'Lancashire Cotton Famine' had thrown out of work some 330,000 men and women – nearly two-thirds of the labour force. But during 1863 Northern victories and President Lincoln's Emancipation Proclamation turned the tide of the war, both militarily and morally. At the same time, Lancashire manu-facturers diversified their supply chains – taking more cotton from Egypt, Brazil and especially India. By 1865, American slavery was dead and King Cotton had been forced to abdicate.[19]

Despite the hubris of Southern planters like Hammond, the transatlantic empire of cotton exemplifies a larger point, namely the economic interdependence of Britain and America. Between 1815 and 1860, almost 50 per cent by value of US exports went to the United Kingdom and 40 per cent of American imports came from the UK, while the US accounted for about 25 per cent of UK exports and roughly 20 per cent of the country's imports. Throughout the nineteenth century Britain's imports alone from the USA usually exceeded in value its whole trade with Asia. 'For all practical purposes the United States are far more closely united with this kingdom than any one of our colonies,' observed a leading article in *The Times* in June 1851 – revealingly at the time of the Great Exhibition staged in London to show off the wonders of the British Empire. 'The United States keeps up a perpetual exchange of the most important good offices; taking our manufactures and our surplus population, and giving us in return the materials of industry, of revenue, and of life.'[20]

As *The Times* indicated, in its ornate prose, the mid-nineteenth century transatlantic relationship was seriously imbalanced: despite political independence the United States remained in many respects an economic colony of Britain. US exports were mostly raw materials, notably cotton, and also foodstuffs such as wheat and meat, whereas British exports to America were mostly manufactured goods. British investment also played a large part in the USA's infrastructural development – largely financing the Erie Canal and the Illinois Central Railroad – and also through buying up large tracts of land in the Plains and the Rockies. Indeed the celebrated Louisiana Purchase of 1803 – the Federal Government's acquisition from Napoleon of 530 million acres extending from the Mississippi to the Rockies (double the area ceded by Britain in 1783) – was funded by a $15 million loan from Baring Brothers in London.[21] After 1865, however, with the South forcibly prevented from setting up as a separate country, the United States developed a huge, continent-sized internal market with prodigious speed and intensity. By 1913 the gross domestic product of the USA comfortably exceeded that of the UK. But, despite the shifting balance, the symbiotic relationship of the two countries continued throughout the twentieth century.

So the legacies of the 'First British Empire' were profound. The slave economy made crucial contributions to Britain's consumer and industrial revolutions; the socio-economic interdependence of America and Britain before the Civil War laid the foundations of the later 'special relationship'. Yet by the mid-nineteenth century another British Empire had developed beyond the Atlantic – global in scope and based on quite different principles.

Britannia Rules: the imperialism of freedom

The British signed away the bulk of their North American Empire in 1783, having lost control of the seas to a French-led coalition of European powers who backed American independence. It was a traumatic national moment, which some saw as divine punishment and others – following Gibbon – blamed on the corrupting effects of imperial power. Within a decade Britain began a life-or-death struggle lasting until 1815 against the French Revolution and Napoleonic imperialism. Yet out of these crisis years, observes historian Boyd Hilton, 'Britons established a second, more dispersed, mainly maritime, and (in their own eyes) moral empire, blessed by providence and devoted to peace, freedom and Christian mission.' By 1850, when about a quarter of the world's population was under some form of British rule, Lord Palmerston – then Foreign Secretary – could credibly boast that a *Pax Britannica* had succeeded the *Pax Romana*. 'As the Roman, in days of old, held himself free from indignity, when he could say *Civis Romanus sum*; so also a British subject, in whatever land he may be, shall feel confident that the watchful eye and strong arm of England will protect him against injustice and wrong'.[22]

The ideology of this mid-Victorian empire revolved around the concept of 'freedom' – especially 'free labour' and 'free trade'. In national memory the ideology's great triumphs were the abolition of slavery in 1833 and the repeal of the Corn Laws in 1846. Yet these assertions of freedom were expressions of power as much as morality – made possible by the magnitude of Britain's wealth and by its naval supremacy after Trafalgar. To foreign rivals, the power seemed more evident than the morality – 'Britannia rules the waves and waives the rules' – but the ideology of freedom was real at the time and has exerted a lasting influence. What we need to appreciate today – in a very different era – is just how far 'Right' depended on 'Might'.

Britain's abolition of slavery provides a good example of this. In the 1940s the Trinidadian historian Eric Williams argued that slavery had been abolished not on grounds of morality but because it had become 'unprofitable': the attack on West Indian slavery was 'only a part of the general attack on monopoly and imperialism which characterised the transition of English economy from mercantilism to laissez faire'.[23] Williams' work set the terms of future debate but on the issue of profitability he is now generally regarded as mistaken. The campaign against the slave trade took off in the 1780s – a decade when British ships transported a third of a million Africans to the plantations of the New World – and although over-planting had exhausted the soil in parts of Jamaica, sugar production was booming in Trinidad and Guyana.

Williams' Marxism inclined him to underplay the religious intensity of the abolitionist campaign, energised by Nonconformists and Evangelical Anglicans who formed the Society for Effecting the Abolition of the Slave Trade in 1787, with intellectual support from Enlightenment writers such as Francis Hutcheson and Edmund Burke. Campaigners did also offer the pragmatic argument that slavery was outdated and economically inferior to free labour, free trade and free enterprise, but their moral passion was undeniable and gained strength from the frenzy about 'liberty' generated by the French Revolution. It has been estimated that between 1787 and 1792 mass petitions against the slave trade were signed by 1.5

million people in Britain – almost one sixth of the country's population. In 1792 a total of 519 petitions were submitted to the
Commons – the largest number ever on a single subject or in a
single session – with every English county represented, as well as
a substantial number from Scotland.[24] Yet the West Indian slave-
owning interest was well entrenched within Britain's unreformed
parliament: in 1792 it blocked in the Lords a Bill proposed by the
abolitionist William Wilberforce. And the conservative backlash in
Britain against France's revolutionary Terror – coupled with the
shock of the slave revolt on France's leading sugar colony of Saint-
Domingue in 1791 – frustrated further efforts by the abolitionists
during the 1790s.

Their success in 1807 owed less to public fervour than to fortuitous shifts in the political and international context. The sudden
death in January 1806 of William Pitt the Younger – an opponent
of slavery in principle but a deeply cautious politician in practice
– opened the way for a cross-party coalition (the 'Ministry of All
the Talents') that brought into office several influential Tory and
Whig politicians who were committed to abolition of the slave trade
on moral grounds. Notable among these were the veteran radical
Charles James Fox and the new Prime Minister, Lord Grenville,
who openly denounced the slave trade as 'an outrage to humanity'
which 'trampled on the rights of mankind'. The Ministry first pushed
through a more narrowly crafted Foreign Slave Trade Bill, sponsored
by Wilberforce, to ban the sale of slaves to other powers. This won
support in Parliament as a patriotic measure against Napoleon.
Having thereby stopped roughly a third of Britain's slave trade, a
general bill for total abolition on moral grounds more easily won
majorities in both Houses – significantly aided in the Commons
by the presence since 1801 of 100 Irish Protestant MPs, most of
whom voted in favour.[25]

Although made possible by ethical politics on an unprecedented national scale, abolition of the slave trade was therefore the result of shrewd politics at an opportune moment. The same is true of the legislation passed in 1833 abolishing the institution of slavery itself within Britain and its empire. After 1807 there was a widespread but erroneous assumption that the practice of slave owning would gradually wither away, now that the supply of new slaves had been cut off. The complete triumph of abolitionism was the product of a new spasm of national reform around 1830 which produced repeal of the Test and Corporation Acts in 1828 and then Catholic Emancipation the following year: these finally allowed non-Anglicans to vote, take up seats in parliament and hold public office. With the Tories divided over these breaches of the old political order, the Whigs won the 1830 election and pushed through the Great Reform Act of June 1832. This enfranchised significant numbers of the middle class and created some forty new seats in middling-size ports and industrial towns. The result was a Commons far more attuned to abolitionist agitation, which was now organised by a younger generation committed to 'immediate, not gradual emancipation'. They organised nationwide lectures in the style of revivalist meetings and drew in Ladies' Anti-Slavery Associations in many of the larger cities. In the parliament elected in September 1832 under the Reform Act, more than 100 MPs were committed to immediate abolition, as were most members of the Cabinet. This gave the movement a new drive at the top. After minor amendments by the Lords, the emancipation bill passed the Commons with a comfortable majority on 31 July 1833 and took effect a year later.

Subsequently, 1807 and 1833 have been incorporated as milestones in narratives of the long march of British freedom. Critics, however, have pointed to the moral limitations of nineteenth-century abolitionism. Most grotesque to modern eyes is that there was absolutely no thought of compensating the 800,000 slaves for systemic denial of their freedom, whereas the 46,000 British slave-owners were compensated for the loss of their 'property' to the tune of £20 million. This was accepted as right even by many ardent abolitionists: 'it would be robbery, under the garb of mercy', wrote the Liverpool pamphleteer Adam Hodgson, 'to compel one class of individuals to atone for the injustice of a nation.' Compensation was certainly deemed to be a political necessity: the 'West India interest' remained powerful – eventually over 100 MPs who sat in the Commons between 1820 and 1835 received compensation payments – and in lengthy negotiations the lobby managed to jack up the total value of the award from £15 million, while also insisting that it must be an outright grant, not a loan. The eventual sum of £20 million represented 40 per cent of the government's current annual spending and would be equivalent today to £13 billion (set against the size of the national debt) or to £76 billion (in relation to GDP). However one assesses it, the compensation to slave-owners constituted 'the largest pay-out in British history' up to that date.[26]

And Britain could afford to pay it. That historical point is often ignored in the recent ethical debate about compensating slave-owners and not slaves. Nineteenth-century Britain had the wealth to end the obscenity of human trafficking by buying out the web of economic and political interests entwined around it. Otherwise the deal would not have got through Parliament. But it is as a noble moral cause that the abolition of slavery has been celebrated in national memory – a source of national pride. And this is perhaps not surprising because the anti-slavery movement inspired a whole ideology of freedom, not just about labour but also trade, as becomes evident from the story of the other great crusade of the time: the repeal of the Corn Laws in 1846.

The Corn Laws had been imposed in 1815 in an effort to protect British agriculture by banning the import of foreign wheat, except from the colonies, until the price of domestic grain had become so high as to threaten famine. Although justified by some theorists as part of a strategy to ensure economic stability, the Corn Laws were widely regarded as a way of maintaining the political supremacy of landowners in an era of radical political reform. Opponents, particularly from the commercial and manufacturing sectors of the economy, argued that repeal of the laws would result in cheaper bread, less pressure on wages and therefore higher profits.

Yet the argument was not merely a clash of interests. The Anti-Corn Law League, founded in Manchester in 1839, picked up on the moral energy and political techniques of the anti-slavery move-ment. Over the next six years 225 affiliates were created – mostly in London, Lancashire and West Yorkshire – under the parliamen-tary leadership of Richard Cobden, a Manchester textile merchant, and John Bright, a mill owner from Rochdale. Tutored by George Thompson – a prominent anti-slavery speaker, who helped organise a celebrated Manchester meeting of 644 ministers in 1841 to proclaim free trade as the 'politics of the Gospel' – they made Repeal into a moral and religious crusade. 'Henceforth,' Cobden noted, 'we will grapple with the religious feelings of the people – their vener-ation for God shall be our leverage to upset their reverence for the aristocracy.' The Anti-Corn Law League developed a starkly Manichean message, linking protectionism with trade wars, arms manufacturing and the aristocratic lust for war, whereas – Cobden declared – 'I see in the Free Trade principle that which shall act on the moral world as the principle of gravitation in the universe – drawing men together, thrusting aside the antagonism of race, and creed, and language, and uniting us in the bonds of eternal peace.'[27]

As with anti-slavery, however, the crusade only triumphed because of political opportunity – in this case the determination of Tory Prime Minister Robert Peel. Peel was the son of a wealthy textile manufacturer in Bury, so it might be thought that he was a natural supporter of free trade. But on this, as on the other 'liberal' causes he eventually championed – Catholic Emancipation, the

Great Reform bill and a peacetime income tax – he started from traditional Tory doctrines and then switched sides. When and why he did so in the case of the Corn Laws remains a matter of dispute – though the appalling human cost of the Irish Famine was clearly a big factor – but Peel was no Cobdenite zealot and may have seen the measure as essentially conservative in intent: 'it would remove the last legitimate popular grievance against the landowners', and thereby shore up his ideal of 'a responsible and respected aristocracy' as the foundation of social order.[28]

Whatever his motives, Peel pushed the measure through the Commons even though he was committing political suicide. The majority of Tories combined against him: Henry Goulbourn, Peel's Chancellor of the Exchequer, warned that Tory unity was 'the only barrier which remains against the revolutionary effects of the Reform Bill' and that repealing the Corn Laws would split the party, exacerbate 'class animosities' and ensure 'the ultimate triumph of unrestrained democracy'. Peel won victory only with the support of most of the opposition Whigs, and his Tory opponents – led among others by the acid-tongued Benjamin Disraeli – exacted revenge by ensuring his defeat on a minor piece of Irish legislation on the very night that the Repeal of the Corn Laws completed its passage through Parliament. Queen Victoria, a fervent Peelite, received both items of news from Westminster in the same box on 26 June 1846. 'In one breath, triumph and defeat,' she wrote in her diary: 'Those abominable, short-sighted and unpatriotic Protectionists.' Peel resigned later that day.[29]

The crusade for free trade – like that for free labour – cannot be separated from Britain's global position. Opponents of the Corn Laws insisted that domestic and colonial agriculture, however well managed, could not support a British population that had nearly doubled from 10.5 million in 1801 (the first census) to 18.5 million in 1841 and whose growth showed no sign of tailing off. And, in the era of the

Pax Britannica, they also argued that Britain no longer needed to operate within old mercantilist definitions of empire because it possessed the capacity to act globally. Since Trafalgar no other power had a navy of comparable size and quality, backed by bases around the world, able to keep open the sealanes. As Palmerston observed with customary directness in 1860, 'It may be true in one sense that Trade ought not to be enforced by Cannon Balls, but on the other hand Trade cannot flourish without security, and that security may often be unattainable without the Protection of physical force.'[30]

His assertion that 'trade cannot flourish without security' – that free trade depended on peace – was a barbed rebuke to Cobden's contrary, and in Palmerston's opinion utterly naïve, belief that the dynamic was the other way round: free trade would foster peace. That is still the vision of today's Cobden Society, whose leading lights include the hard Brexit, anti-EU MP Steve Baker: 'We believe, with Richard Cobden, that with honest money and free trade, international peace and social progress will follow. We endorse Cobden's view that "Peace will come on earth when the people have more to do with each other and governments less."' In nineteenth-century Britain, however, the ideology of freedom – be it the abolition of slavery or the repeal of the Corn Laws – depended on the exercise of Britain's wealth and power.[31]

It is also worth noting that Peel felt able to act in 1846 without requiring any reciprocity. The British market was to be open regardless of whether other countries followed suit, or offered trading concessions in return. 'Peel believed that Britain could afford this unilateral generosity because of her position of competitive advantage.' And, although Peel was not a fluent orator, his speech of 16 February 1846 asking which 'motto' MPs would choose – 'Shall it be "advance" or "recede"? Which is the fitter motto for this great Empire?' – has been described by biographer Douglas Hurd as 'one of the founding documents of globalisation'.[32]

The pattern of British manufactured exports reveals the extent of this new free-trade globalism. In 1700 nearly 84 per cent went to the rest of Europe, but by the 1770s the proportion had dropped to 45 per cent, with 47 per cent to North America and the West Indies. And in the mid-1850s those two regions accounted for just 29 per cent and 28 per cent respectively, while 43 per cent of British manufactured exports went to Asia, Australasia, the Near East, Africa and Latin America. Cotton textiles were overwhelmingly the main export sector, followed by iron goods. And the geographical heart of Britain's new empire was the Indian sub-continent – brought under British control by predatory commerce and brute force but also justified by reference to the ideology of freedom.[33]

The East India Company, which received its royal charter from Queen Elizabeth in 1600, confined itself largely to commerce in its first century of existence. But during the eighteenth century, as Mughal rule in India crumbled and Britain vied with France for global empire, the Company turned to conquest, forming its own private army and bringing under its sway much of the sub-continent, either directly or through client rulers. At the height of the Napoleonic wars the East India Company had an army of over a quarter of million men. Its conquests, however, ran up vast debts and, in the years after Trafalgar, its monopoly of trade with India seemed an unwarranted relic of mercantilism. It was stripped of most of its trade monopoly in 1813, and lost all of it in 1833 – its role now being confined officially to the territorial administration of India.

The assault on the East Indian interest – as with the campaign against the West Indian lobby over slavery – was spearheaded by evangelicals and free traders, arguing that bringing Christian civilisation to India would also boost British commerce. With regard to 'those distant territories . . . providentially put into our hands', argued the evangelical politician Charles Grant in 1797, 'is it not necessary to conclude that they were given to us, not merely that we should draw an annual profit from them, but that we might diffuse among their inhabitants, long sunk in darkness, vice and misery, the light and benign influence of the truth, the blessings of well-regulated society, the improvements and comforts of active industry? . . . In every progressive step of this work, we shall also serve the original design with which we visited India, that design still so important to this country – the extension of our commerce.'[34]

Grant had unbounded confidence in 'the vast superiority even of European laws and institutions, and far more of British institutions, over those of Asia'.[35] Such 'Orientalism', as it would now be dubbed, infused the whole conception of Britain's civilising mission. After the 1833 Act it was embodied in the English Education Act of 1835 to use East India Company funds for education of Indians in the English language, thereby inculcating British values.

The most celebrated exposition of this grand design was articulated in 1833 by Thomas Babington Macaulay – the Whig historian, then an MP for Leeds – who argued that 'as a people blessed with far more than an ordinary measure of political liberty and of intellectual light', the British had no right to 'grudge to any portion of the human race an equal measure of freedom and civilisation'. Macaulay did not baulk at the possible long-term implications of this for British rule over India. 'It may be', he wrote, 'that by good government we may educate our subjects into a capacity for better government, that, having become instructed in European knowledge, they may, in some future age, demand European institutions.' Macaulay did not know whether 'such a day will ever come' but pledged that he would never 'attempt to avert or to retard it', because: 'Whenever it comes, it will be the proudest day in English history. To have found a great people sunk in the lowest depths of slavery and superstition, to have so ruled them as to have made them desirous and capable of all the privileges of citizens would indeed be a title to glory all our own'.[36]

Company rule ended completely in 1858 after its violent suppression of the Indian Mutiny. The Queen's proclamation of a new Government of India stated that race discrimination would have no place in the new order. But by now 'Greater India', a whole sub-empire extending from Aden to Burma, had become hugely important to Britain's global reach, even more so after the Suez Canal was opened in 1869. This cut the voyage from London to Bombay by 40 per cent to 7,200 miles. India's taxes largely paid for a British-officered Indian army and, after the Mutiny, for a large British garrison – with the troops being used to protect or advance British imperial interests in places as far afield as Egypt (1882), the Sudan (1896) and China (1900). After the abolition of slavery, Indian indentured labour worked Britain's plantations in Malaya, South Africa and the Pacific; Indian peasants helped make Burma the rice bowl of Southeast Asia; and trading networks spreading out from regions of South Asia helped develop commerce and retailing around the Indian Ocean. It has been fairly said that 'in much of the tropical world east of Suez, "British" expansion was really an Anglo-Indian enterprise'.[37]

At the same time, the Indian economy, kept open externally by the government to the detriment of native producers, was the largest market for British cotton textiles and for iron and steel. And the commercialisation of the country's agriculture was intensified to boost both the consumption of British goods and the export of primary products. Britain's commercial rivals had not followed along the route to free trade, so India's raw-material exports to the USA and continental Europe became vital for financing Britain's trade deficit with those countries. Because Britain had a surplus with India and a huge deficit with the rest of the world, whereas India had a deficit with Britain and a huge surplus elsewhere, this surplus became 'critical' for the British balance of payments in 1870–1914.[38]

There was, therefore, a yawning gulf between the moral justification for British rule – as presented by apologists such as Macaulay
– and the hard realities of colonial exploitation. This gulf was
exploited by the growing number of 'Anglo-literate' Indians – versed
in both language and culture. Some 700,000 strong by the end of
the nineteenth century, they were active in law and journalism but
were barred from the higher levels of administration in the Indian
Civil Service, which was virtually monopolised by the British,
despite official pledges that there would be no racial discrimination.
This educated Hindu elite, or *bhadralok* (the respectable ones) –
derided by one official report as 'a despotism of caste tempered by
matriculation' – increasingly challenged the Raj status quo on
British ideological terms. Surendranath Banerjea, the leading
Bengali politician of the late nineteenth century, urged Britain to
'regenerate and civilise' India as a liberal society, help form 'a manly,
energetic, self-reliant Indian character' and inculcate the 'arts of
self-government', so that India would become a self-ruling entity
within the British Empire.[39]

These demands were echoed by other provincial politicians, especially in Bombay, led by Gopale Krishna Gokhale. The Indian
National Congress, a political party founded there in 1885 with the
encouragement of a retired Indian Civil Service official Allan
Octavian Hume – who wanted Britain to live up to its principles
– endorsed Banerjea's approach. Indeed, for much of the period
before the Great War, Congress devoted its time and energies to
raising money in order to finance activity in London, rather than
India – setting up a permanent organisation in the empire's capital,
publishing its own newspaper and lobbying MPs. Particular efforts
were made to win support from Gladstonian Liberals, given their
support for Irish Home Rule: after Gokhale's successful visit to
London in 1905, he was hailed back home as India's 'Grand Young
Man'. The 'Congress creed', declared Gokhale in 1914, was 'the

attainment by India of self-government within the empire by constitutional means', rather than by what he called 'a policy of Irish
obstruction'.[40]

Much changed, of course, after 1914. Indian nationalism was
transformed by the two world wars and the consequent mobilisation
of economy and society. It was also revolutionised by M. K. Gandhi's
mass politics founded on non-Western visions of Indian values and
community. But in decisive respects the nationalist project had been
framed within the context of the British Raj by Indian subjects who
not only spoke English but 'knew their Dicey from their Dickens'.
Here is one example of the argument advanced by cultural historian
Priyamvada Gopal, that Britain's colonial subjects were 'not merely
victims of the nation's imperial history' but also 'agents whose resistance not only contributed to their own liberation but also put
pressure on, and reshaped, some British attitudes about freedom.[41]

The politics of Gandhi were very different from those of Banerjea
and Gokhale but they all aimed to hoist Britain by its own ideological petard: empire was the pathway to freedom. And although
Ireland did not prove an encouraging precedent, their case was
strengthened by the peaceful achievement of Dominion self-
government in Canada, Australia, New Zealand and South Africa.

Anglosphere: The fluid solidarities of the English-speaking world

The term 'Anglosphere' became current at the opening of the twenty-
first century and recently gained new purchase among Brexiters as
a putative base for 'Global Britain' once it had left the EU. Yet versions
of the idea have been around since the late nineteenth century:
notably Seeley's 'Greater Britain' but also Joseph Chamberlain's
campaign for Imperial Preference, leading into broader concepts

such as 'Anglo-Saxonism' and the 'English-speaking Peoples'. Linking them loosely together was the search for a larger British polity, extending across much of the world, in response to what were seen as the enervating domestic struggles over democracy, socialism and Irish Home Rule and the concurrent international challenge to Britain's empire from rising powers such as Germany, America and Russia.[42]

The idea of 'Greater Britain' was rooted in the British diaspora of the nineteenth century. Between 1815 and 1914 some 22 million people migrated from Britain and Ireland to the non-European world – the largest efflux from any European or Asian country during that period. Perhaps a third came back or became 'serial migrants' – working for a time overseas – and 65 per cent of the total figure went to the USA. But 19 per cent (4.2 million) ended up in Canada and nearly 11 per cent (2.4 million) in Australasia – followed by another million people in the 1920s.[43] Colonial settlement on such a scale and so far from London raised serious questions of governance, especially given the unhappy precedent of Britain's American colonies and the Canadian rebellions of 1837–8. Although unsuccessful, these Canadian uprisings prompted London's piecemeal concession of 'responsible government' to the separate North American colonies and then their fusion in 1867 into a single 'Dominion', known as Canada, 'with a Constitution similar in principle to that of the United Kingdom'. A comparable process of federation produced the Dominion of Australia in 1901, while the colony of New Zealand – until 1841 a part of New South Wales – also achieved self-government and then Dominion status in 1907.

In these three countries the British diaspora was established by dispossessing the native inhabitants – a human-rights issue that became politically sensitive as the twentieth century progressed. On the other hand, by the 1850s five of the six Australian colonies had adopted the secret ballot – more than a decade before Britain

– and in 1893 New Zealand became the first self-governing country in the world to give women the vote in national elections. 'Many of the central principles of British democracy were experimented with in the colonies of settlement and shipped back to the United Kingdom.'[44] However, the establishment of British control over southern Africa was a much bloodier affair, involving Britain's conquest of the kingdom of Zululand in 1879, and then two wars against the formidable Dutch settlers, the Boers – the second of which in 1899–1902 severely shook British pride before victory was achieved. The Union of South Africa, bringing together the Boer and British colonies, achieved Dominion status in 1910. Although their individual experiences varied, all these four Dominions followed a very different trajectory from that of the French Empire, where the ultimate goal was officially not independence but 'assimilation' – the evolution of colonial 'subjects' into French 'citizens' who elected representatives to the *Assemblée Nationale* in Paris.

Victorian theorists of empire such as Seeley and the radical politician Charles Dilke did not believe that Dominion self-government precluded continued voluntary engagement with the mother country. Although the term 'Greater Britain' was used in various ways, it usually referred to the 'empire of settlement' – meaning those regions inhabited by emigrants from Britain – rather than the racially distinct 'empire of conquest', especially India. 'England in the East is not the England we know,' observed Dilke in 1868: there 'flousy Britannia, with her anchor and ship, becomes a mysterious Oriental despotism.'[45] For Seeley, 'Greater Britain' comprised 'a homogeneous people, one in blood, language, religion, and laws', yet 'dispersed over a boundless space', and it had the potential to be nothing less than what he called 'a United States'. Realising that potential depended partly on technology: the age of steam power and electricity had revolutionised communications and made possible 'highly organised states on a yet larger scale', especially the continent-wide giants, America and Russia. But the right kind of organisation also mattered. The American Revolution had shown the dangers of a colonial system resting on coercion; the need now was for a system of voluntary imperial 'federation'. If Greater Britain became that kind of polity, then it could compete 'on a level with the greatest of these great states of the future'. By 1914 the numbers were substantial: 8 million in Canada, 5 million in Australia and just over 1 million in New Zealand, plus 1.4 million whites in South Africa. The total settler population, predominantly of British stock, was one-third of the UK's 46 million.[46]

Precisely how Greater Britain should be constituted became a matter of intense debate in the years around 1900. The Imperial Federation League (IFL), founded in 1884, aimed to 'secure by federation the permanent unity of the Empire', capped by an imperial parliament. The League collapsed in discord after a decade, but the idea lived on in the Round Table movement, created in the 1900s by disciples of Lord Milner after they had helped to forge the Union of South Africa. Although some of its members gained influence during the Great War – Philip Kerr, for instance, became Lloyd George's private secretary – their aspirations for an 'organic union' proved utopian, reflecting an inability, observed one New Zealander, to 'conceive that London could ever cease to be the centre of the world'. After the failure of the IFL, Joseph Chamberlain focused on economic consolidation in his 1903 campaign for tariff reform. This, he declared, would not apply to India or any other 'native fellow subjects' but to 'our own kinsfolk' – that 'white population that constitutes the majority in all the great self-governing Colonies of the Empire'. But Chamberlain ran up against the rooted commitment of the financial and commercial establishment to free trade, and to their claims that tariff reform would raise the price of food – contrasting the 'big loaf' from free trade with the 'little loaf' that working families would get from imperial preference.

When a detailed federal blueprint for the empire was proposed by Sir Joseph Ward, the New Zealand premier, at the Imperial Conference in 1911, it was dismissed by the other Dominion leaders as 'idiotic' and 'absolutely impractical'.[47]

Despite the failure of such grand designs for imperial coopera-tion, in 1914 the 'British nations' answered the call. Their wartime experience is often depicted as a long stride down the road to independent nationalism, but the story is more circuitous. Certainly there was pride at national heroics (the Anzacs landing at Gallipoli in 1915 or the Canadians storming Vimy Ridge in 1917), coupled with mounting indignation about London's 'bungling' and lack of consultation. 'It can hardly be expected that we shall put 400,000 or 500,000 men in field', complained the Canadian premier Sir Robert Borden, and yet 'willingly accept' being treated as 'toy automata'. Yet London did shift ground by creating an Imperial War Cabinet, which convened for three intensive sets of meetings, each spanning a couple of months, in 1917 and 1918. And Jan Smuts, the South African premier, proposed the term 'British Commonwealth of Nations' as more appropriate to describe the new relationships than the old language of 'empire'. He told the Westminster Parliament in May 1917: 'We are not an empire. Germany is an empire, so was Rome, and so is India, but we are a system of nations, a community of States and nations far greater than any empire which has ever existed.'[48]

In the interwar years, national pride continued to coexist with a transcendent sense of British identity. In 1931 the Statute of Westminster renounced the Imperial Parliament's right to legislate for the Dominions, but the Dominions remained dependent on Britain for defence, trade and investment. And sustained migration from the UK kept the ties with the old country alive. All this helped nurture a feeling of what was sometimes called 'British race senti-ment', a phrase that has been deconstructed to mean 'an aggressive

sense of cultural superiority as the representatives of a global civilisation then at the height of its prestige' because of victory in 1918.
Being a member of the British Commonwealth was therefore 'a
distinctive blend of national status and Imperial identity' and
Dominion nationalism was conceived in familial terms – children
seeking to outstrip a parent, the new British bettering Old England
– rather than as new nations throwing off the imperial yoke.[49]

In Britain's Second World War the Dominions again played their
part. Aside from the Canadian troops who defended London in
1940–1 and the Commonwealth infantry who were integral to
Montgomery's desert victory at Alamein, almost half of the RAF's
newly trained pilots during the war came from the Dominions. By
1945 the RAF had 487 squadrons, of which 100 were provided by
the Dominions. And the Canadian navy played a vital part in winning
the Battle of the Atlantic, without which D-Day and the Normandy
campaign would have been unsustainable. In all, the 2.5 million
service personnel in the wartime Dominion armed forces represented
roughly 8 per cent of their total population.[50]

Even more important, however, was another component of the
Anglosphere: what Churchill called Britain's 'special relationship'
with the United States. This had its roots in the late nineteenth-century rapprochement between the two countries – lubricated by
substantial British investment in the USA and Britain's reliance on
American grain, meat and other imports. Despite anxiety about
Washington's great-power pretensions, especially its navy, British
governments around the turn of the century decided to 'appease'
America in order to concentrate on resisting what seemed greater
threats from Germany and Russia. One example was surrendering
Britain's rights under an 1850 treaty to share in the building of any
canal through the Isthmus of Panama to link the Atlantic and the
Pacific. This left President Teddy Roosevelt with a free hand, which
he exerted to the full. In August 1914, just as the European war

began, America's Panama Canal was opened – 150 miles west of Darien, the site two centuries earlier of the abortive Scottish colony of Caledonia.

Despite the power politics underlying the relationship, however, it was promoted – particularly in Britain – in ideological and cultural terms: as a coming together of the 'Anglo-Saxon races' or the 'English-Speaking Peoples'. The latter idea was particularly in vogue after the wartime alliance of 1917–18: the 'English-Speaking Union' was founded in London in June 1918 and one of its chairmen in the 1920s was Winston Churchill – himself, he liked to say, 'an English-speaking union in my own person', as the offspring of a British father and an American mother.[51] In the 1930s Churchill embarked on a massive *History of the English-Speaking Peoples* – largely about Britain and America, with little on the Dominions (Churchill never once visited Australia or New Zealand). And during the Second World War he frequently extolled the 'special relationship' among the 'English-speaking peoples' as the foundation of post-war peace.

By the end of the war, however, even though Britain remained a great power at the top table with the USA and the USSR, the 'Big Three' was more like the Big '2½' – as one disgruntled senior diplomat put it.[52] The special relationship became increasingly a British diplomatic stratagem, a device by a declining power to harness a rising power to serve its own ends by exploiting the ties of culture and language. In the words of an anonymous verse penned in 1945 when Britain was begging for a post-war American loan:

> In Washington Lord Halifax
> Once whispered to Lord Keynes
> It's true *they* have the money bags
> But *we* have all the brains.[53]

Britain's worldly wisdom from centuries of global power could help tutor the brash but unsophisticated New World giant: that was the underlying conceit. And London's modus operandi was to propitiate in public and manipulate in secret. Never say 'No'; say 'Yes, but' – with the 'Yes' stated loudly and the 'but' urged quietly behind closed doors. Very different from the post-war Gaullist tactic of declaiming 'Non' loudly and repeatedly in an effort to reassert the fading *grandeur* of France. The contrast was particularly evident in the contrasting reactions of Tony Blair and Jacques Chirac in 2003 to George W. Bush's invasion of Iraq.[54]

Yet the special relationship had substance as well. At the end of the Second World War, Britain, though diminished in power, still had much to offer the United States. Successive governments of both main parties continued conscription until 1960, thereby maintaining Britain's military clout. In the 1950s, the UK manufactured nearly a third of the industrial production of non-communist Europe, and its arms output exceeded that of all America's other European partners combined.[55] Despite withdrawal from the Indian sub-continent in 1947, Britain's position in the Middle East and its network of bases around the world were invaluable for Washington as the USA assumed the burdens of global leadership. In these and other ways, the post-war British-American relationship was truly special in *importance* for the United States.

And even when that importance waned in the 1970s, after British withdrawal from East of Suez, the relationship remained special in *quality* in three principal respects. First: the habit of consultation between Washington and London, which stemmed from the wartime years but continued because of the network of contacts facilitated by the shared language and similarity of values. Consultation often produced agreement; sometimes agreement to differ but even then – to quote one Foreign Office official in 1944 – with 'due account of the other's special interests or susceptibilities'.

A second *specialité* was intelligence. Again this grew out of the Second World War but was formalised in the UKUSA agreement of 1947, which also embraced Canada, Australia and New Zealand (the so-called 'Five Eyes'). In recent years the alliance has moved beyond the sharing of signals intelligence into the digital realm. British–American relations are also unique, thirdly, in the area of nuclear weapons. No other state has been such a beneficiary of US nuclear technology, starting with the Polaris agreement signed in 1963 and followed by the Trident deal of 1982. Although successive British governments spoke of Britain's 'independent' deterrent or lauded transatlantic 'interdependence', critics argued that the UK was actually dependent on the USA, and that the nuclear force was an expensive fig-leaf to cover Britain's nakedness as a military power. But however it is judged, the nuclear relationship was another feature of the Washington–London axis that marked it out as special – meaning distinctive – compared with America's other international alliances.[56]

Anglosphere notions of 'Greater Britain' and the 'English-speaking peoples' overlapped in the years before the Great War but, as the twentieth century progressed, the 'special relationship' became much more important to UK policymakers than 'the Commonwealth'. Not just because the Dominions and India went their own ways after 1945, but because the security of the UK itself was seen as dependent on America's nuclear commitment to NATO and the defence of Europe. In the Cold War world of bipolarity, Britain had little choice but to shelter under the US nuclear umbrella; the Commonwealth could offer nothing comparable on an existential issue of national survival. The Tories' turn to Europe from 1961 to 1973 made that starkly clear. The decisive point, in an otherwise evenly balanced argument for and against 'Europe', was that – to quote the Macmillan Cabinet minutes of 26 April 1961 – 'the Common Market, if left to develop alone under French leadership, would grow into a separate political force in Europe.' Eventually this 'might mean that the Six would come to exercise greater influence than the United Kingdom, both with the United States and possibly with some of the independent countries of the Commonwealth', and undermine Britain's position as 'the bridge between Europe and North America'.[57]

Britain's new interest in the EEC was immediately recognised across the Commonwealth as a fundamental reorientation of British priorities. An interdepartmental committee in Canberra warned the Australian government in 1961 that the EEC's purpose would be to 'develop Europe as a world political force' and that 'Australia (and New Zealand) being where they are – out of Europe, out of the Atlantic, and out of Asia – seem to stand to lose most' in terms of 'place and influence in the United Kingdom'. Appeals to the 'Old Country' to respect ties of 'sentiment' (the earlier 'British race patriotism') proved unavailing. During the ensuing decade of uncertainty before de Gaulle's veto was lifted, the Commonwealth countries diversified their trade. In 1962 they took nearly 30 per cent of British exports and provided a similar proportion of Britain's imports; a decade later the figure in both cases was around 20 per cent.[58]

Even so, New Zealand remained heavily dependent on British markets for its butter, cheese and other farm products, and its government played the 'kith and kin' card to particular effect – prompting the Foreign Office's lead negotiator with the EEC to protest that it 'had us over a political barrel' and held almost 'a veto over our entry'. Securing a breathing space for New Zealand farmers cost Britain an extra £100 million in budget contributions over five years. Then Australia and New Zealand signed a bilateral Free Trade Agreement in 1965, which eliminated 80 per cent of tariffs and quantitative restrictions over the next decade. So, by the time Britain entered the EEC in 1973, the Commonwealth was adjusting economically. Yet the emotional sense of betrayal lingered – voiced hyperbolically in 1992 by Australia's Labor premier Paul Keating when urging his countrymen to abandon the 'cultural cringe' towards a country that had 'walked out on you and joined the Common Market'.[59]

After the collapse of the Iron Curtain and the break-up of the Soviet Union, there were predictions that the European Community – soon to become the European Union – and NATO would gradually wither away. Instead, over the next quarter-century both organisations enlarged their membership to embrace most of Europe up to the borderlands of Russia. While in general they were staunch supporters of NATO, Tory Eurosceptics quickly depicted the 2016 vote to leave the EU as a chance to redeem what Boris Johnson called the 'betrayal' of 1973, and to rebuild the old Commonwealth connections and cultivate anew the 'English-speaking peoples'. India was included in some versions of this new Anglosphere (even UKIP's in 2015), but the core was usually the CANZUK quadrilateral of Canada, Australia, New Zealand and the UK. This was envisaged by Churchill biographer Andrew Roberts as a 'Union' based on 'free trade, free movement of people, mutual defence, and a limited but effective confederal structure' which would 'retake' its place as 'the third pillar of Western Civilisation'. The word 'retake' indicated the roots of this idea – the imperial federation championed a century before by the likes of Joseph Chamberlain. And, like earlier advocacy of 'Greater Britain', it was predicated on the idea that technology had transcended geography – with the jet airplane and the internet updating the steamship and the telegraph.[60]

Critics of such ideas, however, depict them as little more than post-colonial nostalgia – 'Empire 2.0'. Decades of Asian immigration into Canada, Australia and New Zealand have rendered them much less 'Anglo' than they were in the 1940s. And Canada's fiercely franco-phone community in Quebec has pulled the country formally into constitutional bilingualism. Strategically, all three nations rely much more on the United States: Canada because of its proximity, Australia and New Zealand because of their growing focus on the Pacific, particularly since the Vietnam War. The deeper agenda for UK enthusiasts for the Anglosphere – mostly English Tories – was a neo-liberal desire to boost innovation, promote 'buccaneers', cut red tape and banish talk of decline. *Britannia Unchained* was the title of one such quick-fix manifesto by five Tory MPs (all from the 2010 intake), which contained caustic observations such as 'once they enter the workplace, the British are among the worst idlers in the world'. Although the book was published in 2012 and seemed to take the EU as a given, after the 2016 referendum its authors became ardent Brexiters and several of them – notably Dominic Raab and Liz Truss – began touting for the premiership as May's authority crumbled.[61]

By 2019, after three years of Tory wrangling and infighting, there was much less talk about CANZUK as a panacea. In any case, the heart of Britain's Anglophone world remained the United States. It was the UK's top trading partner among individual countries (although half the country's overall trade was with the EU), and its security provider because of the American nuclear commitment to NATO. Yet by the time of Brexit, the special relationship was looking more precarious than for years. Although President Donald Trump professed himself an Anglophile and was a fan of Churchill, his propensity for making policy 'on the tweet' created chronic uncertainty abroad, his commitment to NATO was at best grudging, and his aggressive 'America First' philosophy did not bode well for future trade negotiations, especially if the UK was dealing with Trump alone rather than in concert with 27 other EU countries. As Palmerston said, 'trade cannot flourish without security'. Anglosphere sentiment alone has a limited cash value in international commercial bargaining.

And the UK's efforts to exit the EU ran counter to the

predominant view of US policymakers (Trump aside) since the 1960s: Britain was better 'in' than 'out'. That was the main reason Macmillan decided to apply to join in 1961; that's why Obama decided to speak out on the side of 'Remain' in 2016: 'The European Union doesn't moderate British influence – it magnifies it. A strong Europe is not a threat to Britain's global leadership; it enhances Britain's global leadership.' This, of course, ran directly counter to the arguments of 'Leavers' and their fury at being lectured by a foreign leader was perhaps exacerbated in this case by other, darker motives. Writing in the *Sun*, Boris Johnson attacked Obama's 'anti-democratic' intervention in British domestic politics, insinuating that the President's attitude to Britain might be based on his 'part-Kenyan' heritage and 'ancestral dislike' of the British Empire.[62]

The Anglosphere represents a significant legacy of Britain's imperial past – leveraged particularly through the lasting imprint of the English language on America and India – and it unquestionably constitutes a source of 'soft power'. But just how far soft power cuts ice in the hard world of commercial bargaining and international diplomacy is highly debatable. The Brexiters' rhetoric combined an aggressive assertion of national sovereignty with the expectation that the cultural legacies of empire would provide a new framework for interdependence. And it assumed that Britain could afford risking consequent marginalisation from continental power politics – an assumption that runs counter to most of Britain's historical experience, even in the heyday of global empire.

The Empire comes home

A core reason for the Brexiters' assertion of sovereignty was to 'take control of our borders' and restrict the flow of migrants into the UK. 'Vote Leave' made this its key issue in the last stages of the campaign – on 22 May 2016 launching a poster of footsteps walking through an open door shaped like a passport, with the slogan 'Turkey (Population Seventy-Six Million) is Joining the EU'. Leavers warned of the 'threats to UK security' because of Turkey's high rates of crime and gun ownership. In vain Prime Minister David Cameron insisted: 'It's not remotely on the cards that Turkey is going to join the EU. They applied in 1987. At the current rate of progress they will probably get around to joining in the year 3000.' But talk that the Turks were coming had visceral power. And the immigration issue was played up even more crudely by Nigel Farage and UKIP which issued a poster showing a long line of migrants (actually Syrians at the Slovenian border) with the legend, 'Breaking Point. The EU has failed us. We must break free of the EU and take control of our borders.' This appeared on 16 June – a week before polling day, and coincidentally just a few hours before Jo Cox, the vocal pro-EU Labour MP, was stabbed and shot by a man in her constituency. Asked in court to state his name, he said: 'My name is death to traitors, freedom for Britain.' Politicians of all parties hastened to condemn Cox's murder. 'Vote Leave' also sought to distance itself from Farage's 'Breaking Point' ploy, but 'Britain Stronger in Europe' dismissed this as hypocrisy. Its executive director Will Straw observed caustically: 'Michael Gove said he shuddered when he saw the UKIP poster. Did he shudder when he first saw the Turkey poster and signed it off? It's exactly the same: that brown people are coming to this country. That's what both those posters are intended to say.' For his part, Farage was unapologetic: 'At least they're talking about immigration.'[63]

Immigration had long been an obsession of Theresa May – Home Secretary from May 2010 until the start of her premiership in July 2016 – abetted by her political advisers Nick Timothy and Fiona Hill, who acted as zealous enforcers of May's will. As May became

Patrick Blower depicts the 'Windrush Betrayal' in the Daily Telegraph, *18 April 2018. West Indian immigrants disembark from the* Empire Windrush *in 1948, devote their working lives to help maintain essential public services and then are deported to the Caribbean by the Home Office.*

increasingly defensive about failing to keep her promise to cut the annual level of net migration to less than 100,000, she declared in May 2012: 'The aim is to create here in Britain a really hostile environment for illegal migration.'[64] Although the details remain murky, it is clear that immigration officials were directed to zero-in on Caribbean immigrants who had settled legally in Britain in the 1940s and 1950s – the so-called 'Windrush generation' – because their paperwork was often patchy and they were too poor to afford legal assistance. As a result, some lost their homes or jobs and were denied health care. Home Office staff were even given 'targets' for forced deportations – despite claims to the contrary by senior civil servants and by May's successor Amber Rudd, who was eventually forced to resign in April 2018 for misleading the Commons. Rudd was carrying on a policy imposed by her predecessor, though May – like any canny politician – had been careful not to leave many fingerprints. Although the Commons Home Affairs Committee issued damning reports in 2018 about shoddy data, evasion about 'targets', and a 'rigid, rules-based culture' in the Home Office, it seems to have gone out of its way to avoid any mention of May.[65]

Politicians playing the 'race' card, or fixating on immigration, have been a recurrent feature of post-war Britain. But in order to make some sense of the period since 1945, we have to take a longer and more comparative view of the country's immigration history. Most nation states, especially those that took firm shape in Western Europe in the eighteenth and nineteenth centuries, were based on established ethnic majorities, who then decided whether to allow entry and rights to outsiders – a decision usually based on economic interests. Yet those majority populations, if we look back far enough, were in turn the product of earlier migrations – in the British case, from continental Europe and beyond. During the first millennium or so of the Christian era, the migrations across the Channel were generally violent, and took the form of large-scale invasions – Romans, Angles and Saxons, Vikings and then Normans.[66]

Despite their lasting political impact, the Normans had relatively little impact on the demography of England. Comparative DNA analysis of Caucasian British and continental European suggests that in southern and central England the white population owes perhaps 30 per cent to the ancestors of modern Germans, as a result of the Anglo-Saxon invasions of the fifth and sixth centuries and subsequent intermarriage. A further 40 per cent of DNA is shared with the French – not as a result of 1066 but probably from migrations following the end of the last Ice Age nearly 10,000 years ago, before a tsunami triggered by a massive Norwegian landslide created the Channel around 8,000 years ago. All this is a reminder that Victorian notions of a pure English 'race' do not stand up to modern genomics – or even Darwinian science. The same is true for the rest of the UK. Although the inhabitants of the Orkneys are genetically distinct – with 25 per cent of DNA coming from Viking ancestors who settled the islands in the ninth century – there is no single genetic basis for the 'Celtic' regions in Scotland, Northern Ireland, Wales and Cornwall, whatever their similarities of culture. The progressive inter-mixture of various ethnic groups has been the norm over time and, as we shall see, the twenty-first century will probably be no different.[67]

After 1066, migratory movements from the European continent continued, but on a smaller scale. A recurrent pattern may be discerned: migrants were allowed in, usually for economic or religious reasons, but their presence aroused periodic xenophobic outbursts – for instance against the Jews (expelled in 1290) and the Hanseatic Germans (expelled in 1598). In the sixteenth and seventeenth century, Protestant refugees fleeing the continental Counter-Reformation found a home in England – Walloons and Flemings from the Low Countries in the 1560s and 1570s, who settled especially in London and Norwich – and, later, French Huguenots driven out by Louis XIV in 1685. The reception pattern continued: the immigrants brought some economic benefits – Dutch and Germans developed the brewing of beer, the Huguenots promoted silk weaving – but they also attracted hostility and provoked occasional riots. Different in scale and kind were the Irish, especially after the Acts of Union. Between 1800 and 1914 about a million people crossed the Irish Sea to settle in Britain – providing essential labour for the industrial revolution as well as seasonal workers in British agriculture – but also generating ape-like imagery that stereotyped the Irish as a racially 'inferior' to the 'Anglo-Saxons'. 'This wild, reckless, indolent, uncertain and superstitious race have no sympathy with the English character,' declared

Benjamin Disraeli in 1836. 'Their history describes an unbroken circle of bigotry and blood.'[68]

Disraeli, of course, was the offspring of another ethnic group that experienced prejudice and discrimination. But although the child of Jewish parents, he was baptised into the Church of England at the age of twelve and this allowed him to circumvent the barriers to Jewish political advancement. Although Jews had been readmitted to Britain in 1656 by Oliver Cromwell, anti-Semitism remained endemic, and in the early 1900s the influx of Jewish refugees from Tsarist pogroms into the East End of London provoked a housing crisis and an organised backlash in the form of the British Brothers League ('England for the English'). The furore prompted the first modern parliamentary legislation to regulate immigration into the UK.

The story of the Aliens Act of 1905, intended to prevent the arrival of 'undesirables' in the UK, has a certain 'timelessness' about it, when set in the context of subsequent attempts at immigration control right up to the present. For instance: the lack of adequate statistics about the scale and character of the problem. The preoccupation of the Home Office, as the lead department, with aliens as threats to national security and political stability. The vagueness of the Act's criterion of undesirability in an alien, which was the lack of 'the means of decently supporting himself and his dependents'. Officials eventually decided to interpret this as the possession of at least five pounds. The administrative impracticalities of the legislation may also seem familiar, such as the lack of a proper 'receiving house' in the Port of London (like New York's Ellis Island) where new arrivals could be inspected and interrogated. Most recognisable of all is the reluctance of most senior politicians of either main party – the Unionists enacted the law, the Liberals had to enforce it – to associate publicly (though not in private) with measures that polarised opinion around security versus tolerance.[69]

"Britannia: I can no longer offer shelter to fugitives. England is not a free country."

'England is not a free country.' Britannia turns back immigrants
fleeing from the Tsarist pogroms in Eastern Europe after passage
of the Aliens Act of 1905.

Waves of immigration and periodic backlashes have therefore been part of the British *longue durée*. But although 'Britain has for many centuries been both multi-ethnic and multicultural, only recently has it become multiracial' – meaning that 'only in the second half of the twentieth century have groups who are perceived to be different from the existing settled population by the colour of their skin, settled in Britain permanently and in significant numbers.'[70] Although recent research has shown that Afro-Romans garrisoned Hadrian's Wall and people of African descent were living in Tudor London, the black presence in Britain itself (as distinct from the British slave-trading empire) remained small well into the twentieth century – perhaps 20,000 in the 1930s, mostly in port cities such as Liverpool, Glasgow, Cardiff and London.[71] But several thousand black British subjects from the West Indies served in Britain during the Second World War, and they responded enthusiastically to news of the UK's post-war manpower shortage. Attlee's Labour government, however, tried to deter non-white immigration, preferring instead white Eastern Europeans such as Polish ex-servicemen or 'Displaced Persons' (DPs) from refugee camps in Central Europe. The Colonial Secretary, Arthur Creech-Jones, warned his colleagues that people in the West Indies were 'well aware of the labour shortages' in Britain and of plans to use DPs. 'In these circumstances there has been a natural and immediate demand for the employment of British West Indians, who are British subjects and many of whom have had experience of work in Britain during the war years.'[72]

Attlee's Cabinet remained resistant, but on 22 June 1948 the *Empire Windrush* landed at Tilbury with 492 would-be workers from the West Indies. The London *Evening Standard* reported their arrival in the 'mother country' of the empire under the headline 'WELCOME HOME'. Although the government had tried to divert the ship to East Africa, hoping to satisfy the migrants with work on groundnut farming projects, once *Windrush* landed at Tilbury it was impossible to stop them coming ashore: they were British subjects carrying British passports. Within a month, all but twelve had been found work in industries and businesses from Scotland to South Wales.[73]

Another date in the summer of 1948 was also significant. On 31 July the British Nationality Act received Royal Assent. This followed passage in 1946 of a Canadian Citizenship Act and the decision of the 1947 Commonwealth Conference that each member state was free to legislate on its own citizenship. The British Nationality Act created a new status of 'Citizen of the UK and Colonies'. This was intended by London to maintain the fluid two-way traffic of migrants of 'British stock' between the UK and the 'Old Dominions' – one of the residual bonds of empire that shored up Britain's claim still to be a world power. And it reflected the proud boast by Macaulay and others during Britain's imperial heyday that colonial rule was intended to make the colonised people 'desirous and capable of all the privileges of citizens' in the British world. This ideal was reiterated a century later in 1954 by Henry Hopkinson, Minister of State at the Colonial Office: 'In a world in which restrictions on personal movement and immigration have increased we still take pride in the fact that a man can say *Civis Britannicus sum* whatever his colour may be, and we take pride in the fact that he wants and can come to the Mother country'.[74]

When the British Nationality Act was passed in 1948, few expected that citizens of the UK and Colonies from the 'New Commonwealth' would take up their legal right to 'come to the Mother country'. And although the arrival of the *Windrush* is now commemorated as the start of modern British multiculturalism – featured, for instance, in the pageant of British history at the opening of the 2012 London Olympics – it did not in itself represent a major turning point in the history of immigration. Attlee treated the episode as the product of a 'peculiar combination of circumstances' – a troopship returning to the UK and West Indian ex-servicemen who had experienced wartime Britain and had accumulated enough money for the passage.[75] Furthermore, the immediate influx was small – between one and two thousand a year in 1948–52. In any case, politicians and officials since the 1930s had covertly operated racial restrictions by making it difficult for would-be migrants to obtain a British passport – in other words maintaining the right of Commonwealth citizens to *come* to Britain while denying them the right to *leave* their home country. This proved effective in the case of India and Pakistan, even after independence in 1947, but less so in the islands of the British West Indies – facing massive unemployment – which refused London's request to turn down applicants who lacked the means to support themselves in the UK. This economic test was not applied to (white) citizens of the Old Commonwealth. Lord Swinton, the Commonwealth Relations Secretary, told the Cabinet in 1954 that there was 'a continuous stream of persons from the Old Dominions to the United Kingdom who come here, with no clear plans, in order to try their luck; and it would be a great pity to interfere with this freedom of movement'.[76]

The crux of the matter was therefore 'colour', and this issue became a matter of serious debate in the Tory Cabinets of the mid-1950s. Numbers were the primary reason: official figures suggested that West Indian immigration jumped to 10,000 in 1954 and was over 40,000 each year between 1955 and 1957.[77] It was assumed that, given Britain's overwhelmingly white population, there was a limit to how many coloured immigrants could be 'assimilated' without 'racial conflict' – terms that recur in official papers. No clear quantifiable answer was offered; the general view in Whitehall was that 'small' numbers of coloured immigrants were tolerable as long as they were 'dispersed' geographically. Within this official debate there were, of course, many nuances. The Commonwealth Relations and Colonial Offices placed much greater weight on maintaining good relations with the Commonwealth; at the other end of the spectrum the Home Office 'appeared singularly and unrestrainedly opposed to the permanent settlement of "coloured" people from the empire/Commonwealth, believing it likely to lead to social unrest in Britain and, at a time of Cold War tensions, to the growth of communist influence'.[78]

Yet politicians, even from the same party, also took different positions. Churchill was particularly concerned about the matter, and there were no fewer than thirteen separate Cabinet discussions about 'colonial immigration' in less than a year in 1954–5. But the question of formal restriction was shelved in November 1955, partly because his successor, Anthony Eden, was less fixated than Churchill on 'race' and more concerned about Commonwealth solidarity. As Swinton explained to his colleagues, 'Any action which may weaken the ties which help to bind the Commonwealth together is a matter of direct interest to the United Kingdom.' The challenge was that any legislation 'should be non-discriminatory in form' even though 'the problem with which we are in fact concerned is that of coloured immigrants from Colonial territories'. Or as Sir David Hunt, Churchill's private secretary, put it colloquially: 'The minute we said we've got to keep these black chaps out, the whole Commonwealth lark would have blown up'. Unable to find a politically viable solution to this conundrum and persuading themselves that the numbers involved were still 'assimilable', Tory Cabinets of the 1950s did not act, even after racial disturbances in Nottingham and London's Notting Hill in 1958.[79]

The turning point came in 1961 with passage of the Commonwealth Immigration Act. This was partly a response to a new surge in immigration, from a trough of 21,600 (1959) to an unprecedented figure of 136,400 in 1961 – with the bulk now coming from India and Pakistan and therefore overwhelmingly non-white. The 'case for control' was said to rest on two considerations: 'the strain imposed by coloured immigration on the housing resources of certain local authorities and the dangers of social tension inherent in the existence of large unassimilated coloured communities'. The Cabinet decided to go ahead with legislation because it had finally 'solved' the conundrum of non-discriminatory discrimination. Entry would depend on possession of a voucher from the Ministry of Labour. These would be 'issued freely' to those in categories (a) 'those having jobs to go to' and (b) those who had training or qualifications 'accepted as likely to be useful in this country', but would be tightly controlled in the case of category (c) 'Others'. R. A. Butler, the Home Secretary, told his Tory colleagues with some satisfaction:

The great merit of this scheme is that it can be presented as making no distinction on grounds of race or colour, although in practice all would-be immigrants from the old Commonwealth countries would almost certainly be able to obtain authority to enter under either category (a) or category (b). We must recognise that, although the scheme purports to relate solely to employment and to be non-discriminatory, its aim is primarily social and is intended to, and would in fact, operate on coloured people almost exclusively.

Further clarifying the thrust of the legislation, Butler explained that it would not apply to Irish citizens, who would be treated 'as if they were British subjects'. He also rejected the idea that the Bill should include 'provision against discrimination on grounds of race or colour'. Indeed, the whole Cabinet discussion was couched in terms of controlling immigration rather than enhancing resources, such as housing, for those who had arrived. Yet the Treasury had made clear that the immigrants enhanced the GDP because most of them took jobs that native Britons shunned, for instance on the buses or in the National Health Service. The issue, in short, was one of national identity not economics.[80]

The Labour Opposition condemned the Commonwealth Immigration Act as 'a surrender to racialism' and, after narrowly winning the 1964 general election, passed the UK's first Race Relations Act (1965). But although this prohibited incitement to racial hatred and acts of discrimination in public places, it did not apply to housing or employment, nor make violations a criminal offence. At the same time the Government decided that 'tougher' measures were required to control immigration, including a sharp reduction of numbers allowed under the voucher-scheme quotas. A stimulus to this was the shock result of the general election in the West Midlands constituency of Smethwick, where the Tory candidate won on a platform that refused to condemn slogans like: 'If you want a nigger neighbour, vote Labour.' Richard Crossman, Labour's Housing Minister, wrote sadly in his diary: 'We have become illiberal and lowered the quotas at a time when we have an acute shortage of labour.' Nevertheless, he was 'convinced that if we hadn't done all this we would have been faced with certain electoral defeat in the West Midlands and the South-East . . . We felt we had to out-trump the Tories by doing what they would have done and so transforming their policy into a bipartisan policy.'[81]

By the mid-1960s, therefore, the two main political parties had redefined what it meant to hold the status of *Civis Britannicus*. Whereas many continental European countries, dealing with an influx of guest-workers, 'debated the admission of immigrants to citizenship', the UK was unusual in 'discussing the admission of citizens as immigrants'. What had become clear was 'that formal citizenship' mattered less than 'the constructed national identity'. In other words, 'immigrating white aliens were recruited as members and citizens for their perceived potential to become British', and white UK residents were still encouraged to migrate to the Commonwealth in order to 'maintain Britishness abroad as members and citizens of the wider British community'. But immi-grating coloured citizens were shunned as members of British society because, supposedly, 'they had never been and could never become "really" British'.[82]

The 'identity' question was posed with deliberate starkness by Enoch Powell in an emotive speech in Birmingham on 20 April 1968. His intentions were complex. One factor was his underlying belief, rooted in war service in India, that liberal democracy could only flourish in a homogeneous society, free from the 'curse' of 'communalism'. Also potent were the TV images of racial violence in America following the assassination of Martin Luther King two weeks before. But Powell was also an intensely ambitious politician, with his eyes on the Tory leadership, who skilfully wove selective quotation from constituents' letters together with his own inflammatory rhetoric into a speech of malevolent brilliance. This blend of conviction and opportunism has proved typical of demotic figures in later arguments over immigration. Powell described the country as 'mad, literally mad' to allow continued immigration on the current scale. 'It is like watching a nation busily engaged in heaping up its funeral pyre,' he declared. 'As I look ahead, I am filled with foreboding; like the Roman, I seem to see "the River Tiber foaming with much blood"'. That quotation from Virgil's *Aeneid* inspired the speech's familiar, if somewhat inaccurate, title 'Rivers of Blood'.[83]

Amid the ensuing fury – for and against – Tory leader Edward Heath sacked Powell from his Shadow Cabinet for a speech that he called 'racialist in tone, and liable to exacerbate racial tensions'. Yet, according to Heath's biographer John Campbell, 'there is no question that under pressure from Powell he toughened the party's stance on immigration'.[84] Most commentators concur that Powell's rhetoric on race 'encouraged voters to support the Conservatives, which proved crucial in the 1970 general election' that swept Heath to power with a 31-seat majority. In 1971 the Tories' new Immigration Act replaced the traditional dichotomy of 'alien' and 'British subject' with what were effectively 'racially-defined categories'. On the one hand, 'patrials' – essentially, British by place of birth or parentage – were not subject to controls; on the other, 'non-patrials' could apply for a work permit but had no rights of permanent residence or entry for their dependants. The 1971 Act 'abolished the last vestiges of the old empire-embracing concept of British subject or citizen'.[85]

The controls on immigration imposed by both main political parties between 1961 and 1971 were deplored by the left as racist and illiberal. Yet, in an apparent paradox, they also helped make Britain a multiracial and multicultural society. Reports that the

Macmillan government was going to impose the Commonwealth Immigrants Act led to a 'beat-the-ban' rush, exploited by local travel agents. As a result, the UK's Asian and black population doubled in just two years between July 1960 and June 1962, from 250,000 to half a million. The threat of the Act also encouraged many of those who had entered temporarily as visiting workers to decide to remain permanently and to bring over their families. The decision to admit wives, unmarried partners and also children of both existing and future immigrants was 'taken without apparent consideration for the effect it was likely to have' in the future. Despite further attempts to close loopholes, notably in the Thatcher government's British Nationality Act (1981), during every single year except two from 1963 to 1989 between 30,000 and 50,000 Asian and black immigrants arrived for settlement in the UK.[86]

After arrival, they followed the trajectory of earlier waves of immigrants to Britain over the centuries such as Jews and Irish. Initially they tended to huddle together in their own insular communities – encountering suspicion and often hostility from the native population – and lived in the poorest housing, doing menial work. But then subsequent generations began to disperse geographically and move into more remunerative and responsible jobs, especially if they had mastered the English language and adopted British dress. There seems, in short, to be a degree of 'inevitability' about both 'ghettoisation' and then 'integration'. Other variables, of course, retard the speed of the integration process – particularly strict adherence to a religious tradition: be it Catholicism, Judaism or Islam. There are also significant variations among different ethnic communities. 'Most of the crude indicators of success in contemporary Britain – rates of home-owner occupancy and car ownership, distribution between occupational categories and levels of educational achievement – rank African, Indian and Chinese communities as more successful than the average for the country whereas Caribbean, Pakistani and Bangladeshi communities, as yet, enjoy less success than the average.' This divergence speaks to differences in class as much as ethnicity.[87]

The 1971 Immigration Act came into force on 1 January 1973 – the same day that the UK formally joined the EEC and started the process of opening its borders to some 200 million (largely 'white') European citizens. The 'free movement of labour' did not 'cause us much difficulty', according to the UK's chief negotiator, and occasional criticism in the press and parliament failed to ignite any serious campaign. Over the remainder of the twentieth century, thousands of EC citizens came to the UK to live and work, and significant Italian, German and French communities established themselves in London. In fact, European immigration did not become a political issue until the EU's big eastern enlargement in 2004, combined with the decision of Tony Blair's government – unlike most other EU states – to approve immediate freedom of movement, rather than phase it in (see pages 105–6). Between 2004 and 2017, the share of the UK population from the rest of Europe rose from 1.5 per cent to just over 5 per cent. The 900,000 Poland-born residents accounted for 10 per cent of the total non-UK born residents living in the country – more than those born in India. These demographic changes had occurred at the same time that the UK was still absorbing migrants from the Commonwealth who had arrived since the 1950s as well as trying to integrate fully their children and grandchildren who had been born in Britain. This conjuncture of significant immigration from continental Europe *and* from the former empire was unique in British history.[88]

The impact of the Brexit furore on EU residents remains to be determined. What is not going to change is the overall trend towards a more multiracial and more multicultural Britain. Census data over time and across the countries of the UK are not exactly comparable, but the broad pattern is apparent in the evidence from England and Wales. Between 1991, when 'ethnicity' became a category for self-identification, and the census of 2011, the 'White' ethnic group decreased from 94 per cent of the population to 86 per cent, with 80.5 per cent describing themselves as 'White British'. In 2011 'Asian/Asian British' accounted for 7.5 per cent of the population and 'Black/African/Caribbean/Black British' for another 3.3 per cent. Ethnic mixing has also increased over time. Roughly half of British-born black men with a partner live with a white woman; the figure for British-born black women is one-third. Although 'inter-ethnic' marriages are much less prevalent between Muslims and non-Muslims, overall they now amount to 2 per cent of total marriages.[89]

Despite the scale and complexity of recent immigration, the story broadly fits Britain's long-term pattern. 'Over the last two centuries Britain has emerged as a state in which racism remains endemic yet in which migrants, and more especially, their descendants, have often witnessed significant economic and social mobility.'[90] The 2018 'Windrush scandal' aptly illustrates both points. Theresa May's 'hostile environment', the attempted cover-up of how vulnerable non-white citizens were hounded, and the tea party May hosted at 10 Downing Street, at the height of the furore, to celebrate the seventy-fifth anniversary of the arrival of *Empire Windrush* mirrored the blend of deceit, nastiness and hypocrisy displayed by previous British leaders – such as Rab Butler. On the other hand, the man whom May appointed to run the Home Office in the wake of the scandal, Sajid Javid, was the son of a Pakistani immigrant who had arrived in Lancashire in 1961 and started work as a bus driver. Javid said his first reaction to the Windrush revelations was: 'That could be my mum . . . my dad . . . my uncle . . . it could be me.'[91]

* * *

David Cameron wanted to tell the story of global Britain 'warts and all' but also to take pride in 'what Britain has done'. Yet this double act is clearly a challenging task. Any informed account of what made Britain a global force needs to discuss slavepower as well as seapower. It must acknowledge that profits from human trafficking as much as the ingenuity of heroic entrepreneurs and inventors contributed to the country's commercial and industrial revolutions. Yet it should not ignore the ideology of freedom – free labour and free trade – that became inextricably part of Britain's imperial project in its Victorian heyday. Both expressed British values, especially those of evangelical Protestantism, but were turned into political realities by the country's uniquely advantageous position at that moment in terms of wealth and power. Lucrative compensation for slave-owners eased slavery's abolition through Parliament; the imperialism of free trade was enforced by Palmerston's 'cannonballs'. This ideology of freedom – of preparing 'backward races' for self-government – was used to justify colonial rule, even though the reality was very often benign neglect or racist exploitation. Yet that ideology was appropriated by the colonised, for both principled and opportunist ends, to drive home their demands for independence. And *Civis Britannicus sum* – though often a glib phrase whose implications were not appreciated – eventually brought thousands of non-white British 'citizens' to these shores. They, and even more their descendants, are in the process of gradually altering the very meaning of what it is to be British.

How to narrate this historically and morally complex story will challenge scholars and teachers for years to come. Will politicians dare to face the challenge?

Taking Control of Our Past

Is the only lesson of history to be that mankind is unteachable?
Winston S. Churchill, 1946[1]

'Vote Leave. Take Back Control.' After the referendum in June 2016, Brexiters rode high. Over the next three years, however, the UK tied itself in knots as it tried to exit the EU. Those contortions in part mirrored the contorted personality of Theresa May – a theme which forms the opening section of this chapter. But the mayhem of 2016–19 also had deeper roots – especially the historical flaws in the cases for both Remain and Leave and larger issues about how the British, especially the English, understand their past. I reflect on these questions in this 'conclusion' to a story that is only just beginning.

Brexit means Mayhem

When David Cameron abruptly resigned in July 2016, he left a vacuum which Theresa May eagerly filled, professing herself determined to 'deliver' Brexit. But what ensued was captured well by *The Times* in March 2019: she 'may have been dealt a near-impossible hand but each day it becomes clearer that there is no situation so bad that she cannot make worse'.[2] This dénouement was sadly ironic because Theresa Brasier had declared her intention to become Prime Minister as early as her opening term at Oxford in 1974, aged 18, and in 1979 she was reputedly miffed that Margaret Thatcher beat her to it as Britain's first female premier. Given such burning ambition, it seems remarkable that May proved so ineffectual as a politician. Yet her personal limitations point up some of the inherent dilemmas of Brexit.

On the positive side, May had a ferocious work ethic and paid immense attention to detail, but she was also intensely cautious, except for moments of what seemed almost panicked boldness. The only child of a High Anglican vicar, who lost both her parents in her twenties, May was chronically shy and lacked the 'clubbable' manner of most high-flying Tory males. She had virtually no small talk – Cabinet Secretary Jeremy Heywood, who met her occasionally for dinner, said that they had usually 'run out of things to talk about by the main course'. She was also 'quite anti-intellectual' and 'not a great thinker', according to a former minister.[3] May's strong patriotism had its roots in her rather pinched sense of vicarage values and a romanticised nostalgia for Home Counties England in the 1950s. This was all viewed through the prism of the Tory party – her emotional home – and often expressed in a passion for cricket. It is revealing, as things turned out, that her cricketing pin-up as a teenager was Geoffrey Boycott: the dour Yorkshire and England opening batsman who had a reputation for limpet-like occupancy of the crease regardless of the state of the game. Dubbed 'a bloody difficult woman' by one Tory veteran, May adopted the term as a badge of pride.[4]

To compensate for her deficiencies in strategic vision and emotional intelligence, May relied heavily on two political aides: Nick Timothy, a policy intellectual with a Rasputin-like beard who wrote most of her speeches, and Fiona Hill, who attended to May's appearance and boosted her morale. Nick and Fi proved ferocious minders when

May was in the Home Office – widely regarded in Whitehall as bullies – and were eventually forced out by departmental in-fighting. But they continued to pull the strings behind the scenes. During the referendum campaign they persuaded May to adopt a 'submarine' strategy, officially in favour of Remain but staying below the surface and avoiding any high-profile speeches in favour of the EU. This helped her seem like an acceptable compromise candidate after Cameron's resignation, and she was able to move into Number Ten with the duo once more at her side. It was Timothy who came up with the 'Brexit means Brexit' mantra, which May readily adopted. This signalled that she would respect the referendum result, while keeping open her options as to precise policies. In fact, however, those options became tightly circumscribed from early on.[5]

May had a few gut ideas, which her two aides fleshed out. Rather than rejoining the likes of Norway and Switzerland in the European Free Trade Area (EFTA) – which the UK had formed in 1960 and then left to join the EEC – May wanted a 'bespoke' deal for 'Global Britain', befitting its independence, sovereignty and global status. This in turn seemed to require a 'standalone' department to negotiate with Brussels, rather than allowing the Treasury or Foreign Office – the big beasts of the Whitehall jungle, whom May detested – to sabotage the process. Sir Ivan Rogers, the UK's forceful Permanent Representative in Brussels, warned that setting up a new department would wastefully divert staff and energy, and was pushed out for his pains.

May and Timothy, a long-standing Eurosceptic, also agreed that leaving the EU must entail leaving the jurisdiction of the European Court of Justice (ECJ) – hated from her days at the Home Office – which also meant leaving the single market and customs union, over which the ECJ justices held sway. In a speech on Brexit largely written by Timothy she made these priorities clear to the Tory party conference on 2 October 2016, declaring that 'we are not leaving the European Union only to give up control of immigration again'. Since the EU had stated firmly that it would not open any negotiations until the UK had formally notified its intention to leave, thereby triggering Article 50 of the 2007 Lisbon Treaty on European Union, May also told the Tories: 'We shall invoke Article 50 no later than the end of March next year.' Consequently, the UK would have to conclude a deal with the EU by the end of March 2019 in order to facilitate an orderly exit.[6]

May followed this up with her 'Come with Me' keynote address to the conference on 5 October, again largely scripted by Timothy. She presented Brexit as nothing less than 'a turning point for our country': what she called 'a once-in-a-generation chance to change the direction of our nation for good', because the referendum was more than a vote for withdrawal from the EU. 'It was about something broader – something that the European Union had come to represent' – a deep sense that 'many people have today that the world works well for a privileged few, but not for them'. She declared that 'too many people in positions of power behave as though they have more in common with international elites than with the people down the road, the people they employ, the people they pass in the street. But if you believe you're a citizen of the world, you're a citizen of nowhere. You don't understand what the very word "citizenship" means.' That Timothyesque sneer caused particular unease and offence among EU nationals legally resident in the UK.[7]

These two major policy speeches in October 2016 – neither shared in advance with her Cabinet – go a long way to explain what followed. With her instinctive 'thing' about immigrants, May had put the 'control of borders' ahead of everything else, including the economy. This became the most rubicund of her 'red lines'. Anxious to fend off suspicions that she remained a Remainer, she had also committed herself to trigger Article 50 by the end of March 2017. Yet the consequent two-year countdown – as Rogers warned – would hand the initiative in negotiations to the EU 27 unless the British really knew what they were doing. Most striking of all, she had represented the referendum vote as the springboard for a populist crusade, around which she sought to define her premiership.

A different leader, more secure politically and personally, might have decided to treat a 52:48 split in the country as reason to try crafting a compromise – talking to the opposition parties and seeking what became known as a 'soft Brexit'. But such was the polarisation created during the referendum and May's craving to turn the burden of Brexit into a legacy project, that – tutored by Timothy – she cast herself as tribune of the people. In this mode, she was even ready to deny Parliament a significant role in the process. In her speech on 2 October, May declared that those people who claimed that Article 50 could only be invoked by a vote in both houses of Parliament were 'not standing up for democracy, they're trying to subvert it . . . They are insulting the intelligence of the British people.'[8] This was the rhetoric of plebiscitary politics, not representative democracy – yet, constitutionally, sovereignty was vested in Parliament as the people's representatives. And on 3 November a panel of three Justices of the UK Supreme Court rejected the Government's claim that it had sufficient authority under the Crown's prerogative to trigger Article 50. The following day the *Daily Mail*, edited by the Europhobic Paul Dacre, denounced the judges under a banner headline 'ENEMIES OF THE PEOPLE'.

The 'Parliament versus People' furore intensified the populist tone of political debate but May was now obliged to bring Westminster into the Brexit process. The vote to trigger Article 50 was passed by both Houses in February 2017 and the formal letter was delivered in Brussels on 29 March, with contrived theatricality. The two-year countdown had begun, but many civil servants worried that the Government had no idea of what was involved in 'exiting' the EU and was not preparing properly for the likely chaos if it failed in that time to conclude a withdrawal agreement with the EU. In the hope of increasing Britain's leverage, May – prompted by Timothy – had declared in January that 'no deal is better than a bad deal'.[9]

By the spring of 2017, therefore, the core framework for what followed was in place. A secretive and rigid Prime Minister – in thrall to her key advisers and determined to run Brexit from Number Ten – had opted for a hard-Brexit strategy, with little knowledge of what Brussels would accept and remarkable complacency about Britain's bargaining power. Nevertheless, despite the continued feuding within the country about Brexit, May's domestic position was reasonably strong – until, that is, 8 June 2017.

On 18 April the PM had suddenly informed her Cabinet that she intended to hold a general election. In her usual way, there had been virtually no consultation. The driving force behind the decision was again Nick Timothy. May had initially resisted, having told the public from the moment she took power that she had no such intent, but she was currently enjoying a 20-point lead in opinion polls. Holding an election in mid-2017 would avoid the need to have one in May 2020, when it would add further pressure to the Brexit deadline of March 2019. Brexiters were delighted: 'CRUSH THE SABOTEURS' trumpeted the *Mail*. May stated that she wanted to increase the Tory majority and 'strengthen my hand' in Brexit negotiations.[10]

In the event, however, the campaign proved a disaster. Timothy and Hill were now riding high in Downing Street as chiefs of staff. Journalist Tim Shipman observes that 'ministers never knew whether May made decisions or whether the chiefs had done so on her behalf'. She rarely stood up to them and was often described by insiders as their 'captive' or 'prisoner'. Timothy took charge of the manifesto, writing an over-intellectualised statement of the 'Tory revolution' philosophy he had inserted in the 5 October 2016 speech.

When his social-care proposals backfired and the Tories performed an abrupt U-turn, May's shrill insistence that 'Nothing has changed!' revealed her brittleness and exposed the vicar's daughter to charges of bare-faced lying. In other ways, too, the campaign was going badly. Not good at thinking on her feet, she dealt ineptly with questions – mechanically repeating memorised talking points – and her mantra of 'strong and stable' leadership quickly sounded robotic. The nickname 'Maybot', coined by *Guardian* journalist John Crace, stuck – with devastating effect. May's team was clear that she must not risk entering a live debate on BBC TV with the leaders of the other parties, and she sent Home Secretary Amber Rudd instead. Despite the death of Rudd's father only two days before, she performed well, but the fact that Labour leader Jeremy Corbyn agreed at the last minute to appear put the spotlight mercilessly on May's absence. 'The first rule of leadership', declared Caroline Lucas of the Green Party, 'is to show up'. Subjected to relentless personal scrutiny for the first time in her political career, May became depressed and ever more stilted. On election night she lost her majority. One Tory special adviser observed gloomily: 'The manifesto didn't cost us the election, the person did. She didn't connect.'[11]

After 8 June, the Tories remained the largest single party, but instead of a serviceable 17-seat working majority over Labour, they suffered a net loss of 13 seats. May could only stay in power by negotiating a 'confidence and supply' arrangement with Northern Ireland's Democratic Unionist Party (DUP) – which was strongly pro-Brexit and also opposed to the Good Friday agreement. The DUP now effectively held May hostage and the initial pork-barrel payment they extracted amounted to $1 billion, with plenty more to come. Equally important, as a result of the election shambles, Timothy and Hill were obliged to resign. Many in Whitehall were delighted, but their departure left May rudderless and even more isolated.

From this politically weakened position, May began withdrawal negotiations in Brussels less than two weeks later, on 19 June 2017. The EU 27 had hammered out a clear position for their principal negotiator, Michel Barnier, to which they stuck firmly. The British, by contrast, were ill-prepared – the lack of government planning being aggravated by the near two-month diversion for the election. Most of the negotiating rounds in 2017 were taken up with the financial settlement to cover the UK's outstanding obligations – the so-called 'divorce bill' – and in hammering out agreements on the rights of EU citizens living in the UK and British expatriates resident in the EU. May's breezy assumption in the spring that they could start right away to negotiate a post-Brexit UK–EU free-trade deal proved to EU leaders that she was 'living on another galaxy'.[12] It took until December 2017 to achieve an outline settlement about finance and citizens' rights – on terms problematic for many hard Brexiters with regard to the amount of money that the UK would have to pay and also the continuing role of the ECJ – yet these were necessary preconditions for serious discussion on trade and future relations.

Recognising belatedly the impossibility of completing all the necessary negotiations within the two-year timeframe, May had accepted the idea of a 'transition' period after that date. The EU's January 2018 guidelines for the phase-two talks over the next few months made clear its position that, during the transition lasting until 31 December 2020, the UK would continue to be subject to all EU laws and regulations (the *acquis*) and would remain within the customs union and the single market, while having no say in EU decisions.[13] With the Government under attack from many Eurosceptics, intent to 'deliver' a clean and total Brexit on 29 March 2019, Brexit Secretary David Davis preferred to call the transition a strictly limited 'implementation period' for Brexit, allowing both the UK and the EU 'time to build new infrastructure' and 'allow for as free and frictionless trade as possible'.[14] The caveat 'as possible' was crucial. The EU kept asking how the UK intended to resolve 'the incompatibility between wanting to leave the Single Market and customs union and having frictionless trade and full participation in financial-services arrangements'.[15] It resisted the UK's attempts to 'cherry-pick' those aspects of the single market that it liked, insisting on the inseparability of the EU's 'four freedoms': the unrestricted movement of goods, services, capital and persons. May's overriding determination to 'control our borders' breached the last of these principles and cramped her options on the others.

On 12 July 2018, May's government tried to square the circle with its much-delayed White Paper on 'The Future Relationship' between the UK and EU. Having shared virtually nothing in advance with her colleagues, she had tried to ram the proposed deal through her Cabinet at an all-day meeting at Chequers – only to produce a general outcry and then high-profile resignations by David Davis, Steve Baker, one of his junior ministers, and also, after some dithering, Foreign Secretary Boris Johnson. The White Paper's proposal for a 'free trade area for goods' with the EU would depend on maintaining 'a common rule-book' with Brussels – hardly an assertion of independence, especially since the rules would still be open to interpretation by the ECJ. The aim of 'frictionless trade at the border' – May's government had belatedly woken up to the reality of 'just-in-time' supply chains to and fro across the Channel – would supposedly be achieved by the UK acting as customs collector for EU tariffs – something not done anywhere else on a significant scale. And the proposed new 'mobility framework' for work, business and tourism looked to many Brexiters like the thin end of the wedge back to 'freedom of movement'. Across the political spectrum, in fact, there was huge scepticism about the claim in the conclusion of the White Paper that 'this is a Brexit which will deliver in full on the democratic decision of the people of the UK, and work for the whole country'.[16]

Still determined to do it her way, the Prime Minister soldiered on, despite accusations from Johnson that 'a fog of self-doubt' had descended over the original bright Brexit vision of 'Global Britain'.[17] In mid-November 2018, little more than four months before the two-year negotiating period would expire, the UK and EU finally concluded a 'Withdrawal Agreement' together with a non-binding 'Political Declaration' to indicate some of the lines along which both sides hoped to proceed in future negotiations. These were debated in a fraught five-hour Cabinet meeting – when many ministers expressed vocal opposition – and May eventually forced them through as a 'collective' decision, refusing to put matters to a vote.[18] Capping all the earlier fudges was the so-called Irish 'backstop'. Any return of a 'hard border' between Northern Ireland and the Republic was anathema to Dublin and the EU, not least because it would endanger the Good Friday agreement and the peace process. The UK government shared those concerns, but the EU's wording of its 'backstop' provision, if no other arrangements had been agreed by the end of 2020, was unacceptable to the DUP because it would leave Northern Ireland subject to elements of the customs union and the single market, without means of extrication – thereby distinguishing Ulster from the rest of the UK and perhaps pushing it closer to a united Ireland. Dominic Raab, the second of May's Brexit Secretaries – who had just negotiated the withdrawal agreement – resigned over the backstop issue, and joined a bevy of Tory politicians openly angling for the PM's job. With opposition mounting in the party from Brexiters and Remainers alike, May abruptly called off the intended vote on the withdrawal agreement scheduled for 11 December – realising that she did not have enough support to get it through.

After this fiasco, hard-Brexiters of the European Research Group (ERG) – which for several weeks had been running a campaign to topple her as party leader – now got the 48 votes required to trigger a formal vote by Tory MPs. May saw off the challenge, by 200 to 117, but this was hardly a ringing endorsement. To many politicians, the open opposition of over a third of one's party might have been decisive, but the ERGs had misjudged May. Instead of being cowed into resignation, she defiantly reiterated her determination about 'delivering the Brexit people voted for'.[19] Steve Baker, the messianic Brexiter known as Jacob Rees-Mogg's 'shop-steward', had ironically ensured that – under Tory party rules – she was now safe from another formal challenge for 12 months.

On the other hand, the ERGs had shown that they were the Tory power-brokers, ready to put Brexit before party, and May decided that she had to buy their support in order to get her deal through Parliament. And so she shuttled around the European capitals in the hope of securing a legally binding form of words that would satisfy ERGs and DUPs. Otherwise, both groups warned, the UK should leave the EU without a withdrawal agreement. With anger mounting in the Commons about an apparent drift towards 'Mogg Rule', those MPs who wanted to avoid a no-deal Brexit began to push back for Parliament to assert itself and break out of the binary trap now on the table: May's deal or no deal.

Given the muddled state of the Government's belated preparations – hastily moving thousands of civil servants into 'frontline' departments – no deal seemed likely to risk chaos, potentially endangering border security, IT systems, public health and the movement of food, people and goods. Hard Brexiters derided this as more 'Project Fear' scaremongering, but the independent Institute for Government issued a damning report in late January 2019, which concluded that 'the Government's approach to no-deal preparations – being unwilling to talk publicly about plans and developing an adversarial relationship with Parliament' – had made a difficult situation worse.[20]

Battling on with her combination of bludgeon and bribe, May brought the withdrawal agreement and the political declaration to the Commons on two occasions, only to be massively rebuffed – 432 to 202 (15 January 2019) and 391 to 242 (12 March). These were unprecedented humiliations for any British Government in the democratic era, and normally a Prime Minister who had been so roundly defeated on a key policy would have resigned. But May again showed that she was no normal premier. After the second defeat, she indulged in another populist spasm, appealing on television to the public: 'You are tired of the political games and the arcane procedural rows . . . You want this stage of the Brexit process to be over and done with. I agree. I am on your side . . . So far, Parliament has done everything possible to avoid making a choice.'[21] Casting herself as tribune of the people in this way only inflamed the mood of many MPs.

To get around the Speaker's ruling that a government could not keep bringing back legislation that had been defeated, May tried again on 29 March – this time with only the withdrawal agreement. She promised to resign as Prime Minister if that were passed and the UK duly exited. But once again she was defeated, though this time the margin was 'only' 344 votes to 286. Some leading Brexiters – including Johnson, Rees-Mogg and Raab switched their votes, having hitherto damned the withdrawal agreement, now claiming that they saw no other way to Brexit. (It was widely assumed their volte face was in order to bring on a Tory leadership contest.) But there were still enough self-styled 'Spartans' among the ERGs determined to fight to the death against May's deal. One of them, Steve Baker, had told cheering members of the Libertarian Alliance in 2010, 'I think the European Union needs to be wholly torn down.' In March 2019, furious with Parliament, he shouted, 'I could tear this place down and bulldoze it into the river.' For zealots like Baker, there could be no compromise. 'I've known the taste of surrender,' he told the *New Statesman*. 'And I'm never tasting it again.'[22]

By now May had been obliged to ask the EU for a brief Article 50 extension to the 29 March deadline. Meanwhile frustrated MPs, anxious about 'crashing out' with no deal, had voted to take control of some of the parliamentary timetable in order to hold 'indicative votes' – for instance on staying within a customs union – that might reveal a consensual way forward. But party discipline, though now crumbling, held up enough on both sides of the House to prevent any motion gaining a majority. Eventually, on 2 April, May lurched to the left – for the first time opening up discussions with Labour rather than desperately wooing the Tory right, in order to get the withdrawal agreement and political declaration passed by the Commons.

In many ways, this political turn was long overdue. With the country still equally divided, the Prime Minister was finally reaching out to the main opposition party in an effort to achieve some consensus. But her overtures got nowhere, for two main reasons. First, once again, she was determined to do it May Way, ruling out any substantive concessions to Labour. With typical casuistry, she just tried to persuade them that the wording of the documents fitted their political needs. Second, and more important, the Labour leader Jeremy Corbyn seemed even less qualified for his job than May was for hers. A backbench MP since 1983 and a veteran of the hard left, Corbyn was notorious for voting against his own party, especially when Tony Blair was leader. He was a vocal supporter of united Ireland and opposed British membership of both NATO and the EU. But suddenly in 2015, following a quixotic rule change to open up elections for the Labour leadership, Corbyn won a landslide endorsement from members despite the opposition of most Labour MPs. The following year, during the EU referendum campaign, he failed to campaign actively for 'Remain' despite that being the party's avowed policy, and after 'Leave' won he sat on the fence – apparently hoping that May would be left to carry the can for delivering Brexit.

Matt, Daily Telegraph, *30 June 2017, satirises the total failure of political leadership over Brexit.*

Predictably, May's talks with Corbyn went nowhere. But the fact that she was dealing with 'a known Marxist' – in Rees-Mogg's phrase – surrounded by hard-left advisers and tarnished by persistent accusations of anti-Semitism served to alienate Brexiters even further from her. That 'churchgoing diabetic' will be called 'a traitor' and 'she will deserve it,' the *Daily Telegraph* columnist Quentin Letts spluttered. 'Lips will curl at her very name for decades to come. It will be spat to the floor in balls of green-gob spittle.'[23]

On 10 April the EU 27 granted the UK an extension until

31 October. But May frittered away a couple of months in her sham talks with Labour and then again tried abortively to get her withdrawal agreement through the Commons. Faced with near total derision, on 24 May she finally announced that she would stand down as party leader on 7 June 2019 – two years to the day since her pyrrhic election victory. Rivals who had been bad-mouthing her for months now lavished tributes upon her, before using up another two months of the EU extension in their campaign to become party leader and thereby PM.

Theresa May had set herself the dual mission of leaving the EU by 29 March 2019 while keeping the Tory party united. Despite her formidable stamina, she had ended up missing the date, splintering the party and having to hold another round of EU elections nearly three years after the UK had voted to leave. As for David Cameron, who staged a half-baked referendum in 2016 to see off Nigel Farage and UKIP, he now had to watch Farage and his new Brexit party trounce the Tories in the 2019 EU polls.

Since Edward Heath took the UK into the EEC in 1973, all his four successors as Tory premiers – Thatcher, Major, Cameron and May – had been effectively crucified by 'Europe'. Yet in June 2019, no fewer than 10 Tory wannabes seemed eager to follow them along the road to Calvary.

Get Brexit Done

The victor in the leadership race was Boris Johnson, who easily saw off the other challengers, including Michael Gove – the 'Iago' of 2016. Although described by one of the Remain staffers as 'a celebrity, not a leader', Johnson was confident that he had what was needed to escape the Euro-fate of his Tory predecessors. His great hero is Winston Churchill – perhaps the 'greatest man in the history of the world' – and some clues to Johnson's approach to leadership may be found in his book *The Churchill Factor: How One Man Made History* (2014). Chapter fifteen of this entertaining (auto-) biography is entitled 'Playing Roulette with History'. Whereas 'most politicians go with the flow of events' – they 'see what seems inevitable, and then try to align themselves with destiny' – Churchill, by contrast, 'used his Herculean strength to bend the course of events so as to conform' to his ideals. That, Johnson declared, 'was why he was associated with so many epic cock-ups – because he dared to try to change the entire shape of history. He was the man who burst the cabin door and tried to wrestle the controls of the stricken plane. He was the large protruding nail on which destiny snagged her coat'. In 1940, continued Johnson, it 'needed someone with almost superhuman will and courage, to interpose themselves between the world and disaster'.[24]

Perhaps Boris imagined himself in similar vein in 2019: after all, what do a few cock-ups matter when one is about to nail destiny?

Certainly, he played for high stakes from the very start of his premiership on 24 July. His central pledge was Brexit 'do or die' on 31 October – with or without a deal. He later added 'I'd rather be dead in a ditch' than request another extension from the EU.[25] One of his first acts was to appoint as de facto chief of staff Dominic Cummings – the ruthless mastermind of the Leave campaign in 2016. Encouraged by Cummings, Johnson tried to block parliamentary attempts to stop him "crashing out" of the EU by asking the Queen to prorogue (suspend) Parliament from 9 September until the State Opening on 14 October. Among several ministers resigning in protest was his brother Jo Johnson, who said he was 'torn between family loyalty and the national interest."[26] In the Commons, Remainers again voted to take control of business and then passed a bill introduced by Labour MP Hilary Benn to rule out a unilateral Brexit. Johnson, with a mixture of anger and calculation, denounced this repeatedly as nothing less than a "Surrender Act," and 21 Tories who supported Benn were stripped of the party whip and de-selected for future elections. One of them was Sir Nicholas Soames – Churchill's grandson.[27]

An increasingly desperate Johnson tried to get approval for a snap general election to break the deadlock, but on 4 and 10 September he twice failed to get the two-thirds majority needed under the Fixed-Term Parliaments Act (2011). And after a fierce legal battle in Scotland and England, the UK's Supreme Court ruled unanimously on 24 September that Johnson's prorogation was unlawful and therefore void, commenting caustically that the "effect upon the fundamentals of our democracy was extreme."[28]

In short: cock-ups aplenty during Boris' first two months. Frustrated at Westminster, he turned to Brussels – hoping to secure amendments to the EU's deal with Theresa May. The sticking point with Brexiter MPs, especially ERGs and DUPs, had been the Irish 'backstop', intended by the EU to prevent a hard border on the island of Ireland, which would jeopardise the Good Friday agreement. After tough talking with the Irish Taoiseach, who was firmly backed by the EU, Johnson decided on 17 October that he would have to accept a customs border in the Irish Sea instead. Yet less than a year before, on 24 November 2018, he had assured cheering DUP activists at their annual conference in Belfast that 'no British Conservative government could or should sign up to any such arrangement.' The DUP was furious about Johnson's 'betrayal' but, with this small but vital breakthrough, Johnson could claim to have secured from Brussels a 'great new deal'. For its part, the EU was hopeful that this 'beautiful compromise' would 'square the circle' and satisfy the Commons.[29]

On 22 October the Commons did indeed agree to give his revised agreement a second reading but rejected his three-day timetable for approving everything before the 31st. Unable to keep his Ditch

Thursday pledge, Johnson was obliged under the Benn Act to send a letter to the EU requesting an extension until 31 January 2020 – though he petulantly omitted his signature on the grounds that it was 'Parliament's letter, not my letter'.[30] On 24 October he again tried to secure the two-thirds majority needed to call a general election but Corbyn and the Labour party refused until a no-deal Brexit was totally and irrevocably off the table.

Then suddenly, at the end of October, the Remain wall of unity in the Commons cracked. The Liberal Democrats and the SNP broke ranks and proposed a bill to amend the Fixed-Term Parliaments Act and allow an election in December; this would require only a simple majority to become law. Both parties calculated from the opinion polls that they were likely to gain seats and could thereby help overturn Brexit; they also judged that the EU was unlikely to grant any more extensions after January. Their decision gave Johnson the Commons majority he needed to hold an election; Corbyn and Labour were obliged to climb onboard. After some haggling, Johnson got the date he wanted: 12 December.

After that, he never looked back. Let out of the prison of parliamentary politics, he was free to strut the stage he loved as a celebrity performer. Yet he had to follow a tight script. The campaign was run with cynical brilliance by Dominic Cummings and 'election guru' Isaac Levido, who kept Johnson to a simple, endlessly reiterated slogan 'Get Brexit Done'. They minimized the number of difficult interviews and arranged a daily round of photo-opportunities for him to rub shoulders with ordinary voters. 'This week alone', observed a *Guardian* columnist in the last days of the campaign, 'Johnson has dressed up as a fisherman, a digger driver, a milkman, a builder and a baker'.[31] The pantomime clowning conveyed the message that Boris was a fun bloke who would finally get this Brexit horror sorted out so that folks could enjoy Christmas. On 12 December the Tories exceeded their highest expectations and won a huge 80-seat majority. Although David Cameron fumed that in 2016 Johnson had embraced Leave and 'risked an outcome he didn't believe in because it would benefit his political career', the laugh was now on Dave. No cock-ups this time: Boris had nailed destiny and made it into Number Ten.[32]

Tory success was amplified by the abject failure of most of the Remain parties. Labour's campaign was chaotic – with a rambling 'Christmas wishlist' manifesto and a cacophony of mixed messages, especially on Brexit where the party vacillated about a second referendum. Above all, Corbyn himself proved toxic – refusing to apologise for Labour's failure to root out anti-Semitism, seeming like a prehistoric exponent of the nationalization panacea and coming over as a Brexiter who wouldn't dare say so. Johnson, of course, was distrusted and detested by millions, but in a presidential-style contest against Corbyn, he won hands down. The Tories even picked up industrial constituencies that had been Labour for decades.[33]

The outcome was also disastrous for the Lib Dems, whose new leader Jo Swinson had pushed for an early election despite many sceptics in her ranks. She had gambled on Farage's Brexit party splitting the Leave vote with the Tories, opening up the prospect of big gains. Instead, the Farage façade crumbled once again, he pulled out of most constituencies and his party ended up with no Commons seats. Swinson herself sounded too strident and, crucially, her party's hard Remain message – simply revoking Article 50 if in power rather than holding a second referendum – seemed anti-democratic to many Remainers as well as Leavers. Summing up, Cummings declared, with typical venom, that 'educated Remainer campaigner types', having failed to read the country's mood in 2016, had now 'f***ed it up even more'. Tone aside, it was hard to disagree.[34]

The only Remain party to emerge smiling on Friday 13th was

the SNP. Its gamble, unlike Jo Swinson's, had paid off handsomely with thirteen gains which garnered it 48 of Scotland's 59 seats at Westminster. Nicola Sturgeon, the party's leader and Scottish First Minister, claimed this was a mandate for another independence referendum in 2020 and she demanded that the UK Government give the permission she needed constitutionally under the Scotland Act of 1998. Johnson insisted that Scotland's 2014 vote to stay in the UK was definitive for a generation; Sturgeon argued that the 2016 referendum and the 2019 election had transformed the political landscape. Scotland, she told the BBC, 'cannot be imprisoned in the union against its will' by a UK government determined to 'deliver Brexit'.[35] The stage was therefore set for a battle between the two wiliest politicians in the UK – Johnson and Sturgeon – which could decide the future of the Union. At the same time, Johnson's betrayal of the DUP to get a deal with the EU and the party's post-election irrelevance to the Tories now they had such a big majority at Westminster opened the way towards an ever-closer relationship between Northern Ireland and the Irish Republic. The Scottish and Irish dimensions of the 2019 election accentuated the impression that the UK would have to become much more decentralised if it wanted to survive the Brexit era.

Determined that 31 January would not be another ditch too far, Johnson drove his Withdrawal Agreement bill through the Commons in the last week before Christmas – dramatic evidence of how politics had changed since the autumnal paralysis. He added a clause ruling out any extension beyond the end of the transition period in December 2020. This reflected his pledges during the election and pleased his Cabinet, many of whose senior figures were dedicated to a market ideology of free trade, business deregulation and a limited state. They included the authors of the *Britannia Unchained* manifesto of 2012 (p. 200).[36]

Yet most analysts concurred that a full trade agreement between the UK and the EU would take several years to negotiate, which meant that within just twelve months Johnson could hope to reach only a very basic 'zero-tariffs, zero-quotas' deal on trade in goods. This would leave major issues such as financial services unresolved, and he would probably be forced to adhere to EU rules, particularly on the environment and social policy. Or maybe the 2020 deadline would prove to have been bluster because Johnson would see the need for an 'extension' to the 'transition' – though without using such words. There were, of course, more positive readings of the Johnson-Cummings strategy. Perhaps he could exploit the threat of Britain 'crashing out' with no deal – however unsettling for business – as leverage over the EU. Or, alternatively, he might use the no-extension pledge to persuade Brexiters of the need for concessions to Brussels if they wanted a trade deal by the end of 2020. Beyond that, in the longer term, Brexit Britain faced fundamental decisions about whether to align itself with the socio-economic principles of the EU (as Remainers still wanted) or the US (as urged by Cabinet 'free traders'). For the latter, a transatlantic alignment was vital to free 'Global Britain' from European 'vassalage'; whereas Remainers argued that it would 'sacrifice our basic rights' in the hope of 'turning the UK into a Trump-supporting tax haven'.[37]

In short, on policy towards the two 'unions' – the UK and the EU – much would depend on how flexible Johnson turned out to be. Was he a committed hard Brexiter? Or was his betrayal of the DUP a sign, to quote the delicate euphemism of columnist Simon Jenkins, that Johnson was 'a pledge-breaking pragmatist'? In other words, that he could be relied on to renege on his promises so as to maintain political momentum? After all, he once joked that he had no convictions except for speeding.[38]

On 3 February 2020, three days after the UK's formal exit from the EU, Boris Johnson addressed an international gathering of

VIPs in the Painted Hall at Greenwich under an elaborate Baroque ceiling depicting 'The Triumph of Liberty and Peace over Tyranny'. Those able to crick their necks enough might be able to make out Queen Mary and William III – the latter with his foot resting firmly on a scrunched-up Louis XIV, complete with broken sword. The PM did not, however, mention that to 'our European friends'. Instead, his narrative featured the Hall as a celebration of the Act of Union with Scotland in 1707, when the 'newly forged United Kingdom' was 'on the slipway', ready to launch itself into global greatness. Fast forward to 2020 as 'another such moment on the launching pad'. With the 'B' word 'receding into the past behind us', Johnson portrayed Britain 're-emerging, after decades of hibernation, as a campaigner for global free trade'. But, he warned, it was 'not a moment too soon' because 'the mercantilists are everywhere, the protectionists are gaining ground.' His speech ranged across the high seas, marking out the dragons that had to be slain. It was a classic Borisian burlesque – delivered with verve, wit and trademark hyperbole. Among the 'bizarre autarkic rhetoric' now gaining currency, he instanced 'a risk that new diseases such as coronavirus will trigger a panic and a desire for market segregation that go beyond what is medically rational to the point of doing real and unnecessary economic damage'. If things came to that, Johnson proclaimed, humanity would need 'a country ready to take off its Clark Kent spectacles and leap into the phone booth and emerge with its cloak flowing as the supercharged champion of the right of the populations of the earth to buy and sell freely among each other. And here in Greenwich in the first week of February 2020, I can tell you in all humility that the UK is ready for that role.'[39]

Not all the staid VIPs got the allusion to Superman, but Johnson's thrust was clear: the world is now our oyster and nothing will stop us, certainly not some puffed-up little superbug.

Brexit and history

On one level, the story of Brexit from 2016 to 2020 owes much to political contingencies – 'events, dear boy, events', as Harold Macmillan liked to say. Cameron's ineptitude in staging an 'in-out' referendum on the EU and his mishandling of the Remain campaign. Johnson's calculated decision to throw his considerable weight behind Leave. Then Gove's stab in the back when Johnson was about to seize the prize. This unlocked Downing Street for Theresa May, but she proved 'a miniaturist, a details person, when what was needed was a leader with strategic clarity, charisma and intellectual confidence'.[40] Yet, despite May's meanderings after losing her Commons majority, Remainers failed to convert their parliamentary leverage into a coherent and effective policy. And in the 2019 election Johnson-Cummings won hands down, largely thanks to the ineptitude of their (English) opponents.

But the vagaries of politics are only part of the story.

At a deeper level, both Leave and Remain were arguing cases that often flew in the face of history, based on a referendum vote that seemed politically clear but was intellectually vacuous.

The wording on the 2016 ballot paper asked simply: 'Should the United Kingdom remain a member of the European Union or leave the European Union?' As a slogan, 'Leave' was brilliant – implying energy, decision, and action. In contrast, 'Remain' was static: the word implied satisfaction with, or at least acceptance of, the status quo. It lacked dynamism, and offered no vision for the future.

Yet think for a moment about how the word 'leave' might be used in ordinary conversation. If someone says 'I'm leaving', the natural response is to ask, 'Where are you going?' It makes little sense to reply, 'Don't know. I've just got to get out.' Or, when asked 'What's the route map?' to answer: 'Haven't got one. It's just a matter of willpower.'

And it's not just that 'leave' prompts the 'where to?' question. The word itself, when used about 'exiting' the EU, is fundamentally misleading. 'In' or 'Out' may be true as a matter of strict legality, but in terms of historical reality, any form of Brexit was bound to be a process not an event – a process of 'disentangling'. The UK had to be painstakingly disentangled from the EU by individually revoking thousands of regulations and agreements that had accrued over four and a half decades. Then it would have to enact into UK law the thousands of regulations that the government wanted to keep, so as to achieve some degree of smooth interaction with the EU. Not to mention concluding thousands more agreements to construct a new relationship with the 27 and with trading partners that are no longer covered by EU-wide agreements. Equally dishonest was May's reiterated demand that MPs should support her withdrawal bill so her government could 'deliver' Brexit – as if it was a pizza or a parcel.

In other words, we are talking about a messy, complex business that would take years to complete – Deal or No Deal. Brexiters persistently glided over this in their slick propoganda. The exit moment might produce a buzz for some in terms of identity politics – Boris Johnson's eagerly anticipated 'day of jubilation' when 'church bells were rung, coins struck, stamps issued and bonfires lit to send beacons of freedom from hilltop to hilltop'. But the identity mantra about regaining 'sovereignty' ignored the realities of complex interdependence in the modern world. Dominic Raab – a convinced Leaver who served as Brexit Secretary for four months in 2018 – seems to have glimpsed this rather late in the day. He confessed to a technology conference just before he resigned: 'I hadn't quite understood the full extent of this, but if you look at the UK and if you look at how we trade in goods, we are particularly reliant on the Dover–Calais crossing.' Indeed. The port of Dover handles 2.5 million HGVs a year and the traffic is worth £119 billion – about one-sixth of the UK's total trade in goods – all processed by port facilities squeezed into a narrow space of 8 square kilometres between the cliffs and the sea.[41] Quite important statistics for anyone trying to 'deliver' Brexit.

Or take Liam Fox – another ardent Brexiter whose disgraced political career was salvaged in 2016 when May put him in charge of the new Department of International Trade. Fox insisted that concluding a free-trade agreement with the EU should be 'one of the easiest in human history' because 'our rules and our laws are already exactly the same', adding that 'the only reason we wouldn't come to a free and open agreement is because politics gets in the way of economics.'[42] Fox was being doubly disingenuous. First, in what international negotiation does politics *not* play a decisive part? And, secondly, the UK would not be negotiating as a member, within the club, but as an outsider – a third country – seeking 'market access into what is now *their* market', governed by supranational laws and courts of which the UK would no longer be a part.[43] That was almost certainly going to produce a less advantageous trading situation than before. Politically, Britain could no longer play its old game of EU *à la carte*. Brussels would set the menu, and also the price.

The intellectual duplicity of Vote Leave was, however, counterbalanced by the intellectual impoverishment of the Remain campaign. Its modulated case during the referendum debate stated that Britain was, on balance, 'Stronger In'. Yet it was arguing to stay within an increasingly dysfunctional union that had got carried away by the euphoria surrounding European unification after 1989. A union with which successive British leaders had failed to engage seriously, preferring to carp from the sidelines rather than getting stuck into the hard graft of building coalitions and forging compromises. Above all, a union that both political parties in the 1950s had failed to shape at its crucial formative stage – instead, grandly asserting that 'Europe' was for 'them' and not 'us', as a proud victor nation and global power still basking in the lustre of 'our finest hour'. The case made for staying in was therefore more negative than positive. To quote the bullet points in the Cameron government's leaflet sent to all households in April 2016 stating the case for Remain: 'Protecting Jobs. A Stronger Economy. Providing Security.'[44] All far less exciting than Leave's clarion call for a clean break and a fresh start, spiced up with categorical assertions about 'what would happen', such as 'We will save £350 million a week. We can spend our money on our priorities like the NHS, schools, and housing.'[45] Boris Johnson regularly campaigned in front of a bus emblazoned with the words: 'We send the EU £350 million a week. Let's fund our NHS instead. Let's take back control.'[46]

In any case, Cameron never seems to have treated the referendum as a fight for Britain's future – more an irritating party game to outwit his Eurosceptics. He refused to take the gloves off against Johnson and Gove – hoping to heal the party's wounds as soon as possible after Remain had won. That, plus his own tepid Europeanism, explains why he rarely came out with a passionate defence of the EU as being the keeper of the peace since 1945. There was also a deafening silence about the implications for Northern Ireland and the Good Friday agreement. And the issue of the customs union was rarely mentioned (on either side), encouraging lazy assumptions about how Britain could take the bits it liked from the European cake and spit out the rest. Essentially Cameron's version of membership was to be 'just inside' the EU – but 'outside political, monetary, banking, fiscal union' and the Schengen Area of no border controls, and with 'a pick-and-choose approach' to justice and home affairs. Vote Leave also insinuated that the UK could cherry-pick, though in their case from 'outside the EU perimeter fence'.[47]

Crucially, both camps were not being candid about Britain's historical relationship with Europe. About the extent to which the UK after nearly 45 years of membership had become entangled in the EU. About the degree to which the integration process had created a durable institution and fostered European peace. And about the political implications of the referendum vote for an increasingly disunited Kingdom and its constituent peoples.

Both sides tended to use 'history' instrumentally. For David Cameron, it seemed to figure mostly as a reservoir for national pride. Apart from *Our Island Story*, one of his favourite history books was *Reach for the Sky*, the 1954 biography of the paraplegic RAF fighter ace of 1940, Douglas Bader. Cameron said he had been determined as Prime Minister to 'put British history back at the forefront of the curriculum' because he wanted 'children growing up today to be inspired by heroes of history like Douglas Bader – to know about the people who made Britain great'.[48] The image of history as an edifying repository of great lives – a conception that goes back to classical writers such as Plutarch and Suetonius – also inspires Jacob Rees-Mogg, who in 2019 capitalised on his status as a political celebrity by publishing a book about 12 Victorian 'titans' who 'forged Britain'. This rejected the cynicism of Lytton Strachey whose sarcastically titled *Eminent Victorians*, to quote Rees-Mogg, 'took a blow torch to the heroes of the British nineteenth century'. In *The Victorians* Rees-Mogg instead offered what he called 'a parade of public figures from which so much can be learned' – all of them 'heroes' with a 'sense of purpose and destiny so glaringly lacking both in their Hanoverian predecessors and in the beau monde of our contemporary world'. The book was savaged by most reviewers – 'clichéd, lazy history' (*Daily Telegraph*), 'mind-bogglingly banal' (*Sunday Times*), 'an origin myth for Rees-Mogg's particular right-wing vision of history'(*Guardian*) – but, far from troubling its author, these damning verdicts would probably be taken as further proof of contemporary decadence.[49]

For some Brexiters, the past served as a repository of slick historical analogies such as Joseph Chamberlain's 'Imperial Federation' or Churchill's 'English-Speaking peoples', with which to legitimise a turn away from Europe and back to the 'Anglosphere'. To others, it offered sound-bite warnings – 'Suez' for Rees-Mogg, illustrating the need for 'willpower'; 'Hitler' in the case of Boris Johnson talking up the dangers of the EU 'superstate'. Johnson, of course, was a rhetorical showman, who understood the utility of history as entertainment. Indeed, at times during the Brexit saga, the past was reduced almost to vaudeville. In January 2019, Tory MP Mark Francois, an ERG hardliner, denounced Thomas Enders – the German head of the international consortium, Airbus – for warning the British public: 'Please don't listen to the Brexiteers' madness which asserts that "because we have huge plants here we will not move and we will always be here." They are wrong'. In a staged display of indignation at such 'Teutonic arrogance', Francois tore up Enders' statement in front of a TV camera and declared: 'My father, Reginald Francois, was a D-Day veteran. He never submitted to bullying by any German and neither will his son.'[50] Airbus does not seem to have been cowed, but thereafter M. Francois became a regular performer on TV and radio.

Island Stories has taken a very different view of history, arguing that we need to avoid slogans and go beyond a '1940 and All That' caricature of the complexities of 'our island story'. Tracking back over more than a millennium, it has followed four thematic strands, each of which is worth keeping in mind when reflecting on the Brexit debate and on the UK's future.

First, 'Decline'. From a historical perspective, what is remarkable was the rise of Britain to global power, not the fact that it has been overtaken. British greatness was achieved during the era of seapower.

'*It'll whisk you back to the sepia-tinted 1950s*'

Both sides in the Brexit debate were easy targets for cartoonists. Kipper William satirises Leavers as smooth-talking nostalgia salesmen; Grizelda in the New Statesman *sends up gloomy 'Remoaners'.*

The country's geographical insularity conferred a measure of security lacking to most of its continental neighbours, while its navy and merchant fleet provided global reach. Formal colonies and informal trading networks ensured that a kingdom of two small islands off the coast of continental Europe had access to manpower and resources way beyond its own territorial bounds. During the twentieth century, however, the United Kingdom was challenged within Europe by the rising power of Germany and outstripped globally by two continent-sized rivals: the United States and the Soviet Union. What is more, insularity no longer provided security in the era of airpower, long-range missiles and nuclear weapons. Yet, at the very same time, the mentality of an 'island nation' was being accentuated by the saga of 1940 and its progressive inscription into national heritage.

Undoubtedly Britain's refusal to surrender in 1940 was a moment of world-historical importance. Otherwise the United States might well have reverted to Western Hemisphere isolationism. But the elevation of 'our finest hour' in identity politics and national heritage has distracted from other phases of the Second World War. *Pace* some Brexiters, the turning point for Britain's global position was not 'Suez' in 1956 but the ignominious surrender of Singapore in February 1942, which demonstrated to the world the nakedness of the British King Emperor. Although the British regained most of their Asian territories in 1945, their credibility as global rulers had been dealt a fatal blow. Those power realities cannot be willed away by those who hanker after lost 'Greatness'.

Yet the shifting relativities of wealth and power reveal continuity as well as change. The UK, together with France, remains a permanent member of the UN Security Council, and they are the only two European members of the Western Alliance to sustain a capacity for power-projection outside the NATO area. The country remains a major trading nation. It is the fifth-largest national economy, measured by nominal GDP, and around twentieth in terms of GDP per capita. Despite the damage caused by Brexit uncertainty and corporate flight, London remains the second most important financial hub after New York. And so on . . . But what mattered in the referendum debate of 2016 were two other issues, of economics and identity. One was the unequal distribution of that wealth within the UK – largely the result of London's historic domination over the country – which fostered animosity towards the metropolitan elite. The other was the way that some people in Britain seemed to hanker after a sense of lost 'Greatness', without fully understanding how and why the country had become a global power.

The second historical strand in this book was 'Europe': the UK's long-term relationships with the continent. The two invasions of 1066 reoriented England's sense of direction and identity. The Anglo-Saxon defeat of Harald Hardrada's Viking army near York on 25 September ended several centuries of Norse incursions into northern England. But the defeat of the Anglo-Saxons by Duke William of Normandy near Hastings on 14 October 1066 led to England and Wales becoming the northern part of a kingdom that spanned the Channel for nearly four centuries. During that time England's monarchs looked mostly south, fighting to hold on to a French domain that waxed and waned erratically amid the fortunes of war until almost all of it was lost by 1453. The English Reformation in the 1530s then marked the start of another period of over 400 years in which the Channel, guarded by English seapower, became more a barrier than a bridge – protecting the country against invasion from Counter-Reformation Spain in 1588, Napoleonic France in 1803–5 and Nazi Germany in 1940.

Yet during those centuries the rulers of England and then Britain also projected their power onto the Continent in order to maintain some kind of equilibrium to prevent France and then Germany from gaining European hegemony. Since the Second World War new technologies of warfare – airpower and nuclear missiles – have overridden the Channel barrier, and a rail tunnel under the Channel was opened in 1998 – more than a century after the first trial borings. In terms of security, the UK's membership of an alliance that embraces Europe and North America remains axiomatic to this day. The country played a defining role in the creation of NATO, which it joined at the start in 1949. Yet, partly in consequence, Britain spurned the politico-economic community established in Western Europe in the 1950s. Because of this and then de Gaulle's two vetoes, it did not become a member until the EC had set firm in ways that were at odds with basic British interests. To some degree the 'Leave' majority in 2016 is therefore historically understandable. But if and when Britain does finally Brexit, the country will find it even more important yet even more difficult to play a balancing role in the affairs of Europe.

Turning, thirdly, to 'Britain', we need to understand English history in relationship to that of Scotland, Wales and Ireland – in particular, taking seriously that 'other' island story across the Irish Sea. The United Kingdom grew out of the project of English empire-building across both islands, which intensified after England's continental ambitions had been frustrated by the failure of the Hundred Years' War. Although Wales was brought relatively easily under English rule by Henry VIII, the struggle against Scotland – the most developed of the other three kingdoms – was far more demanding. After several centuries of on-off conflict it gradually became clear that the English could punish Scotland militarily but never completely subdue it. Union – first of the crowns in 1603 and then of the parliaments in 1707 – eventually seemed the best way to pacify Britain. Catholic Ireland, however, proved more intractable, and its frequent insurgencies were regularly supported by continental powers. In 1640s, civil war in Ireland sparked similar devastating conflicts in Scotland and England, and in the 1790s a nationalist uprising backed by Revolutionary France finally pushed the government in London into a parliamentary union with Dublin.

During the nineteenth century many Scots and Irish profited from participation in the 'British Empire' and played a major part in conquering and administering the imperial domains. But 'Britishness' never papered over the sectarian divide in Ireland, and the Home Rule crisis of the 1910s resulted successively in a war of independence, civil war and partition, followed later by three decades of sectarian violence in Ulster. By contrast, the two world wars served to strengthen the bonds of Britishness in Scotland and Wales, which had also been fraying before 1914, and this sense of unity did not wane until the late twentieth century. But then in 1998 the Troubles ended in an agreement that eliminated the militarised border between Northern Ireland and the Republic, presaging a more cooperative relationship, and in 1999 new devolved parliaments were inaugurated in Scotland and Wales. A referendum on Scottish independence was lost in 2014, but 45 per cent of voters wanted to leave the Union.

So the United Kingdom was forged and sustained in large measure by war – both internally and against others. The close parliamentary union, run from London, was a reaction to security crises in 1707 and 1801, but it has proved increasingly problematic over the last century or so. The 1990s process of devolution to Scotland and Wales was an attempt to loosen metropolitan control, but this was thrown into confusion by the result of the Brexit referendum, with Scotland and Northern Ireland voting to remain in the EU, and England and Wales opting to leave. Since the bulk of the UK population live in England, the overall result of the referendum was a narrow but clear majority to leave the European Union. In fact, a striking correlation may be discerned in attitudes to *both* unions – the UK and the EU – especially among Leave voters in England. A 2018 opinion survey by the Centre on Constitutional Change concluded: 'Theresa May's "precious Union" has little in the way of meaningful support from her own supporters or self-professed Unionists in other parties.' In particular, as a price for Brexit at least three-quarters of English Tory voters said they would support Scottish independence and accept the collapse of the Northern Ireland Peace Process, and nearly half did not think that Scottish MPs should sit in the UK Cabinet. In general, there was a regular correlation in opinion polls between Euroscepticism in England and so-called 'devo-anxiety' – a feeling that 'England was being neglected or left behind by benefits awarded to devolved territories'.[51] Yet the process of UK devolution is unlikely to be reversed; indeed it is being extended within England itself. Perhaps this might help address the sense of alienation among pro-Brexit voters. Giving English regions, especially in the north, greater autonomy and proper budgets would allow them to make decisions about crucial issues such as infrastructure, transport and investment with less dictation from London.

Moving beyond an Anglocentric 'us and them' view of history is equally important in the case of the fourth major thematic strand: 'Empire'. The encounter of Britain and the world has traditionally been written from the perspective of the metropole, as an account of what 'we' did to (and for) 'them'. But the emergence of 'subaltern studies' gave voice and agency to the colonised; and the development of 'world' or 'global' history has 'created the challenge of studying colonial and metropolitan history through the same lens', exploring a multitude of 'connections across the globe, albeit in the context of unequal relations of power'. These developments encourage historians of Britain to 'open up national history and imperial history', bridging that binary, and serve to underline both 'our dependence on and exploitation of others'.[52]

As a prospectus for innovative history, this is demanding. But how can it be squared with the yearning of the likes of David Cameron or Michael Gove for a history that reinforces 'national values' and British pride? Is that kind of history always going to be simplistic and even dishonest? Take, for instance, Britain's profits from the slave trade. This is, at last, a matter of public debate, and has also been given a place, albeit locally, in the municipal museums of cities such as Bristol and Liverpool, which made much of their wealth from people trafficking. But it will take years of research and discussion to incorporate the slave trade into a broader rewrite of Britain's commercial and industrial revolution. And doing that should not obscure a more traditional story of the grass-roots moral and religious crusade against slavery, eventually pushed through Parliament – like free trade – by nineteenth-century Britain's exceptional wealth and power. National pride is an essential element of a country's identity, yet can that be squared with historical honesty?

Equally testing historically is the modern story of mass immigration. Governments of both main parties – Tory and Labour – after 1945 did little to manage the process or mitigate the human consequences until social problems became almost toxic. Yet, despite persistent racism and the recent radicalisation of fringe elements of Muslim youth since 9/11, over time a degree of multiculturalism has developed. Many 'non-white' Britons in this country have developed their own sense of roots and identity – redefining to some degree what it means to be 'British'. In short, taking 'empire' seriously is one of the major challenges for those concerned with our history.

History, trauma and opportunity

Yet a country's history is not simply the domain of scholars. It's also a public matter – arousing feelings of pride and shame, optimism and anxiety – which can affect the whole sense of national identity. At the end of the twentieth century it seemed possible to narrate a relatively clear, simple and coherent story about Britain's place in the world over the course of that century. A story of two great wars to defeat German hegemonic militarism, the rapid end of global empire after 1945 and the acceptance of a primarily European identity since 1973. However, the Brexit furore has torn up that sequential narrative. In 1973, as Britain prepared to join the European Community, the commentator Andrew Schonfield dubbed entry a *Journey to an Unknown Destination*. In 2017, the historian and politician Julie Smith called the UK's journeys into *and* out of the EU *Destinations Unknown*.[53]

In any case, the 'losing an empire, finding a role' motif was always problematic. Not just because some of the legacies of empire had been brushed under the carpet – with Ireland, slavery and immigration top of the list – but, more pressingly for Brexit, because of Britain's complex about the two world wars. As the Second became elevated as a narrative of triumph, centred on Churchill and 1940, so the First – especially since the fiftieth anniversary in the 1960s – became a narrative of trench-bound tragedy, told from the bottom-up through the voices of a few 'war poets'. In Britain's version of both great conflicts 'Europe' remained at a distance: in 1914–18 the fighting was mostly 'over there', across the Channel, while in 1939–45 the fulcrum was supposedly fighting on 'alone' in 1940 and then winning victory with non-European allies, above all the United States and the 'English-speaking peoples'. The UK brought this version of history to the European table in 1973. That, so to speak, was Britain's historical *acquis*.[54]

And it is still with us. The emotional intensity of the 2014–18 centenary of the Great War made that clear: far from the British gently 'letting go' of the dead, attachment to the 'lost generation', the trenches and the 'unknown soldier' has only intensified. Equally apparent is the country's abiding passion for 'finest hour' movies and the cult of Churchill. Addressing the problem of the Tories' ageing membership, Cabinet minister Matthew Hancock remarked in April 2019: 'We have got to sound like we actually like this country. We have got to be patriots of the Britain of now and not the Britain of 1940.'[55]

Perhaps the gross political mismanagement of Brexit will make it harder to luxuriate in the glories of the past. Even if, almost inconceivably, the UK changed its mind and returned to the fold – assuming the EU wanted it back – the damage done by the years of Mayhem to Britain's international image would take time to overcome. The country's 'soft power' had relied on a reputation for stability, prudence and common sense, whereas the Brexit mess prompted phrases like 'political farce' and 'banana republic' – to mention only the more polite examples. A tweet from a man in India warned: 'I can tell you that Brits take forever to leave.' An Israeli journalist proposed no longer wishing people 'the best of British luck'. One Australian commentator likened the Brexit malaise to the gradual decline of a senile relative: 'You care for them deeply. You appreciate all they have done for you. But each day they become more inwardly focused. Their world contracts. They seem increasingly incoherent.' The international cover of *Time* magazine on 17 June 2019 featured familiar faces from the long-running Whitehall farce – headed by May, Johnson, Corbyn, Farage, and a top-hatted Rees-Mogg – aboard a classic London red double-decker bus marked 'Out of Service', with articles inside on 'The Brexit Fiasco' and 'How Britain Went Bonkers'.[56]

To move on from the May era will require far better leadership, and a much less amateur approach to negotiating with the EU 27. But it also demands greater historical honesty. This does not mean denigrating Britain's achievements but developing a more inclusive and less nostalgic sense of 'our' past – moving out of a tightly 'islanded' sense of identity and recognising the intricately 'storied' character of the UK's various pasts.

Political leaders want a clear, simple and uplifting version of history to inspire visions of the future – usually orated in heroic tones. Yet there are always many competing accounts, with the orthodox version often simply echoing the verdict of the political victors. Around the world in recent years a process of telling and listening to such competing stories has been deliberately developed in the hope of promoting 'truth and reconciliation'. Pioneered in post-apartheid South Africa and then followed in more than 40 countries, usually in fraught situations after civil war, colonial rule or authoritarian regimes, this practice has also been adopted by Canada, Australia and New Zealand to start addressing their historical treatment of indigenous peoples. Results have been varied, and grand schemes of 'restorative justice' have proved utopian. Yet the device of talking across divides at times of transition has gained some successes at the less ambitious but important level of damage limitation.[57] Talking, particularly across barriers that no longer exist physically but endure mentally – what East and West Germans, following the fall of the Berlin Wall in 1989, referred to as the continuing *Mauer im Kopf* ('the wall in the head').

Post-1945 France and West Germany addressed the historical dimension explicitly and deliberately as part of their process of reconciliation after three ruinous wars in three-quarters of a century. In 2006 the publication of *Histoire/Geschichte* was lauded as the world's first secondary school history textbook produced jointly by two countries, with virtually the same text in each language set out on opposite sides of each two-page spread. The book has since been studied as a possible model in other parts of the world where present tensions have their roots in conflicted pasts, such as Central Europe, the Balkans and East Asia. Although the French and German authors were praised for seeking 'historical truth', the textbook project was 'more a product of cultural negotiation' than of 'objective historical examination' and often involved some degree of 'prescriptive forgetting' in order to find common ground. The nature of that common ground is indicated by the subtitle of the book: 'Europe and the World since 1945'. In other words, *Histoire/ Geschichte* took shape against a shared vision of France and Germany's future within the European Union, and this influenced judgments about the past. Such a vision is not, of course, shared by Brexit Britain. But another aspect of the book *is* relevant. The idea of writing a binational history textbook actually emanated not from politicians or even historians, but from young people participating in a Franco-German student conference. They were the generation who would have to create something positive out of the mess made of the past by their predecessors.[58]

The United Kingdom is now at such a moment of pained transition, one that is unique in living memory. The referendum split the country down the middle and Brexitoxicity has poisoned public life. Instead of declaiming 'our island story' we need to talk and listen across the Leave/Remain divide, trying to grasp conflicting visions of how 'Britain' related to 'Europe'. There is also need for conversations about the UK's national and often nationalistic histories. That might help all concerned to comprehend why how the Union came about – by thinking in a more rounded way about 1707 and 1801. To appreciate that the form of the Union reflected English security panics during wars with France, but also that an enduring outcome was to create a common market of huge mutual benefit. Particularly important for the English is to understand more fully the history of Ireland, its images of England and its tangled sectarianism, especially at a moment when the Partition of 1922 is in flux because of the Good Friday agreement and the Brexit EU withdrawal deal. Rather than trumpeting a glorious heritage of global greatness, we should try to appreciate why the increasingly diverse citizens of modern Britain understand the legacies of empire. And instead of smug complacency about the 'Mother of Parliaments', the mismanagement of Brexit suggests that the 'Westminster Model' needs far more radical reconstruction than simply a facelift for its crumbling Victorian fabric.

Whatever the outcome of Brexit – leading on to 'bright shining uplands' or down into the abyss – the process is a national trauma. Getting through it will entail a protracted odyssey, involving the generation now coming of age more than the people who voted Leave or Remain. It is a journey to an unknown destination by a country in search of a new identity. And along the way, talking about conflicting versions of the past will be more constructive than preaching 'our island story'. As we set out into the unknown, we need an unconventional approach to the British past – treating it not as an excuse to sink into nostalgia or history-onics but as a spur to future action.

As 2020 progressed, an even bigger trauma than Brexit offered a possible opportunity to see British history differently. Boris Johnson's breezy aside about the coronavirus in the Painted Hall at Greenwich soon came back to haunt him. A month later, on 3 March, he was obliged to promulgate an 'action plan' for Covid-19, but his tone was still boisterous: 'for the vast majority of the people of this country, we should be going about our business as usual'. The key point, he emphasised, was 'wash your hands with soap and hot water for the length of time it takes to sing Happy Birthday twice'.[59] On 23 March, however – as the official UK death toll passed 300, with thousands more predicted – Johnson had to take the 'bizarre autarkic rhetoric' seriously and announce a national lockdown under emergency powers not used since the Second World War. On 27 March he admitted that he, too, had developed Covid-19 symptoms; by 6 April he was in an intensive care bed at London's St Thomas' Hospital. By the time the PM returned to work at Number Ten on 27 April the UK officially stated death toll from Covid-19 had passed 20,000.

As the pandemic took hold, the crisis was sometimes described in 1940 language – the need for improvisation being likened, for instance, to the 'little ships' at Dunkirk. But wartime analogies

worked only so far. There was no visible enemy, no physical destruction – just an eerie silence as planes were grounded, trains and
buses ran skeleton services, and schools, pubs and restaurants
closed. People had to work from home, with tight legal restrictions
on when and why they could venture out. Yet the lockdown was
generally accepted. Meanwhile medical staff – often without protection – battled to save lives, while other workers kept shops and
essential services open. They were hailed as national heroes and
those who died on the 'frontline' were remembered in a one-minute
silence akin to Remembrance Day for the dead of the two world
wars. Britain's Black, Asian and minority ethnic communities
(BAME) were disproportionately represented among the front-
liners – groups targeted by Theresa May's 'hostile environment'
policy. The crisis required unprecedented government action. Over
20,000 members of the armed forces were redeployed as a Covid
Support Force. To avoid total economic collapse the Government
offered unprecedented support to businesses, including a Job
Retention Scheme that covered 80% of wages if companies kept
staff on their payrolls. Economists forecast a global depression on
a par with the 1930s.

It became clear that even when lockdown was gradually eased,
some restrictions – such as social distancing – would have to
continue for months, or even years. Indeed, life would probably
never 'return to normal.' In March historian Peter Hennessy
predicted that his successors, writing in 2050 about Britain since
1945, would divide the story into 'BC and AC – Before Corona
and After Corona'. Here was an experience that would indelibly
mark those who lived through it. But also, perhaps, a stimulus for
fresh thinking and a new focus for national identity? On 18 June
1940, after the Fall of France, Winston Churchill urged his shaken
people to 'so bear ourselves that if the British Empire and
Commonwealth last for a thousand years, men will still say, "This

was their finest hour.'" On 5 April 2020, Queen Elizabeth II, aged 93, made a special broadcast to the UK and the Commonwealth. Her talk reminded listeners that she had lived through 1940 and, although not mentioning Churchill by name, seemed to have his words in mind. 'I hope in the years to come everyone will be able to take pride in how they responded to this challenge. And those who come after us will say that the Britons of this generation were as strong as any.'[60]

Trauma *and* opportunity. Perhaps the pandemonic year 2020 will serve as a new 'finest hour' by which Britons of the twenty-first century can make sense of their history and benchmark their future.

Acknowledgments

This book had its roots in a talk entitled '"Decline" and Alternative Grand Narratives for Modern British History' which I gave to a conference about Britain and the world after 1945 at the Foreign and Commonwealth Office on 11 April 2016. This gave me the opportunity to reflect anew on some of the ideas I had previously developed in *Britannia Overruled* and *The Long Shadow*. I am grateful to Professor Patrick Salmon, head of FCO Historians, for inviting me to speak and for his continued interest in the themes I raised – though of course he bears no responsibility for anything written here.

For making the book possible, I thank my long-standing agent Peter Robinson and more recently his successor Natasha Fairweather. Also warm appreciation to Arabella Pike, my editor at HarperCollins, and her production team, especially Katy Archer, Jo Thompson and copy-editor Luke Brown. Amanda Russell helped me source the illustrations.

My wife Margaret has tolerated another book with her customary patience – understanding it as my way of trying to cope with what Brexit Britain is going through, just as she was anguishing about the travails of her own country across the Atlantic. Thanks, also, to Jim and Emma, plus grandsons Jake and Toby – who give us hope and fun in troubled times.

My customary acknowledgment to the staff of three outstanding Cambridge libraries: the University Library, the Seeley Historical Library and the library of Christ's College.

For comments on draft chapters I am immensely grateful to several friends and fellow historians – particularly Kristina Spohr, and also John A. Thompson and John Morrill.

When I spoke at the FCO it was some ten weeks before the 2016 referendum and at that point I never imagined taking those ideas much further. To explain why a talk became a book, I must make mention of two quite incredible old Etonians:

Dave and Boris – without whom . . .

DR
Cambridge, July 2019

For the paperback edition, the subtitle has been altered. I have made a few updates to the opening chapter and also included a new section in chapter five on Boris Johnson's premiership up to the UK's exit from the EU. At the very end of the book, I have added some paragraphs about the possible implications of the 2020 Covid-19 pandemic for the way the British think about their past – especially 'our finest hour' in 1940.

DR
May 2020

Notes

Introduction: Brexit Means . . . ?

1. Dean Acheson, 'Our Atlantic Alliance: The Political and Economic Strands', *Vital Speeches of the Day,* 29/6 (1 Jan. 1963), 162–6.
2. Stephen George, *An Awkward Partner: Britain in the European Community* (Oxford, 1990).
3. '"Insecurity is fantastic," says billionaire funder of Brexit campaign', *Reuters*, 11 May 2016,
   https://uk.reuters.com/article/uk-britain-eu-donations-hargreaves/insecurity-is-fantastic-says-billionaire-funder-of-brexit-campaign-idUKKCN0Y22ID
4. Tim Ross, 'Boris Johnson interview: We can be the "heroes of Europe" by voting to Leave', *Daily Telegraph*, 14 May 2016, and Tim Ross, 'Boris Johnson: The EU wants a superstate, just as Hitler did', *Daily Telegraph*, 15 May 2016 https://www.telegraph.co.uk/news/2016/05/14/boris-johnson-interview-we-can-be-the-heroes-of-europe-by-voting/ and https://www.telegraph.co.uk/news/2016/05/14/boris-johnson-the-eu-wants-a-superstate-just-as-hitler-did/
5. Andrew Roberts, 'CANZUK', The Telegraph, 13 Sept. 2016 https://www.telegraph.co.uk/news/2016/09/13/canzuk-after-brexit-canada-australia-new-zealand-and-britain-can/; Theresa May, 'The Government's negotiating objectives for exiting the EU', 17 Jan. 2017, https://www.gov.uk/government/speeches/the-governments-negotiating-objectives-for-exiting-the-eu-pm-speech
6. Michael Gove, speech, 5 Oct. 2010 https://conservative-speeches.sayit.mysociety.org/speech/601441 Tom Holland, 'Our Island Story . . .', the *Guardian*, 7 Feb. 2014, https://www.theguardian.com/books/booksblog/2014/feb/07/our-island-story-conservative-david-cameron
7. A theme of much stimulating work over the last few decades: for example,

see the pioneering essays collected in J. G. A. Pocock, *The Discovery of Islands: Essays in British History* (Cambridge, 2005); the provocative grand narrative by Norman Davies, *The Isles: A History* (London, 1999); and the posthumously published second volume of radical historian Raphael Samuel's 'Theatres of Memory' trilogy entitled *Island Stories: Unravelling Britain* (London, 1998).

8. For this theme, and interesting parallels, see Sujit Sivasundaram, *Islanded: Britain, Sri Lanka, and the Bounds of an Indian Ocean Colony* (Chicago, 2013).

9. Robert Tombs, *The English and Their History* (London, 2014).

Chapter One – Decline

1. Edward Gibbon, *The History of the Rise, Decline and Fall of the Roman Empire* (6 vols, London, 1776–88), 6: 645.

2. *The Times*, 17 July 1897, 13.

3. A theme suggestively developed by David Cannadine, 'Apocalypse when? British politicians and British 'decline' in the twentieth century' in Peter Clarke and Clive Trebilcock, eds, *Understanding Decline: Perceptions and Realities of British Economic Performance* (Cambridge, 1997), 261–84.

4. Quotations from Peter Clarke, *A Question of Leadership: From Gladstone to Thatcher* (London, 1992 pbk), 75–6, 78.

5. Leopold Amery, *The Life of Joseph Chamberlain* (London, 1951), 421 ('titan'); Charles W. Boyd, ed., *Mr Chamberlain's Speeches* (2 vols, London, 1914), 2: 181, 368.

6. Boyd, ed., *Chamberlain's Speeches*, 2: 248.

7. A point noted in Barry Supple, 'Fear of Failing: Economic History and the Decline of Britain', *Economic History Review*, 47 (1994), 448.

8. Speeches on 23 Feb. 1931 (Epping) and 5 March 1931 (Edinburgh) in Robert Rhodes James, ed., *Winston S. Churchill: His Complete Speeches* (8 vols, New York, 1974), 5: 4985–6, 4990.

9. Speech on 5 March 1931 (Liverpool) in Winston S. Churchill, *India: Speeches and an Introduction* (London, 1931), 84–5. A slightly different text of this speech is published in Rhodes James, ed., *Churchill Speeches*, 5: 4972, and dated 2 Feb. 1931.

10. Robert Rhodes James, *Churchill: A Study in Failure, 1900–1939* (Harmondsworth, 1973), 275.

11. Christopher Thorne, *Allies of a Kind: The United States, Britain, and the War against Japan, 1941–1945* (London, 1978), 244–5.

12. Speech of 10 Nov. 1942 in Martin Gilbert, *Winston S. Churchill, vol. 7* (London, 1986), 254.

13. Speeches of 12 Dec. 1946 and 6 March 1947 in Martin Gilbert, *Winston S. Churchill, vol. 8* (London, 1988), 295, 301

14. Speech at Woodford, 12 Oct. 1951, in Rhodes James, ed., *Churchill Speeches*, 8: 8262–3.

15. Quotations that follow come from Labour Party, *Let Us Face the Future* (1945) – http://www.labour-party.org.uk/manifestos

16. *Daily Mirror*, 5 July 1945, 1.

17. Margaret Thatcher, *The Downing Street Years* (London, 1993), 5–6.

18. Thatcher, *Downing Street Years*, 8.

19. General Election Address, Dartford, Kent, 3 Feb. 1950 https://www.margaretthatcher.org/document/100858

20. BBC TV interview, 27 April 1979, https://www.margaretthatcher.org/document/103864

21. Speech to a Tory rally, Bolton, 1 May 1979 https://www.margaretthatcher.org/document/104065

22. Party election broadcast, 30 April 1979 https://www.margaretthatcher.org/document/104055

23. Thatcher, *Downing Street Years*, 10.

24. Hugo Young, *One of Us: A Biography of Margaret Thatcher* (London, 1989), 242.

25. Speech at Cheltenham, 3 July 1982, https://www.margaretthatcher.org/document/104989

26. UPI report 14 June 1982, https://www.upi.com/Archives/1982/06/14/Thatcher-Great-Britain-is-great-again/9487119078212/

27. Charles Moore, *Margaret Thatcher: The Authorized Biography, Vol. 2: Everything She Wants* (London, 2015), quoting 163, 151, 704–05.

28. Quotations that follow come from speech by Jacob Rees-Mogg, London, 27 March 2018 https://www.leavemeansleave.eu/jacob-rees-mogg-speech-brexit-one-year-go-full-text/

29. Quotations from Gibbon, *The History of the Rise, Decline and Fall of the Roman Empire*, 3: 631; François Crouzet, *The Victorian Economy* (London, 1982), 379.

30. David Olusoga, *Black and British: A Forgotten History* (London, 2016), 199.

31. William Shakespeare, *Richard II*, Act 2, Scene 1, Line 48; *King John*, Act 2, Scene 1, Line 27; [W. E. Gladstone], 'Germany, France, and England', *The Edinburgh Review*, 132 (Oct. 1870), 588.

32. Arthur J. Marder, *From the Dreadnought to Scapa Flow: The Royal Navy in the Fisher Era, Vol. 1, The Road to War, 1904–1914* (London, 1961), 41.

33. Crouzet, *Victorian Economy*, 4–8; David Cannadine, *Victorious Century: The United Kingdom, 1800–1906* (London, 2017), 266.

34. Quotations from C. J. Bartlett, *Great Britain and Seapower, 1815–1853* (London, 1963), 68, 95n.

35. Christopher Ricks, ed., *The Poems of Tennyson* (London, 1969), 84.

36. *Manchester Guardian*, 23 June 1897, 5; *Daily Mail*, 23 June 1897, 5.

37. Elizabeth Longford, *Victoria R.I.* (London, 1964), 549; Max Beloff, *Britain's Imperial Sunset, Vol. 1* (London, 1969), 20–1.

38. Paul Kennedy, *The Rise and Fall of the Great Powers: Economic Change and Military Conflict from 1500 to 2000* (London, 1988), xvi.

39. See statistical tables in David Reynolds, *Britannia Overruled: British Policy and World Power in the Twentieth Century* (2nd edn, London, 2000), 11.

40. Malcolm Chalmers, *Paying for Defence: Military Spending and British Decline* (London, 1985), 23–4.

41. David Edgerton, *Warfare State: Britain, 1920–1970* (Cambridge, 2006), esp. 43, 46, 68.

42. A point emphasised in P. J. Cain and A. G. Hopkins, *British Imperialism: Innovation and Expansion, 1688–1914* (London, 1993), 19–22.

43. John Darwin, *The Empire Project: The Rise and Fall of the British World-System, 1830–1970* (Cambridge, 2009), 10–11.

44. Ian Drummond, *British Economic Policy and the Empire* (London, 1972), 18.

45. P. J. Cain and A. G. Hopkins, *British Imperialism: Crisis and Deconstruction, 1914–1990* (London, 1993), 293.

46. Ranald Michie, 'The City of London and the British Government: The Changing Relationship', in Ranald Michie and Philip Williamson, eds, *The British Government and the City of London in the Twentieth Century* (Cambridge, 2004), 45.

47. See Office of National Statistics data at https://www.ons.gov.uk/economy/investmentspensionsandtrusts/bulletins/ownershipofukquoted-shares/2016

48. Paul W. Schroeder, *Austria, Great Britain, and the Crimean War: The Destruction of the European Concert* (Ithaca, NY, 1972), 401.

49. House of Lords, *Debates*, Series 3, Vol. 204: 1364–5; Paul Kennedy, *The Rise and Fall of British Naval Mastery* (London, 2004), 201.

50. P. R. Ghosh, 'Disraelian Conservatism: A Financial Approach', *English Historical Review*, 99 (1984), 289.

51. D. P. Crook, *The North, the South, and the Powers, 1861–1865* (London, 1974), 227–30.

52. Michel Chevalier, 'La Guerre et la Crise Européenne', *Revue des Deux*

Mondes, 1 June 1866, 784–5; Constantin Frantz, *Die Weltpolitik unter besonderer Bezugnahme auf Deutschland* (3 vols, Osnabruck reprint edn, 1966), 1: 89.

53. Kennedy, *Rise and Fall of British Naval Mastery*, 209.

54. International Institute for Strategic Studies, *The Military Balance, 1972–73* (London, 1972), 74.

55. D. K. Fieldhouse, *The Colonial Empires: A Comparative Survey from the Eighteenth Century* (London, 1982), 242, 303.

56. Denis Judd and Peter Slinn, *The Evolution of the Modern Commonwealth* (London, 1982), 38.

57. Iain E. Johnston-White, *The British Commonwealth and Victory in the Second World War* (London, 2017), 25; Yasmin Khan, *The Raj at War: A People's History of India's Second World War* (London, 2015), 18.

58. Correlli Barnett, *The Collapse of British Power* (London, 1972), 143.

59. Frantz, *Die Weltpolitik*, 1: 106–7.

60. Cf. T. O. Lloyd, *The British Empire, 1558–1983* (London, 1984), 403. On 'Britannic nationalism', see Darwin, *Empire Project*, ch. 4.

61. B. R. Tomlinson, *The Political Economy of the Raj, 1914–1947: The Economics of Decolonization in India* (London, 1979), 179.

62. Hilaire Belloc, *Complete Verse* (London, 1970 edn), 184.

63. Ronald Hyam, *Britain's Imperial Century, 1815–1914* (London, 1976), 158.

64. Entry of 24 Sept. 1938 in David Dilks, ed., *The Diaries of Sir Alexander Cadogan, 1938–1945* (London, 1971), 104.

65. B. R Tomlinson, *The Political Economy of the Raj*, 140.

66. G. C. Peden, 'Suez and Britain's Decline as a World Power', *The Historical Journal*, 55/4 (2012), 1073–96, quoting p. 1095.

67. Winston S. Churchill, *The Second World War* (6 vols, London, 1948–544), 3: 551 and 4: 81.

68. Commons, *Debates*, 27 Jan. 1942, 377: 601.

69. Darwin, *Empire Project*, 13–14.

70. David Edgerton, *Britain's War Machine: Weapons, Resources and Experts in the Second World War* (London, 2011), 85.

71. A. J. P. Taylor, *English History, 1914–1945* (Harmondsworth, 1970 pbk), 727

72. Cannadine, 'Apocalypse When?', 284.

73. Jim Tomlinson, 'Thrice Denied: "Declinism" as a Recurrent Theme of British History in the Long Twentieth Century', *Twentieth Century British History*, 20/2 (2009), 240; cf. Angus Maddison, *The World Economy: A Millennial Perspective* (Paris, 2001), 276–7.

74. Supple, 'Fear of Failing', 444.

75. Christina Beatty and Steve Fothergill, 'The Long Shadow of Industrial Britain's Demise', *Regions*, 308/4 (Autumn 2017), 5.

76. Francesca Carnevali and Julie-Marie Strange, eds, *Twentieth-Century Britain: Economic, Cultural and Social Change* (2nd edn, London, 2017), 11–13.

77. Jim Tomlinson, 'De-industrialization not Decline: A New Meta-narrative for Post-war British History', *Twentieth Century British History*, 27/1 (2016), 76–99, quoting p. 79.

78. Tomlinson, 'De-industrialization not Decline; see also Maarten Goos and Alan Manning, 'Lousy and Lovely Jobs: The Rising Polarization of Work in Britain', *The Review of Economics and Statistics*, 89/1 (2007), 118–33.

79. Ian Budge, 'Relative Decline as a Political Issue: Ideological Motivations of the Politico-Economic Debate in Post-War Britain', *Contemporary Record*, 7/1 (Summer 1993), 4–6.

80. Quoted in Robert Hewison, *The Heritage Industry: Britain in a Climate of Decline* (London, 1987), 136–7.

81. This aspect of heritage has been emphasised by Raphael Samuel, *Theatres of Memory: Past and Present in Contemporary Culture* (2nd, edn, London, 2012), 238.

82. Jerome de Groot, *Consuming History: Historians and Heritage in Contemporary Popular Culture* (London, 2009), 163–80.

83. Nicholas Pronay, 'The British Post-Bellum Cinema: A Survey of the Films Relating to World War II Made in Britain between 1945 and 1960', *Historical Journal of Film, Radio and Television*, 8 (1988), esp. pp. 39–41; John Ramsden, 'Refocusing "The People's War': British War Films of the 1950s, *Journal of Contemporary History*, 33 (1998), esp. pp. 36–8, 45; Wendy Webster, *Englishness and Empire, 1939–1965* (Oxford, 2005), ch. 3, esp. p. 91.

84. See Jay David Bolton and Richard Grusin, *Remediation: Understanding New Media* (Cambridge, Mass, 2000); also David Reynolds, *In Command of History: Churchill Fighting and Writing the Second World War* (London, 2004), esp. 506–27.

85. Commons, *Debates*, 18 June 1940, 362: 60–1.

86. Patrick Wright, 'Misguided Tours', *New Socialist*, July/August 1986, 34.

87. Hewison, *Heritage Industry*, 146.

Chapter Two – Europe

1. Gaitskell, speech at Labour party conference, 3 Oct. 1962, quoting 8, 10. https://www.cvce.eu/content/publication/1999/1/1/05f2996b-000b-4576-

8b42-8069033a16f9/publishable_en.pdf. For background see Philip M. Williams, *Hugh Gaitskell* (2nd edn, Oxford, 1982), ch. 23. Many of the negative passages were drafted by Peter Shore, head of research at Labour party HQ, a lifelong opponent of British membership of the EC/EU right through to 2016.

2. Gaitskell, speech of 3 Oct. 1962, quoting 6–7.
3. Dean Acheson, 'Our Atlantic Alliance: The Political and Economic Strands', *Vital Speeches of the Day*, 29/6 (1 Jan. 1963), 162–6, quoting pp. 163–4.
4. Quoted in Alan Brinkley, 'Dean Acheson and the "Special Relationship": The West Point Speech of December 1962', *Historical Journal*, 33/3 (1990), 599–608 at p. 602.
5. Harold Macmillan, *At the End of the Day, 1961–63* (London, 1973), 339–40.
6. 'Hard Words . . . from Dean Acheson', *The Listener*, 18 June 1970, 827.
7. Also taken up by historians: Sir Brian Harrison, for instance, entitled his two post-war volumes of the 'New Oxford History of England' *Seeking a Role: The United Kingdom, 1951–1970* and *Finding a Role? The United Kingdom, 1970–1990* (Oxford, 2009–10).
8. Helmut Kohl, *Vom Mauerfall zur Wiedervereinigung: Meine Erinnerungen* (Munich, 2009), 137.
9. Dominic Lawson, 'Saying the Unsayable about the Germans', *Spectator*, 14 July 1990, 8–10; Tim Ross, 'Boris Johnson: The EU wants a superstate, just as Hitler did', *Daily Telegraph*, 15 May 2016 https://www.telegraph.co.uk/news/2016/05/14/boris-johnson-the-eu-wants-a-superstate-just-as-hitler-did/
10. Renaud Morieux, *The Channel: England, France and the Construction of a Maritime Border in the Eighteenth Century* (Cambridge, 2016), 65–6.
11. Malcolm Vale, *The Origins of the Hundred Years War: The Angevin Legacy, 1250–1340* (Oxford, 1996), 35.
12. Vale, *Origins of the Hundred Years War*, 52.
13. For a stimulating overview see Brendan Simms, *Britain's Europe: A Thousand Years of Conflict and Cooperation* (London, 2016), though I do not agree with some of his conclusions.
14. David Scott, *Leviathan: The Rise of Britain as a World Power* (London, 2013), 62.
15. Elizabeth Evenden and Thomas S. Freedman, *Religion and the Book in Early Modern England: The Making of Foxe's 'Book of Martyrs'* (Cambridge, 2011), esp. 16, 32, 67, 102–04, 322; Colin Hayden, *Anti-Catholicism in Eighteenth-Century England* (Manchester, 1993), 28–30.

16. https://www.britishmuseum.org/research/collection_online/collection_object_details.aspx?objectId=1451076&partId=1&subject=16602&page=311

17. Alexandra Walsham, *Providence in Early Modern England* (Oxford, 1999), 243–50, 255–6; Linda Colley, *Britons: Forging the Nation, 1707–1837* (London, 1992), 19–20, 46.

18. Andrew C. Thompson, 'The Development of the Executive and Foreign Policy, 1714–1760', in William Mulligan and Brendan Simms, eds, *The Primacy of Foreign Policy in British History, 1660–2000* (Basingstoke, 2010), 65–79, quoting 70.

19. Brendan Simms, '"Ministers of Europe": British Strategic Culture, 1714–1760', in Hamish Scott and Brendan Simms, eds, *Cultures of Power during the Long Eighteenth Century* (Cambridge, 2007), 110–32, quoting from 117–18.

20. Simms, *Britain's Europe*, 59.

21. Anonymous pamphleteer, quoted in Michael Sheehan, 'The Sincerity of the British Commitment to the Maintenance of the Balance of Power, 1714–1763', *Diplomacy and Statecraft*, 15 (2004), 494.

22. 'The Idea of a Patriot King' (1738) in David Armitage, ed., *Bolingbroke: Political Writings* (Cambridge, 1997), 274, 279.

23. P. J. Marshall, 'A Nation defined by Empire, 1755–1776', in Alexander Grant and Keith J. Stringer, eds, *Uniting the Kingdom? The Making of British History* (London, 1995), 208–22.

24. Daniel Baugh, 'Great Britain's "Blue-Water" Policy, 1689–1815', *International History Review*, 10 (1988), 53–4.

25. Colley, *Britons*, 368.

26. Colley, *Britons*, 286; Andrew Roberts, *Napoleon the Great* (London, 2014), 331–2; H. M. Scott, 'The Second "Hundred Years War", 1689–1815', *Historical Journal*, 35/2 (1992), 469.

27. Morieux, *The Channel*, 326–7.

28. François Crouzet, 'The Second Hundred Years War: Some Reflections', *French History*, 10/4 (1996), 443.

29. Paul Kennedy, *Strategy and Diplomacy, 1870–1945* (London, 1983), 15–16.

30. Memo of 10 Jan. 1914, quoted in Arthur J. Marder, *From the Dreadnought to Scapa Flow: The Royal Navy in the Fisher Era, Vol. 1, The Road to War, 1904–1914* (London, 1961), 322–3; cf. Winston S. Churchill, *The World Crisis, 1911–14* (London, 1923), 176.

31. Margaret MacMillan, *The War that Ended Peace* (London, 2013), 554–6

32. Christopher Clark, *The Sleepwalkers: How Europe went to War in 1914* (London, 2012), 527–37.

33. T. G. Otte, *July Crisis: The World's Descent into War, Summer 1914* (London, 2014), 498–9, 521.

34. Zara S. Steiner and Keith Neilson, *Britain and the Origins of the First World War* (2nd edn., London, 2003), 243.

35. Otte, *July Crisis*, 502.

36. Paul Kennedy, *The Rise and Fall of the Great Powers: Economic Change and Military Conflict from 1500 to 2000* (London, 1988), 267.

37. Northcliffe quoted in Kathleen Burk, 'Great Britain in the United States, 1917–1918: The Turning Point', *International History Review*, 1 (1979), 228; Cecil, memo, 18 Sept. 1917, GT 2074, CAB 24/26 (The National Archives, Kew, Surrey – henceforth TNA).

38. Neville Waites, ed., *Troubled Neighbours: Franco-British Relations in the Twentieth Century* (London, 1971), 67.

39. David Dutton, *Austen Chamberlain: Gentleman in Politics* (London, 1985), 238–9; Vansittart, memo, 1 Jan. 1932, para. 5, CP 4 (32), CAB 24/227.

40. P. M. H. Bell, *France and Britain, 1900–1940: Entente and Estrangement* (London, 1996), 157–8; Keith Wilson, *Channel Tunnel Visions, 1859–1945: Dreams and Nightmares* (London, 1994), 150.

41. House of Commons, *Debates*, 5th series, 292: 2339, 30 July 1934; Uri Bialer, *The Shadow of the Bomber: The Fear of Air Attack and British Politics, 1932–1939* (London, 1980), 129–30; Basil Collier, *The Defence of the United Kingdom* (London, 1957), 528, gives a casualty figure of 146,777, including 60,595 dead.

42. House of Commons, *Debates*, 5th series, 270: 632, 10 Nov. 1932.

43. David French, *Raising Churchill's Army: The British Army and the War against Germany, 1919–1945* (Oxford, 2000), 14; B. J. C McKercher, 'Deterrence and the European Balance of Power: The Field Force and British Grand Strategy, 1934–1938', *English Historical Review*, 123 (2008), 128–9.

44. Neville Chamberlain to Hilda Chamberlain, 17 Dec. 1937, Neville Chamberlain papers, NC 18/1/1032 (Birmingham University Library).

45. Minutes by Sargent, 28 Feb. 1940, and Chamberlain, 1 March 1940, FO 371/24298, C4444/9/17 (TNA).

46. 'Schools in Wartime' memo no. 18, 'France and Ourselves', April 1940, Board of Education papers, ED 138/27 (TNA); for the text of the declaration see House of Commons Debates, 2 April 1940, Vol. 359, Cols 40–1.

47. Bell, *France and Britain, 1900–1940*, 229.

48. The figure cited by Churchill to the Commons on 4 June – Commons, *Debates*, 361: 788.

49. Commons, *Debates*, 4 and 18 June 1940, 361: 795 and 362: 60–1.

50. Mark Connelly, *We Can Take It! Britain and the Memory of the Second World War* (Harlow, 2004), 63–7; 'Little Gidding' in *The Collected Poems and Plays of T. S. Eliot* (London, 1969), 197; Peter Ackroyd, *T. S. Eliot* (London, 1985), 263–4.

51. Paul Readman, *Storied Ground: Landscape and the Shaping of English Identity* (Cambridge, 2018), 3, 5, 27–51.

52. Winston S. Churchill, *The Second World War* (6 vols, London, 1948–54), 2: 529.

53. The Greeks also held the Italians at bay for six months in what became known there as 'the Epic of 1940', until overwhelmed by the Germans in April 1941.

54. Memo of 25 May 1940, para. 1, WP (40) 168, CAB 66/7, italics in original; Halifax to Hankey, 15 July 1940, FO 371/25206, W8602/8602/49 (TNA).

55. Churchill, *Second World War*, 2: 4–6; Churchill to Smuts, 3 Dec. 1944, CHAR 20/176 (Churchill Archives Centre, Cambridge).

56. Julian Lewis, *Changing Direction: British Military Planning for Post-war Strategic Defence, 1942–1947* (2nd edn, London, 1988), 232–5; Commons, *Debates*, 15 Feb. 1951, 484: 630.

57. Peter Hennessy, *Cabinets and the Bomb* (London, 2007), 43–8.

58. Quotations from Nigel J. Ashton, *Kennedy, Macmillan and the Cold War: The Irony of Interdependence* (Basingstoke, 2002), 17, 179, 183–4.

59. Extract from Cabinet ministers' discussion with Prime Minister, 10 Feb. 1981, PREM 19/417 (TNA).

60. Quotations from Hennessy, *Cabinets and the Bomb*, 343.

61. Jean Monnet, *Memoirs* (London, 1978), 306.

62. 'Policy towards Europe', note of meeting on 5 Jan. 1949, in Richard Clarke, *Anglo-American Economic Collaboration in War and Peace, 1942–1949* (Oxford, 1982), 209; Martin Gilbert, *Winston S. Churchill, vol. 8* (London, 1988), 265–6; Churchill, 'United Europe', C (51) 32, 29 Nov. 1951, CAB 129/48.

63. Alec Cairncross, *Years of Recovery: British Economic Policy, 1945–51* (London, 1985), 278.

64. Michael Charlton, *The Price of Victory* (London, 1983), 307, appropriating a phrase from Jean Monnet.

65. Alan Bullock, *Ernest Bevin, Foreign Secretary, 1945–1951* (London, 1983), 659; Pierson Dixon, memo, 23 Aug. 1950, FO 800/517, US/50/35 (TNA).

66. CM 19 (55) 9, 30 June 1955, CAB 128/29; Butler, 'European Integration', CP (55) 55, 29 June 1955, CAB 129/76.

67. Charlton, *Price of Victory*, 190, 195; Simon Burgess and Geoffrey Edwards, 'The Six plus One: British policy-making and the question of European economic integration, 1955', *International Affairs*, 64 (1988), esp. 407, 413.

68. Roland Vogt, *Personal Diplomacy in the EU: Political Leadership and Critical Junctures of European Integration* (London, 2017), ch. 3, esp. 54–60; Alan S. Milward, *The European Rescue of the Nation State* (London, 1992), 196–223; Wm. Roger Louis and Roger Owen, eds, *Suez 1956: The Crisis and its Consequences* (Oxford, 1989), 336–7.

69. Miriam Camps, *Britain and the European Community* (London, 1964), 169.

70. N. Piers Ludlow, *Dealing with Britain: The Six and the First UK Application to the EEC* (Cambridge, 1997), 32.

71. Harold Macmillan, *At the End of the Day, 1961–1963* (London, 1973), 365.

72. Ludlow, *Dealing with Britain*, 247–52.

73. *Britain's Entry into the European Community: Report by Sir Con O'Neill on the Negotiations of 1970–1972* (London, 2000), 38, 441, quoting Dr K. O. Nass of the European Commission staff.

74. Stephen George, *An Awkward Partner: Britain in the European Community* (3rd edn, Oxford, 1998), 56; Paul Taylor, *The Limits of European Integration* (New York, 1983), 238.

75. Ali El-Agraa, 'Mrs Thatcher's European Community Policy' in David S. Bell, ed., *The Conservative Government, 1979–1984* (London, 1985), 165; Geoffrey Howe, 'The future of the European Community: Britain's Approach to the Negotiations', *International Affairs*, 60 (1984) 187–8.

76. For the text and background documents see https://www.margaret-thatcher.org/archive/1988CAC5

77. Margaret Thatcher, *The Downing Street Years* (London, 1995), 555; Commons Foreign Affairs Committee, 1989–90, 2nd report, 82:1: xiv.

78. Patrick Salmon et al, eds, *Documents on British Policy Overseas: Series III, Vol. VII: German Unification, 1989–1990* (London, 2010), 165, 217.

79. *Guardian*, 29 Oct. 1990, 1; Commons, *Debates*, 30 Oct. 1990, 178: 876–7; Geoffrey Howe, *Conflict of Loyalty* (London, 1995), 644–5, 691.

80. John Major, *The Autobiography* (London, 1999), 268–9; Julie Smith, *The UK's Journeys into and out of the EU* (London, 2017), 37; Stephen Castle, 'Wrapped in the Flag', *Independent*, 27 March 1994 https://www.independent.co.uk/news/uk/wrapped-in-the-flag-struggling-to-survive-john-major-has-played-the-patriotic-card-stephen-castle-1431989.html

81. Sarah Hogg and Jonathan Hill, *Too Close to Call: Power and Politics – John Major in No. 10* (London, 1995), 157.

82. Michael Spicer, *A Treaty too Far: A New Policy for Europe* (London, 1992), viii.

83. Hugo Young, *This Blessed Plot: Britain and Europe from Churchill to Blair* (London, 1998), 448, 469; Castle, 'Wrapped in the Flag'.

84. Oliver Daddow, 'The UK media and "Europe": From Permissive Consensus to Destructive Dissent', *International Affairs*, 88 (2012), 1219–36.

85. Young, *Blessed Plot*, 485.

86. Smith, *The UK's Journey*, 45–6; cf. 'The Impact of EU Enlargement on Migration Flows', Home Office Online Reports, 25/03 (2003) http://discovery.ucl.ac.uk/14332/1/14332.pdf

87. Craig Oliver, *Unleashing Demons: The Inside Story of Brexit* (London, 2016), 9.

88. Tim Shipman, *All Out War: The Full Story of Brexit* (2nd edn., London, 2017), 3–4, 126, 173–4, 613–22.

89. Shipman, *All Out War*, 395–6.

90. Smith, *UK's Journey*, 1.

91. Shipman, *All Out Wars*, 538.

92. https://www.theguardian.com/politics/2017/apr/26/david-cameron-brexit-vote-ended-poisoning-uk-politics

93. Nick Clegg, *How to Stop Brexit (and Make Britain Great Again)* (London, 2017), 120–1.

94. 'We must not play by the EU's stifling rules', *Daily Telegraph*, editorial, 6 May 2018, 17; Robert Tombs, *The English and their History* (London, 2015), 877; Boris Johnson, 'My vision for a bold, thriving Britain enabled by Brexit', *Daily Telegraph*, 18 Sept. 2017, 6–7.

Chapter Three – Britain

1. J. G. A. Pocock, 'British History: A Plea for a New Subject', in Pocock, *A Discovery of Islands* (Cambridge, 2005), 27.

2. These and subsequent quotations from Gordon Brown, speech to Fabian Society, 14 Jan. 2006 http://www.britishpoliticalspeech.org/speech-archive.htm?speech=316

3. John Morrill, *'Uneasy Lies the Head that Wears a Crown': Dynastic Crises in Tudor and Stewart Britain, 1504–1746* (Reading, 2005), 14.

4. Linda Colley, *Acts of Union and Disunion* (London, 2014), 6.

5. A. J. P. Taylor did so in 1965 when publishing *English History, 1914–1965* – but that was before the Northern Irish 'Troubles', the Good Friday

agreement, devolved parliaments in Scotland and Wales and the Scottish independence referendum. The distinguished historian of nineteenth-century France, Robert Tombs, did not have such excuses in 2014 when he published *The English and their History*.

6. In, for example, Eric Hobsbawm, *Nations and Nationalism since 1780: Programmes, Myth, Reality* (Cambridge, 1990); Anthony D. Smith, *Nationalism and Modernism: A Critical Survey of Recent Theories of Nations and Nationalism* (London, 1998); Paul Lawrence, *Nationalism: History and Theory* (London, 2005).

7. Jörn Leonhard, 'Nation-States and Wars', in Timothy Baycroft and Mark Hewitson, eds, *What is a Nation? Europe 1789–1914* (Oxford, 2006), 235.

8. 'Am Amfang war Napoleon.' Thomas Nipperdey, *Deutsche Geschichte, 1800–1866: Bürgerwelt und starker Staat* (München, 1983), 1.

9. See Baycroft and Hewitson, eds, *What is a Nation?*, esp. chs 4 and 8; Marteen Prak, *Citizens without Nations: Urban Citizenship in Europe and the World c. 1000–1789* (Cambridge, 2018).

10. Andrea Ruddick, *English Identity and Political Culture in the Fourteenth Century* (Cambridge, 2013), chs 1–2, esp. 61, 63, 130.

11. R. R. Davies, 'The Peoples of Britain and Ireland, 1100–1400: Part 1. Identities', *Transactions of the Royal Historical Society*, 4 (1994), 1–20, quoting 9, 16–17.

12. Ruddick, *English Identity*, ch. 1, esp. 67–81 and 99 (quotation).

13. Krishan Kumar, *The Making of English National Identity* (Cambridge, 2003), 30–6, quoting 36.

14. Robin Frame, *The Political Development of the British Isles, 1100–1400* (Oxford, 1995), ch. 2, quoting 25.

15. G. R. Elton, ed., *The Tudor Constitution: Documents and Commentary* (Cambridge, 1968), doc. 177, 344.

16. David Armitage, *The Ideological Origins of the British Empire* (Cambridge, 2000), 36–40, quoting John Elder, a Scottish advocate for union, on 38.

17. Armitage, *Ideological Origins*, 51 (Smith); Jane E. A. Dawson, 'William Cecil and the British Dimension of Early Elizabethan Foreign Policy', *History*, 74, no. 241 (June 1989), 196–216.

18. Cf. John Elliott, 'A Europe of Composite Monarchies', *Past and Present*, 137 (1992), 48–71.

19. Susan Doran and Paulina Kewes, eds, *Doubtful and Dangerous: The Question of Succession in late Elizabethan England* (Manchester, 2014), 4.

20. Roger A. Mason, 'Scotland, Elizabethan England and the Idea of Britain', *Transactions of the Royal Historical Society*, 14 (2004), 290–1.

21. Judith M. Richards, 'The English Accession of James VI: "National"

Identity, Gender and the Personal Monarchy of England', *English Historical Review*, 118 (2002), 514–18.

22. John Morrill, 'Dynasties, Realms, Peoples and State Formation, 1500–1720', in Robert von Friedeburg and John Morrill, eds, *Monarchy Transformed: Princes and their Elites in Early Modern Western Europe* (Cambridge, 2017), 25.

23. Derek Hirst, *Dominion: England and its Island Neighbours, 1500–1707* (Oxford, 2012), chs 5–6, quoting 143, 145.

24. Quotations in this paragraph from Richards, 'The English Accession', 513–15. See also Bruce Galloway, *The Union of England and Scotland, 1603–1608* (Edinburgh, 1986).

25. See Jenny Wormald, 'James VI, James I and the Identity of Britain', in Brendan Bradshaw and John Morrill, eds, *The British Problem, c. 1534–1707* (Basingstoke, 1996), ch. 6, esp. 159–65, 170–1. James IV died on the field of Flodden; James V after a nervous breakdown following his defeat at Solway Moss.

26. Colley, *Acts of Union*, 87.

27. Morrill, 'Dynasties, Realms, 19–20; J. G. A. Pocock, 'The Limits and Divisions of British History: In Search of the Unknown Subject', *American Historical Review*, 87 (1982), 317.

28. Hirst, *Dominion*, 190. See also Joseph Cope, *England and the Irish Rebellion* (Woodbridge, 2009), esp. ch. 5.

29. See Steven G. Ellis and Sarah Barber, eds, *Conquest and Union: Fashioning a British State* (London, 1995), 31–3, 38, 195–221.

30. Hirst, *Dominion*, 220–6, 236; also John Morrill, 'The Rule of Saints and Soldiers: The Wars of Religion in Britain and Ireland, 1638–1660', in Jenny Wormald, ed., *The Seventeenth Century* (Oxford, 2008) 112–13.

31. Hirst, *Dominion*, 218; Michael Braddick, *God's Fury, England's Fire: A New History of the English Civil Wars* (London, 2008), xii. The 'billiard-ball' metaphor comes from Conrad Russell, 'The British Problem and the English Civil War', *History*, 72 (Oct. 1987), 408.

32. David Hayton, 'Constitutional Experiments and Political Expediency, 1689–1725' in Ellis and Barber, eds, *Conquest and Union*, 276–305, quoting p. 279.

33. John Robertson, 'Empire and Union: Two Concepts of the Early Modern European Political Order', in Robertson, ed., *A Union for Empire: Political Thought and the British Union of 1707* (Cambridge, 1995), 4.

34. Figures from Christopher A. Whatley, with Derek J. Patrick, *The Scots and the Union* (Edinburgh, 2006), 167–8, 173.

35. T. M. Devine, *The Scottish Nation, 1700–2007* (London, 2006), 1.

36. The international dimension is stressed by Bob Harris, 'The Anglo-Scottish Treaty of Union, 1707 in 2007: Defending the Revolution, Defeating the Jacobites', *Journal of British Studies*, 40 (2010), esp. 30, 41, 46.

37. Whatley, *The Scots and the Union*, 141–2; Allan I. Macinnes, *Union and Empire: The Making of the United Kingdom in 1707* (Cambridge, 2007), 318; T. M. Devine, *The Tobacco Lords: A Study of the Tobacco Merchants of Glasgow and their Trading Activities, c. 1740–1790* (Edinburgh, 1975), v.

38. Macinnes, *Union and Empire*, 325–6.

39. Joanna Innes, 'Legislating for three kingdoms: How the Westminster parliament legislated for England, Scotland and Ireland, 1707–1830', in Julian Hoppitt, ed., *Parliaments, Nations and Identitities in Britain and Ireland, 1660–1830* (Manchester, 2003), 23–8.

40. Hayton, 'Constitutional Experiments', 276–80, 296; see also James Kelly, 'The Origins of the Act of Union: An Examination of Unionist Opinion in Britain and Ireland, 1650–1800', *Irish Historical Studies*, 25 (1987), 236–63.

41. Roy Foster, *Modern Ireland, 1600–1972* (London, 1988), 237, 241.

42. Nancy J. Curtin, 'The Transformation of the Society of United Irishmen into a Mass-Based Revolutionary Organisation, 1794–6', *Irish Historical Studies*, 24 (1985), 463–92, quoting 463.

43. J. Holland Rose, *William Pitt and the Great War* (London, 1911), 364, quoting Las Casas.

44. William Hague, *William Pitt the Younger* (London, 2004), 436–7; Rose, *Pitt*, 411.

45. Curtin, 'Transformation', 492.

46. Ian McBride, 'Reclaiming the Rebellion: 1798 in 1998', *Irish Historical Studies*, 31 (1999), 410.

47. Rose, *Pitt*, 389.

48. Innes, 'Legislating for Three Kingdoms', 15.

49. Linda Colley, *Britons: Forging the Nation, 1707–1837* (New Haven, 1992), ch. 5, esp. 208–9, 219, 232.

50. Devine, *The Scottish Nation*, 290; Robert Colls, *Identity of England* (Oxford, 2002), 49 (quote).

51. Bryan S. Glass, *The Scottish Nation at Empire's End* (New York, 2014), 26.

52. Foster, *Modern Ireland*, 323–4, 345.

53. Quoted in F. S. L. Lyons, *Culture and Anarchy in Ireland, 1890–1939* (Oxford, 1982), 42.

54. See generally Patricia Jalland, 'United Kingdom Devolution 1910–1914: Political Panacea or Tactical Diversion?', *English Historical Review*, 94 (1979), 757–85.

55. Quoted in Devine, *The Scottish Nation*, 308.

56. House of Commons Debates, 53: 481–2, 30 May 1913 (William Cowan).

57. Speeches by Law (27 July 1912) and Churchill (14 March 1914) in Randolph S. Churchill, *Winston S. Churchill, Vol. II* (London, 1967), 469–70, 489.

58. David Powell, *The Edwardian Crisis: Britain 1901–1914* (London, 1996), ch. 5, quoting 149. On Ulster Catholics see A. C. Hepburn, 'Irish Nationalism in Ulster, 1885–1921', in D. George Boyce and Alan O'Day, eds, *The Ulster Crisis, 1885–1921'* (London, 2006), esp. 105–11.

59. John Horne and Alan Kramer, *German Atrocities, 1914: A History of Denial* (New Haven, 2001), 419 (statistics); see also Alan Kramer, *Dynamic of Destruction: Culture and Mass Killing in the First World War* (Oxford, 2007), ch. 1.

60. Jalland, 'United Kingdom Devolution', 759; Richard Toye, *Lloyd George and Churchill: Rivals for Greatness* (London, 2007), 22; John Grigg, *Lloyd George: From Peace to War, 1912–1916* (London, 1997), 161–7; *The Times*, 21 Sept. 1914, 12.

61. Kenneth O. Morgan, *Rebirth of a Nation: Wales, 1880–1980* (Oxford, 1982), ch. 6, quoting 163.

62. Trevor Royle, *The Flowers of the Forest: Scotland and the First World War* (Edinburgh, 2007), 195.

63. Gregory, *Last Great War*, esp. 81–7, 120–1, 228.

64. Jack Brand, *The National Movement in Scotland* (London, 1978), ch. 4, quoting 49; see also Atsuko Ichijo, 'Civic or Ethnic? The Evolution of Britishness and Scottishness', in Helen Brocklehurst and Robert Phillips, eds, *History, Nationhood and the Question of Britain* (London, 2004), 119.

65. Keith Jeffrey, *Ireland and the Great War* (Cambridge, 2000), 2.

66. Joseph P. Finnan, *John Redmond and Irish Unity, 1912–1918* (Syracuse, NY, 2004), 86, 88–9, 141.

67. Charles Townshend, *Easter 1916: The Irish Rebellion* (London, 2005), 72.

68. Jeffrey, *Ireland*, 51.

69. Thomas Hennessey, *Dividing Ireland: World War I and Partition* (London, 1998), 142.

70. Townshend, *Easter 1916*, 310–14; Grigg, *Lloyd George, 1912–1916*, 349–55.

71. Martin Gilbert, *Winston S. Churchill, vol. 4* (London, 1975), 471.

72. Adrian Gregory, 'Peculiarities of the English? War, Violence and Politics: 1900–1939', *Journal of Modern European History*, 1 (2003), 53–4; Colls, *Identity of England*, 93, note 1.

73. Foster, *Modern Ireland*, 506.

74. Diarmaid Ferriter, *The Border: The Legacy of a Century of Anglo-Irish Politics* (London, 2019), 9–10, 18.

75. Patrick Buckland, *The Factory of Grievances: Devolved Government in Northern Ireland, 1921–1939* (Dublin, 1979), ch. 10; Northern Ireland Parliamentary Debates, Vol. 16, Col. 1095, 24 April 1934.

76. Devine, *The Scottish Nation*, 558.

77. Morgan, *Rebirth of a Nation*, 367–8, 384, 414–15.

78. Stuart Allan and Allan Carswell, *The Thin Red Line: War, Empire and Visions of Scotland* (Edinburgh, 2004), 40.

79. Alvin Jackson, *The Two Unions: Ireland, Scotland, and the Survival of the United Kingdom, 1707–2007* (Oxford, 2012), 174, 278.

80. Paul Bew and John Bew, 'War and Peace in Northern Ireland, 1965–2016', in Thomas Bartlett, ed., *The Cambridge History of Ireland, vol. 4* (Cambridge, 2018), 474.

81. Ferriter, *The Border*, 81–3, 87; 105–6; Bew and Bew, 'War and Peace', 442–3, 446.

82. *Belfast Telegraph*, 18 Dec. 2015, https://www.belfasttelegraph.co.uk/news/ northern-ireland/arlene-foster-relives-horror-of-fathers-shooting-by- ira-and-tells-how-bus-blast-could-have-killed-her-34297350.html

83. Sebastian Whale, 'Karen Bradley: "I'm not here for the headlines."' *The House: Parliament's Magazine*, 6 Sept. 2018, https://www.politicshome. com/news/uk/uk-regions/northern-ireland/house/house-magazine/98026 /karen-bradley-%E2%80%9Cim-not-here-headlines; Johnson as reported in the *Guardian*, 7 June 2018 https://www.theguardian.com/politics/2018/ jun/07/pm-confident-david-davis-will-stay-in-job-no-10-says

84. Speech in Belfast, 20 July 2018, https://www.gov.uk/government/speeches/ pm-belfast-speech-20-july-2018

85. Colley, *Acts of Union*, 147.

86. See Prak, *Citizens without Nations*, 305–6; also Philip Rycroft, 'Place policy after Brexit', lecture, 26 June 2019 http://www.centreonconstitu- tionalchange.ac.uk/publications/books-articles/place-policy-after-brexit

Chapter Four – Empire

1. David Cameron, *Mail on Sunday*, 15 June 2014, reprinted on 10 Downing Street website, https://www.gov.uk/government/news/british-values- article-by-david-cameron

2. J. R. Seeley, *The Expansion of England* (London, 1883), 296 and 50–1.
3. Seeley, *Expansion of England*, 8.
4. Seeley, *Expansion of England*, quoting 45, 302 and 192.
5. D. A. Low, *The Contraction of England* (Cambridge, 1985).
6. Powell, speech, 22 April 1961, J. Enoch Powell papers, POLL 4/1/1, file 6 (Churchill Archives Centre, Cambridge – henceforth CAC).
7. David Olusoga, *Black and British – A Forgotten History*, (London, 2016), 15 – also quoting words written by Stuart Hall in 2008.
8. 'The history of Britain and the history of the British Empire cannot easily be separated' – P. J. Marshall, 'No fatal impact?: The elusive history of imperial Britain', *Times Literary Supplement*, 12 March 1993, 8.
9. John Darwin, *Unfinished Empire: The Global Expansion of Britain* (London, 2012), xii–xiii.
10. The title of the book by Ian K. Steele, *The English Atlantic, 1675–1740: An Exploration of Communication and Community* (Oxford, 1986).
11. Joseph E. Inikori, *Africans and the Industrial Revolution in England: A Study in International Trade and Economic Development* (Cambridge, 2002), ch. 6, esp. 227–8, 237.
12. Richard S. Dunn, *Sugar and Slaves: The Rise of the Planter Class in the English West Indies, 1624–1713* (London, 1973), 226.
13. Peter H. Wood, *Black Majority: Negroes in Colonial South Carolina from 1670 through the Stono Rebellion* (New York, 1974), 152.
14. Letter of 1779 quoted in Samuel W. Mintz, *Sweetness and Power: The Place of Sugar in Modern History* (New York, 1985), 119.
15. See Mintz, *Sweetness and Power* , ch. 3, quoting 148; Elizabeth Abbott, *Sugar: A Bittersweet History* (London, 2009), ch. 2, esp. 56–70.
16. Winthrop D. Jordan, *White over Black: American Attitudes toward the Negro, 1550–1812* (Baltimore, 1969), 71.
17. Neil McKendrick, 'The Consumer Revolution of Eighteenth-Century England', in Neil McKendrick, John Brewer and J. H. Plumb, *The Birth of a Consumer Society: The Commercialization of Eighteenth-Century England* (London, 1982), 28.
18. Sven Beckert, *Empire of Cotton: A New History of Global Capitalism* (London, 2014), chs 3 and 9, esp. 73 and 244 (Marx, Merivale); Olusoga, *Black and British*, ch. 9, esp. 340, 343–6.
19. Speech of 4 March 1858 in *Selections from the Letters and Speeches of the Hon. James H. Hammond of South Carolina* (New York, 1866), 317; D. P. Crook, *The North, the South, and the Powers, 1861–1865* (New York, 1974), 199–206.
20. Crook, *The North, the South, and the Powers*, 6–7; Darwin, *Unfinished*

Empire, 168; 'The prosperity of the United States . . .' *The Times*, 4 June 1851, 4.

21. Kathleen Burk, *Old World, New World: The Story of Britain and America* (London, 2007), 311–24.

22. Quotations in this paragraph from Boyd Hilton, *A Mad, Bad, and Dangerous People? England 1783–1846* (Oxford, 2006), 1.

23. Quotations from Eric Williams, 'Laissez Faire, Sugar and Slavery', *Political Science Quarterly*, 58 (1943), 67; see more fully Eric Williams, *Capitalism and Slavery* (London, 1944).

24. Kenneth Morgan, *Slavery and the British Empire: From Africa to America* (Oxford, 2006), 157; see also J. R. Oldfield, *Popular Politics and British Anti-Slavery: The Mobilisation of Public Opinion against the Slave Trade, 1787–1807* (Manchester, 1995), 61.

25. See Roger Anstey, *The Atlantic Slave Trade and British Abolition, 1760– 1810* (London, 1975), chs 14–17, quoting 374.

26. Nicholas Draper, *The Price of Emancipation: Slave-Ownership, Compensation and British Society at the End of Slavery* (Cambridge, 2010), 106–7, 112, 156; Olusoga, *Black and British*, 230. Adult slaves were also compelled to work for six years after Emancipation as 'apprentices' for their former masters – a provision revoked only in 1838 after another mass petitioning campaign.

27. Hilton, *A Mad, Bad, and Dangerous People?* 502–3; Simon Morgan, 'The Anti-Corn Law League and British Anti-Slavery in Transatlantic Perspective, 1838–1846', *Historical Journal*, 52 (2009), 90–1.

28. David Cannadine, *Victorious Century: The United Kingdom, 1800–1906* (London, 2017), 219.

29. Douglas Hurd, *Robert Peel: A Biography* (London, 2008), 344, 368.

30. Darwin, *Unfinished Empire*, 60.

31. The Cobden Centre, 'Our Vision', https://www.cobdencentre.org/about/ our-vision/

32. Quotations from Hurd, *Robert Peel*, 333, 340, 359.

33. N. F. R. Crafts, *British Economic Growth during the Industrial Revolution* (Oxford, 1985), 143, 145.

34. Quoted in Eric Stokes, *The English Utilitarians and India* (Oxford, 1959), 34. Grant was a Company employee, using free trader arguments.

35. Stokes, *The English Utilitarians*, 35.

36. House of Commons, *Debates*, 10 July 1833, third series, vol. 19: 503–36, quoting from columns 535–6.

37. John Darwin, *The Empire Project: The Rise of the British World-System, 1830–1970* (Cambridge, 2009), 183. See also Claude Markovits, 'Indian

Merchant Networks outside India in the Nineteenth and Twentieth Centuries: A Preliminary Survey', *Modern Asian Studies*, 33 (1999), 883–911.

38. Sugata Bose and Ayesha Jalal, *Modern South Asia: History, Culture, Political Economy* (1998), 100; more generally, B. R. Tomlinson, *The Political Economy of the Raj: The Economics of Decolonization in India* (London, 1979), ch. 1.

39. Darwin, *The Empire Project*, 194–6.

40. Gordon Johnson, *Provincial Politics and Indian Nationalism: Bombay and the Indian National Congress, 1880–1915* (Cambridge, 1974), 33–4, 130–1, 187–8.

41. Sunil Khilnani, *The Idea of India* (London, 1998), 23. Priyamvada Gopal *Insurgent Empire: Anticolonial Resistance and British Dissent* (London, 2019), 5–6.

42. See Duncan Bell, *The Idea of Greater Britain: Empire and the Future of World Order, 1860–1900* (Princeton, 2007), ch. 1.

43. Darwin, *Unfinished Empire*, 90, 95. In 1815 the UK population was about 16 million, by 1914 around 39 million.

44. Carl Bridge and Kent Fedorowich, eds, *The British World: Diaspora, Culture and Identity* (London, 2003), 5.

45. Miles Taylor, 'Imperium et Libertas? Rethinking the Radical Critique of Imperialism during the Nineteenth Century', *Journal of Imperial and Commonwealth History*, 19 (1993), 12.

46. Seeley, *Expansion of England*, 158–9, 301; Robert Holland, 'The British Empire and the Great War, 1914–1918', in Judith M. Brown and Wm. Roger Louis, eds, *The Oxford History of the British Empire Vol. 4* (Oxford, 1999), 117.

47. Michael Kenny and Nick Pearce, *Shadows of Empire: The Anglosphere in British Politics* (Cambridge, 2018), 17, 28; John E. Kendle, *The Round Table Movement and Imperial Union* (Toronto, 1975), 302; W. David McIntyre, *Historians and the Making of the British Commonwealth of Nations, 1907–1948* (London, 2009), 116.

48. Martin Thornton, *Sir Robert Borden* (London, 2010), 46; W. K. Hancock, ed., *Selections from the Smuts Papers, vol. 3* (Cambridge, 1966), 510–11.

49. Brown and Louis, eds, *Oxford History of the British Empire*, 4: 71–2.

50. Ian E. Johnston-White, *The British Commonwealth and Victory in the Second World War* (London, 2017), 92, 143, 270–1. India also raised about 2.5 million troops, mostly volunteers, but this was less than one percent of the total population of 315 million.

51. John Ramsden, *Man of the Century: Winston Churchill and his Legend since 1945* (London, 2002), 326–9.

52. David Dilks, ed., *The Diaries of Sir Alexander Cadogan, OM, 1938–1945* (London, 1971), 778.

53. Richard Gardner, *Sterling-Dollar Diplomacy in Current Perspective* (3rd edn, New York, 1980), xiii.

54. On this, see Peter Riddell, *Hug Them Close: Blair, Clinton, Bush and the 'Special Relationship'* (London, 2003).

55. John Baylis, *Anglo-American Defence Relations, 1939–84: The Special Relationship* (2nd edn, London, 1984), 43.

56. See David Reynolds, 'A "Special Relationship": America, Britain and the International Order since the Second World War', in Reynolds, *From World War to Cold War* (Oxford, 2006), 308–30; Alex Danchev, *On Specialness: Essays on Anglo-American Relations* (London, 1998).

57. CC (61) 24, 26 April 1961, CAB 128/35 (TNA).

58. Stuart Ward, *Australia and the British Embrace: The Demise of the Imperial Ideal* (Melbourne, 2001), 81; Kenny and Pearce, *Shadows of Empire*, 78–81.

59. Sir Con O'Neill, *Britain's Entry into the European Community: Report on the Negotiations of 1970–1972* (London, 2000), 146; Paul Keating, Australian House of Representatives, 27 Feb. 1992, http://australianpolitics.com/1992/02/27/keating-blasts-liberal-party-fogies.html

60. Andrew Roberts, 'CANZUK' *The Telegraph*, 13 Sept. 2016 https://www.telegraph.co.uk/news/2016/09/13/canzuk-after-brexit-canada-australia-new-zealand-and-britain-can/; and Andrew Lilico, 'From Brexit to CANZUK', *Financial Post*, 1 Aug. 2017, https://business.financialpost.com/opinion/from-brexit-to-canzuk-a-call-from-britain-to-team-up-with-canada-australia-and-new-zealand. See also Boris Johnson, 'The Aussies are just like us', *Daily Telegraph*, 25 Aug. 2013, https://www.telegraph.co.uk/news/politics/10265619/The-Aussies-are-just-like-us-so-lets-stop-kicking-them-out.html

61. Duncan Bell, 'Empire of the Tongue', *Prospect*, February 2017, 42–5; Annabelle Dickson, 'Ex-colonies to UK: Forget Brexit "Empire 2.0"', *Politico*, 26 Feb. 2018 https://www.politico.eu/article/commonwealth-summit-wont-be-empire-2-0-for-brexit-uk/; Kwasi Kwateng, Priti Patel, Dominic Raab, Chris Skidmore, Elizabeth Truss, *Britannia Unchained: Global Lessons for Growth and Prosperity* (London, 2012), 61, 78. See generally Kenny and Pearce, *Shadows of Empire*, chs 6–7.

62. Barack Obama, 'Barack Obama: As your friend, let me say that the EU makes Britain even greater', the *Telegraph*, 21 April 2016, https://www.telegraph.co.uk/news/2016/04/21/as-your-friend-let-me-tell-you-that-the-eu-makes-britain-even-gr/; Jon Stone, 'Boris Johnson suggests

"part-Kenyan" Obama may have "ancestral dislike" of UK', *Independent*, 22 April 2016, https://www.independent.co.uk/news/uk/politics/boris-johnson-suggests-part-kenyan-obama-may-have-an-ancestral-dislike-of-britain-a6995826.html

63. Tim Shipman, *All Out War: The Full Story of Brexit* (London, 2017), 297–302, 386–92; Owen Bennett, *The Brexit Club: The Inside Story of the Leave Campaign's Shock Victory* (London, 2016), 323.

64. James Kirkup and Robert Winnett, 'Theresa May interview', the *Telegraph*, 25 May 2012, https://www.telegraph.co.uk/news/uknews/immigration/9291483/Theresa-May-interview-Were-going-to-give-illegal-migrants-a-really-hostile-reception.html

65. HC 500 and 990 (15 Jan. and 3 July 2018), quoting HC 500, 3; see also Amelia Gentleman, *The Windrush Betrayal: Exposing the Hostile Environment* (London, 2019).

66. Panikos Panayi, *An Immigration History of Britain: Institutional Racism since 1800* (London, 2010), 11–13.

67. Stephen Leslie, et al., 'The fine-scale genetic structure of the British population', *Nature*, 19 March 2015, 309–14; cf. Hannah Devlin, 'Genetic Study reveals . . . ', *Guardian*, 18 March 2015.

68. Panayi, *An Immigration History of Britain*, 13–26; Robert Blake, *Disraeli* (London, 1960), 152–3.

69. Jill Pellew, 'The Home Office and the Aliens Act, 1905', *Historical Journal*, 32 (1989), 369–85, quoting 369 ('timelessness'). The Act is 5 Edw. 7, cap 13.

70. Ian R. G. Spencer, *British Immigration Policy since 1939: The Making of Multi-Racial Britain* (London, 1997), xiii.

71. Olusoga, *Black and British*, 29–33, 467; Miranda Kaufmann, *Black Tudors: The Untold Story* (London, 2017).

72. Winston James and Clive Harris, eds, *Inside Babylon: The Caribbean Diaspora in Britain* (London, 1993), 22.

73. Olusoga, *Black and British*, 493–4.

74. *HC Debs* 5 November 1954, 532: 827.

75. Spencer, *British Immigration Policy*, 52–3, 55.

76. Spencer, *British Immigration Policy*, 23–31, 67 (Swinton), 89–90.

77. Kathleen Paul, *Whitewashing Britain: Race and Citizenship in the Post-war Era* (London, 1997), 132, 234.

78. Spencer, *British Immigration Policy*, 42–6.

79. Swinton, memo, 23 Nov. 1954, C (54) 356, CAB 129/72; Andrew Roberts, *Eminent Churchillians* (London, 1994), 225, quoting Sir David Hunt, 31 Dec. 1992; and generally Spencer, *British Immigration Policy*, 58–87.

80. Spencer, *British Immigration Policy*, 87–91, 115; Butler, memo, 'Commonwealth Migrants', 6 Oct. 1961, C (61) 153, CAB 129/107; Cabinet meeting, 10 Oct. 1961, CC 55 (61) 3, CAB 128/35. See also Dennis Dean, 'The Conservative Government and the 1961 Commonwealth Immigration Act: The Inside Story', *Race and Class*, 35/2 (1993), 57–74.

81. Paul, *Whitewashing*, 168, 174–5; Richard Crossman, *The Diaries of a Cabinet Minister, vol. 1* (London, 1975), 2 Aug. 1965, 299.

82. Quotations from Paul, *Whitewashing*, xiv–xv.

83. Speech to AGM of the West Midlands Area Conservative Political Centre, 20 April 1968, POLL 4/1/3 (CAC); Peter Brooke, 'India, Post-imperialism and the Origins of Enoch Powell's "Rivers of Blood" Speech', *Historical Journal*, 50 (2007), 669–87; Camilla Schofield, *Enoch Powell and the Making of Postcolonial Britain* (Cambridge, 2013), 208–37.

84. Schofield, *Enoch Powell*, 237; John Campbell, *Edward Heath: A Biography* (London, 1993), 245.

85. Quotations from Nicholas Hillman, 'A "Chorus of Execration"? Enoch Powell's "Rivers of Blood" Forty Years On', *Patterns of Prejudice*, 42 (2008), 104, and Spencer, *British Immigration Policy*, 144.

86. Spencer, *British Immigration Policy*, 129–34, 154–5; Neil MacMaster, *Racism in Europe, 1870–2000* (London, 2001), 181. In 1972 the total was over 60,000 because of the decision to admit Asians, mostly holding British passports, driven out of Uganda by the government of Idi Amin.

87. Panayi, *An Immigration History of Britain*, 94, 121, 183; Spencer, *British Immigration Policy*, 158.

88. Con O'Neill, *Britain's Entry into the European Community* (London, 2000), 232; Office of National Statistics, 'UK Population by Country of Birth and Nationality: 2016', esp. section 7 https://www.ons.gov.uk/people populationandcommunity/populationandmigration/international migration/bulletins/ukpopulationbycountryofbirthandnationality/2016# poland-remains-the-most-common-non-uk-country-of-birth-and-non-british-nationality

89. Office of National Statistics, 'Ethnicity and Nationality Identity in England and Wales: 2011', https://www.ons.gov.uk/peoplepopulationandcommunity/ culturalidentity/ethnicity/articles/ethnicityandnationalidentityinenglan-dandwales/2012-12-11#changing-picture-of-ethnicity-over-time; Miri Song, 'Is Intermarriage a Good Indicator of Integration?' *Journal of Ethnic and Migration Studies*, 35 (2009), 332, 344.

90. Panayi, *An Immigration History*, 316.

91. Edward Malik, 'Sajid Javid's Windrush fury', *Sunday Telegraph*, 28 April 2018,

https://www.telegraph.co.uk/politics/2018/04/28/sajid-javids-windrush-fury-could-have-mum-dad/

Chapter Five – Taking Control of Our Past

1. Speech in Zurich, 19 Sept. 1946, http://www.churchill-society-london.org.uk/astonish.html
2. 'Strategic Failure', *The Times*, leading article, 22 March 2019, 29.
3. Tim Shipman, *Fall Out: A Year of Political Mayhem* (London, 2017), xxvi, 5–6.
4. BBC interview, 2 May 2017, https://www.bbc.co.uk/news/uk-politics-39784170
5. Shipman, *Fall Out*, 3.
6. Speech to Conservative party conference, 2 Oct. 2016, https://www.politicshome.com/news/uk/political-parties/conservative-party/news/79517/read-full-theresa-mays-conservative
7. Speech to Conservative party conference, 5 Oct. 2016, https://www.telegraph.co.uk/news/2016/10/05/theresa-mays-conference-speech-in-full/
8. Speech to Conservative party conference, 2 Oct. 2016, https://www.politicshome.com/news/uk/political-parties/conservative-party/news/79517/read-full-theresa-mays-conservative
9. Shipman, *Fall Out*, 96.
10. *Daily Mail*, 19 April 2017, 1.
11. Shipman, *Fall Out*, 160, 172, 345, 353.
12. Dan Roberts, *Guardian*, 1 May 2017, https://www.theguardian.com/politics/2017/may/01/jean-claude-juncker-to-theresa-may-on-brexit-im-10-times-more-sceptical-than-i-was-before
13. European Council, General Secretariat, Supplementary Directives, 29 Jan. 2018, https://www.consilium.europa.eu/media/32504/xt21004-ad01re02en18.pdf
14. David Davis, speech in Teesport, 26 Jan. 2018, https://www.gov.uk/government/news/david-davis-teesport-speech-implementation-period-a-bridge-to-the-future-partnership-between-the-uk-eu
15. House of Commons Library, Briefing Paper 8238, 23 February 2018, 7,
16. Cmd. 953, 'The Future Relationship between the United Kingdom and the European Union', July 2018, quoting 2, 14 (para 7a), 97, https://assets.publishing.service.gov.uk/government/uploads/system/uploads/attachment_data/file/786626/The_Future_Relationship_between_the_United_Kingdom_and_the_European_Union_120319.pdf

17. Johnson, resignation speech, 18 July 2018, https://brexitcentral.com/full-text-boris-johnsons-resignation-speech-house-commons/

18. Heather Stewart, 'Theresa May's Brexit plan', *Guardian*, 14 Nov. 2018, https://www.theguardian.com/politics/2018/nov/14/theresa-may-wins-cabinet-backing-for-brexit-deal

19. Heather Stewart, 'Theresa May defeats leadership challenge', *Guardian*, 13 Dec. 2018, https://www.theguardian.com/politics/2018/dec/12/theresa-may-defeats-leadership-challenge-by-83-votes

20. Institute for Government, 'Brexit: Two Months to Go', 2, https://www.instituteforgovernment.org.uk/sites/default/files/publications/brexit-two-months-to-go-final-web.pdf. See also Beckie Smith, 'Ready, aim, hire: how is Brexit reshaping the civil service?', *Civil Service World*, 28 Jan. 2019.

21. https://www.gov.uk/government/speeches/pm-statement-on-brexit-20-march-2019

22. https://www.independent.co.uk/news/uk/politics/brexit-european-union-eu-steve-baker-theresa-may-wholly-torn-down-libertarian-alliance-a7820721.html; Patrick Maguire, 'I'm never tasting surrender again', *New Statesman*, 5 April 2019, 24–5.

23. https://www.theguardian.com/politics/2019/apr/02/i-fear-for-brexit-erg-dismayed-by-may-plan-to-talk-to-corbyn; Quentin Letts, 'In years to come . . . .' *Daily Telegraph*, 5 April 2019, 4.

24. Remain staffer Ryan Coetzee, quoted in The Guardian, 18 July 2019, 13; Boris Johnson, *The Churchill Factor: How One Man Made History* (London, 2014), 201, 224, 353.

25. Kate Devlin et al., 'I'd rather die in a ditch…' *Times*, 6 Sept. 2019, https://www.thetimes.co.uk/article/id-rather-die-in-a-ditch-than-ask-for-brexit-delay-says-boris-johnson-mprnrrdg0

26. 'PM's brother quits as Tory MP and minister', BBC News, 5 Sept. 2019, https://www.bbc.co.uk/news/uk-politics-49594793

27. Chris Stokel-Walker, '"Traitors," "Betrayals" and "surrenders," *Prospect*, 1 Oct. 2019, https://www.prospectmagazine.co.uk/politics/boris-johnson-surrender-bill-parliament-language-brexit-division Some of the 21 were later readmitted to the party in time for the December election.

28. R (on the application of Miller) (Appellant) v The Prime Minister (Respondent), [2019] UK 2019/0192, 24 Sept. 2019, https://www.supremecourt.uk/cases/docs/uksc-2019-0192-summary.pdf

29. Sam Fleming et al., 'Can Boris Johnson "get Brexit done"?' *Financial Times*, 19 Oct. 2019, p. 9 – quoting, for the EU, Dutch PM Mark Rutte.

30. 'Brexit: PM sends letter to Brussels seeking further delay', BBC News, 20 Oct. 2019, https://www.bbc.co.uk/news/uk-politics-50112924

31. Marina Hyde, 'Lost in politics', *Guardian*, 11 Dec. 2019, https://www.theguardian.com/politics/2019/dec/11/fridge-hiding-the-final-frontier-in-election-wtf-ery

32. David Cameron, *For the Record* (London, 2019), 654-5.

33. BBC News, 16 Dec. 2019, quoting Labour MP Stephen Kinnock https://www.bbc.co.uk/news/election-2019-50811026

34. Oliver Wright, 'Educated Remainer types failed to read mood of the country, says Cummings', *Times*, 14 Dec. 2019, p. 5.

35. BBC News, 15 Dec. 2019 https://www.bbc.co.uk/news/av/election-2019-50801743/nicola-sturgeon-scotland-cannot-be-imprisoned-in-uk

36. Felicity Lawrence et al, 'How the right's radical thinktanks reshaped the Conservative party', *Guardian*, 29 Nov. 2019, https://www.theguardian.com/politics/2019/nov/29/rightwing-thinktank-conservative-boris-johnson-brexit-atlas-network

37. Jonathan Portes, 'So Boris Johnson is going to "do" Brexit – but what are the actual options?' *Guardian*, 16 Dec. 2019, https://www.theguardian.com/commentisfree/2019/dec/16/boris-johnson-do-brexit-options-rhetoric-uk-single-market https://www.bbc.co.uk/news/election-2019-50818134 quoting Labour's John McDonnell.

38. Rachel Sylvester, 'Johnson's weakness is his need to be loved', *Times*, 23 July 2019, 21; Simon Jenkins, 'A Conservative manifesto? No, it's the Boris Johnson show', *Guardian*, 25 Nov. 2019, Opinion, p. 3.

39. https://www.gov.uk/government/speeches/pm-speech-in-greenwich-3-february-2020

40. Anthony Seldon, with Raymond Newell, *May at 10* (London, 2019), xi.

41. Boris Johnson, 'The people's day of jubilation highjacked by spineless pirates', *Daily Telegraph*, 27 March 2019, 1; Raab comments of 8 Nov. 2018 https://www.bbc.co.uk/news/uk-politics-46142188 See also Institute for Government, 'Implementing Brexit: Customs', Sept. 2017, 12, https://www.instituteforgovernment.org.uk/sites/default/files/publications/IfG_Brexit_customs_WEB_0.pdf

42. Fox, interview on BBC Radio 4 'Today' programme, 12 July 2017, https://www.bbc.co.uk/news/av/uk-40667879/eu-trade-deal-easiest-in-human-history

43. Ivan Rogers, *9 Lessons in Brexit* (London, 2019), 14, 18.

44. https://webarchive.nationalarchives.gov.uk/20160813202542/https://www.gov.uk/government/publications/why-the-government-believes-that-voting-to-remain-in-the-european-union-is-the-best-decision-for-the-uk/why-the-government-believes-that-voting-to-remain-in-the-european-union-is-the-best-decision-for-the-uk

45. http://www.voteleavetakecontrol.org/why_vote_leave.html

46. Challenged in 2018 about the accuracy of these assertions, Johnson declared defiantly, 'We grossly underestimated the sum over which we would be able to take back control,' and upped the figure to £438 million. https://www.theguardian.com/politics/2018/jan/15/leave-campaigns-350m-claim-was-too-low-says-boris-johnson

47. Rogers, *9 Lessons in Brexit*, 14–15.

48. David Cameron, 'My history hero', *BBC History Magazine*, August 2016, 98.

49. Jacob Rees-Mogg, *The Victorians: Twelve Titans who Forged Britain* (London, 2019), quoting x, xiii. See, for instance, https://www.telegraph.co.uk/books/what-to-read/victorians-jacob-rees-mogg-review-cliched-lazy-history-often/ https://www.thetimes.co.uk/article/rees-mogg-bores-for-britain-with-victorians-book-zn9qdqrng https://www.theguardian.com/politics/2019/may/19/jacob-rees-mogg-book-the-victorians-12-titans-who-forged-britain

50. 'Brexiter Tory MP accuses Airbus boss of "German bullying"', 25 Jan. 2019 https://www.bbc.co.uk/news/av/uk-politics-47004688/brexiter-tory-mp-mark-francois-accuses-airbus-boss-of-german-bullying

51. Centre on Constitutional Change, 'May's "Precious Union" has little support in Brexit Britain', 8 Oct. 2018, https://www.centreonconstitutionalchange.ac.uk/news/press-release-may%E2%80%99s-%E2%80%98precious-union%E2%80%99-has-little-support-brexit-britain; J. G. A. Pocock, *The Discovery of Islands: Essays in British History* (Cambridge, 2005), 309.

52. Quotations from Robert Gildea, *Empires of the Mind: The Colonial Past and the Politics of the Present* (Cambridge, 2019), 9, and Catherine Hall and Sonya O. Rose, eds, *At Home with the Empire: Metropolitan Culture and the Imperial World* (Cambridge, 2006), 5. As Priyamvada Gopal observes, 'Slavery and empire shape Britain's material and discursive inheritance; so, undoubtedly, do antislavery and anticolonialism' *Insurgent Empire*, 453.

53. Andrew Schonfield, *Europe: Journey to an Unknown Destination* (London, 1973); Julie Smith, *The UK's Journeys Into and Out of the EU: Destinations Unknown* (London, 2017), also 3, 111.

54. David Reynolds, 'Britain, the two world wars, and the problem of narrative', *Historical Journal*, 60 (2017), 197–231, esp. 230–1.

55. *PoliticsHome* report, 9 April 2019, https://www.politicshome.com/news/uk/political-parties/conservative-party/news/103150/cabinet-ministers-hail-kick-arse-tories

56. 'From a bad joke to a banana republic, how other countries see Brexit Britain', *Guardian*, 6 April 2019, 11; *Time*, 17 June 2019.

57. https://theconversation.com/do-truth-and-reconciliation-commissions-heal-divided-nations-109925

58. Peter Guiss, Guillaume Le Quintrec, et al., *Histoire/Geschichte* (Paris and Leipzig, 2006); Mona Siegel and Kirsten Harjes, 'Disarming Hatred: History Education, National Memories, and Franco-German Reconciliation from World War I to the Cold War', *History of Education Quarterly*, 52 (2012), 370–402, quoting 373, 401. See also Karina Korostelina and Simone Lässig, eds, *History Education and Post-Conflict Reconciliation* (London, 2013).

59. https://www.gov.uk/government/speeches/pm-statement-at-coronavirus-press-conference-3-march-2020

60. https://www.bbc.co.uk/news/stories-52066956 (Hennessy); broadcast on 5 April 2020, https://www.royal.uk/queens-broadcast-uk-and-commonwealth; for Churchill, see above p. 84.

Index

CENTRAL   13-11-2020